ANGELA BIRD

G000039799

THE VENDÉE

An English Family Guide

Illustrations by Michaël Jallier

Ⱶ.

Editions Hécate
3 bis, rue Dumaine
85400 Luçon

Thanks to
Josette, Carole, David, Sue, Adrian
and, of course . . . my family

The right of Angela Bird to be identified as the author of this work has been asserted
in accordance with the Copyright, Designs and Patents Act, 1988.

Cover picture:
Le Passage du Gois
This unique phenomenon is a 4.5km stretch of road along the sea bed,
linking the island of Noirmoutier to the mainland twice a day, at low tide.
The platform is a refuge for stranded motorists or pedestrians,
who face a draughty 10-hour wait for the waters to subside (see page 37).
© Angela Bird.

© 2000, Editions Hécate
Tous droits réservés pour tous pays
ISBN 2-86913-109-7

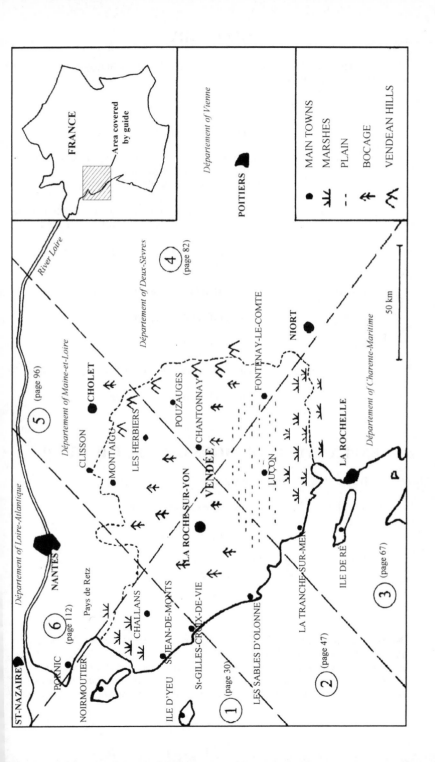

GLOSSARY

To save repetitive explanations, here are some French words you may come across in the following pages, or in life:

biologique, or bio	organic.
bocage	undulating, wooded areas of the Vendée.
coëfficient	figure in tide-tables indicating magnitude of tide on a particular day - the higher the *coëfficient*, the higher (and lower) the high and low tides.
dégustation	tasting, for example a free tasting of wine (though the provider obviously hopes you will make a purchase)
donjon	castle keep (not "dungeon", despite similarity in sound).
location	rental - as in *location de vélos,* cycle rental.
mairie	council offices in village or small town.
marais	fens, marshes, marshland.
mogette/mojette	white haricot bean, a favourite Vendean vegetable.
VTT	mountain-bike (*vélo tout-terrain*).

EXPLANATION OF SIGNS USED IN THE GUIDE

i	=	tourist information office
✳	=	open for a short summer season only
▲	=	open during a longer period of the year
●	=	open all year (if no other details are shown, the site is accessible at all times without charge)

While every care has been taken in the compiling of this book, neither the author nor the publisher can accept responsibility for any inaccuracies, and visitors are advised to check details in advance before making a special journey. Prices, usually based on 1999 rates, are given as a guide only and do not constitute a guaranteed admission charge. The author welcomes any comments, corrections or suggestions.

CONTENTS

INTRODUCTION

Nobody needs advice about how to soak up the 2,500 annual hours of sunshine that beam down on the 140km of sandy beaches lining the coast of the Vendée - a large *département* (or county) of western France, about the size of Devon. Yet inland, visited by only a few of the half-a-million foreign tourists who arrive each year, lies a land of legend and troubled history among the marshes, plains and rolling wooded hills that make up this area of western France.

I have been in love with the Vendée for 30 years, slowly uncovering its mysteries and finding offbeat outings for family and friends. I aim to share my enjoyment and give you a taste of the towns, villages, waterways and countryside that lie beyond the campsite or the rural *gîte*. Leaving aside any discussion of camping establishments, hotels or restaurants, my guidebook will concentrate essentially on culture and fun and lead you into lesser-known corners, or even slightly beyond the boundaries to other places within easy reach: the Pays de Retz and Nantes to the north; Cholet and the cinema park of Futuroscope at Poitiers; and historic La Rochelle.

If you are staying near the seaside you will almost certainly be familiar with the *marais*, the marshland dredged out of the sea by 12th-century monks and 16th-century Dutch engineers. You may have already crossed the Marais Breton (famed for salt production and duck-breeding), a patchwork of fields divided by watery ditches and canals that stretches from the mouth of the Loire southwards to St-Gilles-Croix-de-Vie. Perhaps you have glimpsed the salt-marshes north of Les Sables-d'Olonne, or the oyster-rich marshland that lies between Talmont-St-Hilaire and Jard-sur-Mer. Or maybe you know the Marais Poitevin, consisting of the flat, treeless *marais desséché* (dry marsh) south of Luçon and the idyllic *marais mouillé* (wet marsh), a network of tree-lined waterways south of Maillezais.

The *bocage* covers most of the rest - the *haut-bocage* being the hilly, wooded region down the eastern fringe of the *département*, and the *bas-bocage* the gently undulating land that surrounds La Roche-sur-Yon and continues towards the coast. This area is dotted with small farmhouses and cottages - their doorways often outlined in white and topped by a painted cross to keep witches and ill-fortune at bay. Here, Neolithic man built dolmens and raised the enormous standing-stones known as menhirs; more than 4,000 years later - after the French Revolution - 18th-century guerrillas hid in the forests to escape the flames and bayonets of Republican troops.

Blending into the Marais Poitevin and the *bocage* is the *plaine*, a series of vast, rolling prairies that stretches between Ste-Hermine and Fontenay-le-Comte and provides the Vendée's crops of maize, wheat and sunflowers. The red-roofed houses here exude prosperity - tall and substantial, they are built of fine, white stone, unlike the more primitive, ground-hugging cottages of the marshes.

I shall not linger on the coast, except to suggest some of its alternative attractions and to recommend serious seaside-lovers to obtain tide-tables (*horaires des marées*), free from tourist offices. To enjoy the maximum personal space, aim for the period around *basse mer* (low tide). In July and August the sands are often extremely crowded and the smarter town beaches like those of Les Sables-d'Olonne and St-Gilles-Croix-de-Vie can become unbearably congested at high tide (*pleine mer*), particularly when this occurs in mid-afternoon. A little research pays off if you want to avoid the crush.

For a bit of variety, get out a good map and head inland; there you can walk in the forests, rent a mountain-bike, look for dolmens and canoe through the marshes, or admire the Vendée's rich legacy of Romanesque architecture, ride on a steam train, go birdwatching or visit a submarine. And, if you are unfortunate enough to wake up to a spot of rain, you can dip into this book to find museums, castles, aquariums and junk shops in which to spend the time until the sun comes out again. I have included at-a-glance symbols as an indication of opening periods to help out-of-season visitors easily home in on what to do in autumn, winter and spring, as well as high summer.

Sports-lovers and night-owls will have no difficulty discovering riding establishments, casinos and discos, which are well documented in tourist offices. I have attempted to point out some of the Vendée's other resources - unusual museums, rural events and market-days - and to throw in a seasoning of things that I find irresistible on holiday like flea markets, crafts fairs, and getting acquainted with local customs and food - you haven't lived until you've tried the region's ham and *mogettes* (white haricot beans), barbecued quail, grilled sardines, or eels that have been cooked over cowpat fires.

Village festivals, heavily advertised on posters and banners throughout the neighbourhood, are great fun. Usually low-key affairs held on a Sunday, they tend to promote different, often food-related local traditions - from oyster-fishing to the baking of brioche. While the older men drink steadily at a long trestle bar, the youngsters bowl for a pig and folk dancers swirl through the hot summer afternoons. Be warned: in spite of Brigitte Bardot's efforts, animals at circuses and fêtes in France are often accorded far fewer rights than they would be in Britain. Tossing a hoop over a duck can mean just that; if you succeed, then you get to take the bewildered bird home. Events are usually rounded off with a *bal populaire* where you can find yourself dancing a conga with the local butcher, baker and clog-maker.

Bonfires are often lit to celebrate the Feast of St John the Baptist around 24 June, which makes a further excuse for festivities. The Fête Nationale (Bastille Day) is marked by parades and fireworks on the evening of either 13 or 14 July, though events are sometimes low-key in this region, which was decidedly anti-Republican after the 1789 Revolution (see page 25). The circus remains a much-loved tradition in France, and travelling companies large and small still pitch their big tops in holiday towns and villages. In mid-September a weekend of *journées du patrimoine* (Heritage Days) gives you a chance to visit historic properties at reduced rates - including some that are normally closed to the public. You can pick up a brochure from tourist offices or from the Conseil Général offices in La Roche-sur-Yon during the few weeks beforehand. From mid-September to mid-January is the eagerly-awaited season for *la chasse* (shooting). On Sundays and on one weekday, that varies from village to village, the locals pick up their guns and lurk among the hedgerows from dawn to dusk, firing at anything from rabbits to wild boar. It is probably wise to resist taking country walks on those days if you want to avoid being peppered with shot - or at least make sure you are noticed, by wearing bright clothes.

The heritage has its melancholy side, too. Western France was torn by the Hundred Years War (against the English) and the Wars of Religion (that pitched Catholics against Protestants). But the area suffered most cruelly during the bitter civil war waged immediately after the French Revolution of 1789 by the strongly Catholic Vendean peasants - who supported the deposed French monarchy - against the Republicans' new ideas and well-armed forces. To understand the soul of the region you should skim through the section on the Vendée Wars (see pages 25-28), which outlines the savage events that are indelibly stamped on collective memory. In just three years from March 1793 the uprising cost more than 250,000 lives. Almost every village was destroyed, castles and manor houses were reduced to ruins, and a ruthless extermination policy cut down the population by one third - in some villages by up to a half. So it is no surprise that most pre-19th-century castles, houses and churches are in various stages of ruination - the miracle is that any are left at all. Since those days the Vendean emblem has featured two intertwined hearts topped with a cross and a crown to symbolise the region's twin loyalties to church and king, though in keeping with republican sentiment the crown is becoming less apparent.

As befits a *département* whose major industry is now tourism, the Vendée has begun to rescue its heritage of crumbling Romanesque churches, feudal strongholds, Renaissance castles and industrial relics from layers of ivy and centuries of neglect. Houses connected with local celebrities like politician Georges Clemenceau, painter Charles Milcendeau and military hero Marshal Jean de Lattre de Tassigny give fascinating insights into provincial French life. No less intriguing are museums that have evolved from private passions such as collecting kitchen utensils, perambulators or vintage cars.

I have usually given titles of museums and events in French, since this is how you will see them advertised or signposted. Most of the smaller establishments have tours and details only in French, so I have tried to explain enough historical background to give non-French speakers a little understanding of displays or events. Opening details may be varied on public holidays (see page 19). More attractions are beginning to offer family tickets and all-day opening. The cut-off point for children's admission rates varies between about 12 and 16 years and, if anyone in your party is aged over 60, it is worth enquiring in the larger museums about possible reductions for "*troisième-âge*". Keep an eye open also for *passeport* cards or leaflets, which give reductions on admission to other sites in an area once you have visited a first one.

Whenever you stop in a town or village, try and spend a few minutes strolling around the back streets - particularly the area around an ancient church, where you frequently find interesting buildings and hidden corners invisible to those who whizz by on the through roads or bypasses. Oh, and if your child is taking a turn on a roundabout, tell him or her to watch out for the monkey's tail. The ride operator often releases a soft toy towards the end of the ride, dangling it above the children until one of them grabs the tail and pulls it off - winning a second, free ride.

I wish you a wonderful, interest-filled holiday, though I am certain you will find - as I have even after 30 years of Vendée summers - that it will not be long enough.

PLANNING YOUR TRIP

WHEN TO GO
The Vendée's climate is generally considerably warmer than that of southern England, with very hot summers and mild, damp winters (see Weather, page 21). Peak French holiday months are July and August - especially from 14 July to 15 August. Apart from seaside and purely child-orientated activities, there is still plenty to visit between May and October; many attractions are gradually extending their seasons, and most museums and cultural sites are open - at weekends at least - almost all year round.

HOW TO GET THERE
By sea
Brittany Ferries operates Portsmouth to St-Malo, Portsmouth to Caen, Poole to Cherbourg, Plymouth to Roscoff and Cork to Roscoff.
P&O operates Portsmouth to Cherbourg, Portsmouth to Le Havre.
Irish Ferries operates Rosslare to Cherbourg.
By air
Air France, with regional French airline Brit Air, operates London (Gatwick) to Nantes.
By train
SNCF (French Railways) operates direct services by TGV (high-speed train) from Paris-Montparnasse to Nantes, La Roche-sur-Yon and Les Sables-d'Olonne. Regular rail services also operate from Paris to St-Gilles-Croix-de-Vie.
Eurostar trains from London-Waterloo to Lille-Europe connect with a direct TGV service from Lille-Europe to Nantes.

WHERE TO STAY

The Vendée has almost 400 classified camp sites, plus numerous *campings à la ferme* - small sites on working farms where children can play in the meadows, fish in farm ponds or help feed the animals. At a more sophisticated level, many British companies offer luxury camping in tents or mobile homes at four-star sites both on the coast and inland, backed up by the services of cheerful couriers. Prominent among these are Canvas, Carisma, Keycamp, Eurocamp, Eurosites, French Country Camping, Haven Europe, Matthews, and Sunsites. Useful advice for independent travellers can also be obtained in the UK from the Caravan Club and the Camping and Caravanning Club.

Holiday cottages can be rented through through many British organisations such as Brittany Ferries, Chez Nous, Martin Sturge, Vacances en Campagne and VFB, and also through Gîtes de France. (Contact the French Government Tourist Office, 178 Piccadilly, London W1V 9DB or, for a wider selection, the Vendée's own Gîtes de France office at 124 Boulevard Aristide-Briand, 85000 La Roche-sur-Yon; tel: 02 51 47 87 00; fax: 02 51 62 15 19.)

Further tourist information from:

Comité Départemental du Tourisme de la Vendée, BP 233, 85006 La Roche-sur-Yon Cédex (tel: 02 51 47 88 20; fax: 02 51 05 37 01); web site: www.vendee.com/

Regional Tourist Board of Pays de la Loire (Western Loire), 2 Rue de la Loire, BP 20411, 44204 Nantes Cédex 2 (tel: 02 40 48 24 20; fax: 02 40 08 07 10).

USEFUL INFORMATION

ACCESSIBILITY

Things in France are slowly improving for people with limited mobility (*à mobilité réduite*, or *handicapé*), and the Vendée is no exception. The traditional single-storey construction of many Vendean buildings means that museums are often on ground level only - though unfortunately those that are not sometimes have no lift (*ascenseur*).

Obviously all new establishments are designed with accessibility in mind, and feature such facilities as toilets for the disabled.

In the text I have tried, where relevant, to mention steps and other obstacles that might pose particular problems for less mobile visitors, but it is best to contact the local tourist office for specific up-to-date information.

Wheelchair-bound fishing enthusiasts are well catered for: many riverbanks and lakesides have specially-designed pontoons jutting out into the water. Disabled parking spaces are provided at supermarkets - though, regrettably, many able-bodied French drivers seem to think they are there for all. State-of-the-art trams in the city of Nantes have special ramps that enable wheelchair-users to board easily.

If you need to check wheelchair access or the existence of disabled toilets, *"Est-ce que c'est accessible aux fauteuil roulants?"* or *"Y a-t-il des toilettes pour handicapés?"* are useful phrases.

BEACHES

Many of the beaches - including Noirmoutier, Barbâtre, La Barre-de-Monts, Notre-Dame, St-Jean, St-Hilaire, St-Gilles, Brétignolles, Olonne, Talmont, Longeville, La Tranche and L'Aiguillon - receive regular European Blue Flag accolades for their cleanliness and for their water quality. Best surfing beaches are reckoned to lie between St-Gilles and Les Sables/Tanchet and between Longeville and La Tranche, with surf shops at St-Jean, St-Gilles, Brétignolles, Les Sables and La Tranche.

BIRDWATCHING

Ornithologists are spoiled for choice. The Vendée is on migratory routes for many species, so large numbers of birds are seen in spring and autumn. The region is a popular nesting area for avocets, terns and lapwings and, between April and September, for storks, who favour sites in the marshes of Châteauneuf and Velluire. The mudflats of the Bay of Bourgneuf provide an incredible wintertime spectacle at high tide when thousands of wading birds advance with the rising water, probing the mud for food. Herons, egrets and other marshland birds are often seen on the salt-meadows, and brent geese arrive in large numbers during December on the Marais Breton. Other wetland areas that attract migrant species include the lake of Grand-Lieu, and L'Aiguillon Bay.

BOATING

Canoeing

Guided tours are available through open marshland at Sallertaine and Bois-de-Céné. Canoes may also be rented on many of the Vendée's rivers, canals and lakes, or on the signposted waterways of the Marais Poitevin ("Green Venice" marshes).

Traditional craft

You can be taken out on a punt-like *yole* at Le Perrier, paddle a flat-bottomed *plate* along tree-lined waterways in the Marais Poitevin (Green Venice), or enjoy guided tours by traditional *chaland* in the marshland national park of the Grande Brière.

Pedaloes, windsurfers, rowing and sailing dinghies

The above may be rented on various inland lakes such as Apremont, Jaunay, Moulin-Papon, Mervent-Vouvant, Rochereau, Bellenoue and La Tricherie.

CASINOS

French holiday resorts are, by tradition, well-endowed with casinos. Far less exclusive than in the UK, they are welcoming establishments with a casual atmosphere, pleasant restaurants and bars open to non-players, and occasional evenings of entertainment by well-known names. The fruit machines are usually in operation all day for over-18s. A rather more serious approach is necessary for the gaming rooms (open from 10 or 11pm to about 4am); potential roulette or blackjack players must pay the equivalent of several pounds to gain admission, and produce a valid passport or other satisfactory *pièce d'identité*. You will find casinos at St Jean-de-Monts, St-Gilles-Croix-de-Vie, Les Sables-d'Olonne (two), La Faute-sur-Mer, and also at Pornic and at St-Brévin-les-Pins.

CHURCHGOING

Worshippers are always welcome to attend Mass at local Catholic churches - services on Saturday evening or Sunday morning. Fontenay-le-Comte, Mouchamps and La Roche-sur-Yon have *églises réformées*, or Protestant churches, with weekly services known as *cultes*. From mid-July to the end of August, a resident Anglican chaplain conducts a regular Sunday service in English at one of the seaside campsites or churches. You will find details on a small information slip from tourist offices, or from the Intercontinental Church Society in Warwick (UK tel: 01926 430347).

CYCLING

Many local trails (*pistes cyclables*) are signposted; details of them, as well as of cycle hire (*location de vélos*), are obtainable from tourist offices. Guided tours are available around the Marais Breton - the open marshland near Challans - by *VTT* (mountain-bike) from Sallertaine; other guided trips are offered through the marshland and countryside surrounding Les Sables-d'Olonne (mountain-bikes provided in each case).

Many sections of a 150km Atlantic cycleway, which will eventually run the whole length of the Vendée's coastline - from Bouin to L'Aiguillon-sur-Mer - are now in place. Among other popular bike routes that will connect with it are a super-smooth cycle track that runs along a disused railway line from La Roche-sur-Yon via Aizenay and Coëx, soon to reach St-Gilles-Croix-de-Vie, and a canalside trail due to link La Tranche with Maillezais.

The most unusual form of cycling is unquestionably the *vélo draisine*, a flat-bed wagon that runs along a disused railway line from Commequiers, carrying four or five people, two pedalling and three "resting".

DIVING

If you have internationally-recognised diving certificates, you can join local divers exploring wrecks off Noirmoutier or the Ile d'Yeu. Enquire about *la plongée* at tourist offices.

ELECTRICITY

The electric current is usually 220 volts, so British equipment should function successfully if you have brought an adaptor to convert your plug to fit a French socket. These are widely available in British shops, on ferries and at airports, but you are unlikely to find them once you are in France. A couple of warnings: power supplies may be interrupted during storms; and the voltage in many *gîtes* does not allow you to run several major items - e.g. oven and dishwasher - at once.

ENTERTAINMENT

Concerts

Probably the most accessible form of entertainment for non-French speakers is music.

A free quarterly brochure, *Musique Danse*, lists fixtures - from rock to classical - in concert halls, churches and other venues. The Logis de la Chabotterie organises a baroque music festival in summer, and a festival of romantic music is held at Luçon.

11

Theatres

Theatrical performances in France tend to rely heavily on words, and anyone with limited command of French may find them difficult to follow. There are theatres at La Roche-sur-Yon and Fontenay-le-Comte, and within the new Atlantes centre at Les Sables-d'Olonne. Outside the *département* you will find theatres at La Rochelle and Nantes (where opera performances are also given between October and June at the Théâtre Graslin). It is usual to slip 10F to the usherette who shows you to your seat.

The best thing is to go for spectacle, and for this the night-time Cinéscénie at the Puy-du-Fou cannot be beaten. Other good *son-et-lumière* productions are performed at Olonne-sur-Mer and at Machecoul. They tend to be popular, so book in advance through local tourist offices. In July and August at seaside towns some highly original street-theatre artistes are often engaged to give free open-air evening performances.

Cinemas

The French are great movie-goers and most towns, even quite small ones, have cinemas. In July and August a programme of free open-air film shows, known as Cinésites, is organised outside castles and other venues. Details are usually given in local newspapers (be sure you pick up the appropriate edition - a copy bought at some distance from your base may cover different towns from the one you are interested in). With the exception of showings in a few Nantes cinemas, films will always be in French - English-language ones being dubbed rather than subtitled, so entertainment value for non-French-speakers is restricted. The letters "V.O." (*version originale*) indicate a movie is being shown in its original language, with French subtitles - not much help, of course, if a film was in Swedish or German in the first place.

FISHING

Freshwater fishing

The inland lakes and rivers yield bream, perch, roach, tench, pike, zander, black-bass and, occasionally, carp; in rivers of the *haut-bocage* around Pouzauges, on the eastern side of the county, are some trout; marshland canals may harbour eels; while the sluggish lower reaches of rivers like the Vie contain more than their fair share of small catfish.

A holiday licence (*Carte Pêche-Vacances*), from many tackle shops, allows you to fish in all non-private waters - which include rivers, and also areas on them where lakes have been created by dams - of the Vendée and surrounding *départements* (though Charente-Maritime, to the south, requires a separate permit). It is valid on 15 consecutive days between 1 June and 30 September and costs around 150F. Information from *mairies* and tourist offices, or from La Fédération de Pêche de Vendée, 10bis Rue Haxo, BP 673, 85016 La Roche-sur-Yon Cédex (tel: 02 51 37 19 05/fax: 02 51 05 54 13). "*Pêche Interdite*" means No Fishing; ask if in any doubt about whether a stretch of water is included in the pass. Tackle and bait are on sale in sports and watersports shops and hypermarkets, though maggots are, for some reason, extremely expensive.

Some places of special interest to fishermen are: the Maison de la Rivière at St-Georges-de-Montaigu, the tourist office at Chaillé-les-Marais, and a huge new fishing project due to be unveiled in 2001 at Moncoutant, just beyond Pouzauges.

Traditional fishing

Annual event on 15 August and the first Sunday after, at Passay on the lake of Grand-Lieu. On these two days you can wade waist-deep in water, through the mud and reeds, to help the fishermen haul in the long seine nets.

Sea fishing

Boat trips may be taken from Les Sables-d'Olonne or from St-Gilles-Croix-de-Vie.

Shrimping and shellfish-collecting

At low water, push a shrimping net through the shallows and the rock-pools or join the locals digging for cockles, clams and other shellfish. You need to consult tide-tables to find the days with the highest figure in the *coëfficient* column, showing extra-low low tides (*coëfficients* of more than 90 are best). Rarely-uncovered sandbanks - the Pont d'Yeu, for example, south of Notre-Dame-de-Monts - or the mudflats alongside the causeway leading to Noirmoutier island are popular spots, but keep an eye on the time, and stay away from any dubious outflow pipes as well as from commercial oyster-beds or mussel-posts. It goes without saying that you should not collect anything too tiny, nor harvest more shellfish than you can eat at a sitting.

FOOD

Traditional local specialities are hearty, peasant food like cabbage, and the white haricot beans known as *mogettes* that used to be simmered slowly in the embers of the fire while the family toiled in the fields. With such a long coastline and active fishing industry, fish and shellfish are an important part of the repertoire, especially mussels from L'Aiguillon-sur-Mer, oysters from the Bay of Bourgneuf, sardines from St-Gilles-Croix-de-Vie and sole from Les Sables-d'Olonne.

The idea of buying organic foods is slowly taking root in the region. Look for the words *bio* or *biologique*, indicating foodstuffs that conform to the same "organic" regulations as in the UK. It's also worth knowing that the "Label Rouge" (Red Label) designation indicates produce - from meat to melons - that has been farmed subject to stringent rules governing natural conditions and feeding. The phrase "*sans OGM*" on an item means it contains no genetically-modified organisms.

Shellfish

When you buy fish and shellfish in a shop, don't hesitate to ask for advice on cooking them. Shrimps and prawns are usually sold cooked (the little brown shrimps known as *crevettes grises* have much more flavour than their pretty pink cousins). *Langoustines* (salt-water crayfish) can be bought ready-cooked (*cuites*) or raw (*crues*) - if uncooked, they should be plunged into a large saucepan of well-salted boiling water flavoured with pepper and a little vinegar, brought back to the boil and then cooked briskly for just three minutes, before being cooled rapidly under cold water.

Crabs can be bought cooked, but most often are still clambering over one another, blowing bubbles, in the fishmonger's tray. The non-squeamish can steel themselves to place the creature in a large saucepan of cold water, heavily salted and flavoured with pepper and a *bouquet garni* of available herbs, bringing it to the boil and cooking for 12 minutes per kilo (about six minutes per pound). Plunge the crab into cold water immediately it is cooked. The only parts you should not eat are the fleshy, grey, finger-shaped gills and the stringy intestine. A pair of nutcrackers (or pliers, hammer, or even, at a pinch, a couple of good, flat stones) is invaluable for smashing your way into the better-protected parts - try to buy some pointed, metal shellfish-picks in a supermarket to dig out the best bits. Spider crabs (*araignées*) should be put into boiling water flavoured with a little cayenne pepper and cooked for 20 minutes per kilo (about 10 minutes per pound), then allowed to cool in the cooking water. If you can't face any of this, you can always order cooked crabs or lobsters from a fishmonger at a day's notice.

Mussels and other shellfish need to be well scrubbed and scraped, using a sharp knife to remove barnacles and any whiskery bits of "beard". Discard any that are not tightly closed. You can sometimes buy ready-scraped mussels (*moules grattées*) which saves a bit of work, but you should still look them over carefully. To cook a kilo of mussels, heat 125ml of Muscadet, Gros-Plant or other dry white wine with a chopped onion, a chopped clove of garlic, 2 teaspoonsful of chopped parsley, and seasoning. When it is boiling, add the mussels, cover the pan and steam for five to 10 minutes until they open (throw out any that remain closed). Remove the mussels, and stir a little butter or cream into the juice before pouring it over them. You can do something similar with cockles (*coques*) and other shellfish, though the French usually eat them raw.

Oysters - usually the long, knobbly *portugaise* variety - are in season all year and are, to British minds, incredibly inexpensive. To open, attack the hinged end of the creature using one of the cheap, stubby blades with a special shield around the handle from hardware shops or supermarkets, avoiding getting flakes of shell mingled with the delicate flesh. Wrap your other hand in a tea-towel for protection! If you are going to open many, you may want to treat yourself to an electric, vibrating oyster-knife.

Fish

A wonderful fish soup in large glass jars, sold under the label of "La Vendéenne", can be eaten with a little spicy *rouille* sauce stirred in, and then sprinkled with *croûtons* and grated gruyère cheese.

Fresh sardines are a real, yet inexpensive, treat. Gut and wash them well. For barbecuing it is easiest to cook them in a metal, double tennis-racquet arrangement, if you can lay your hands on one. Sprinkle them with olive oil and some coarse Noirmoutier sea-salt and grill for about three minutes each side (depending on thickness). Eat with something plain, like boiled potatoes or crusty bread, and butter. You can also barbecue steaks of fresh tuna (*thon*). The red-tinged meat is very filling, and particularly delicious with a horseradish and cream sauce - if you are British enough to have brought horseradish with you.

Vegetables

Mogettes (haricot beans), introduced to the area by monks in the 16th century after Pope Clement VII had been presented with some from South America, need to be soaked overnight before cooking and then simmered for an hour or two in water with no salt, just bouquet garni. Salt them only *after* they are cooked. You can stir in some *crème fraîche* (slightly soured cream) after draining them. If this sounds too much trouble, there are some excellent, home-cooked versions "*à l'ancienne*" - with tasty bits of bacon and carrot included - available in supermarkets. The beans - also known as *lingots* - are traditionally served with ham (*jambon*), another Vendean speciality, cured using a mixture of sea salt, spices and *eau-de-vie*. In late summer you sometimes see the new season's beans, called *demi-secs*, on sale still in their withered pods; these need no pre-soaking, and are supposed to be more digestible.

If you find strange mushrooms irresistible, you can take any that you gather in forests and hedgerows to a chemist for identification and advice on whether they can be eaten. On the whole it is probably safer to stick with those you can buy in the markets around October: chanterelles, ceps and horns of plenty (*trompettes de la mort*) look quite adventurous enough for most people.

Sea salt - grey and chunky, known as *sel de mer* or *gros-sel*, and the finer, white *fleur de sel* - made the fortunes of the monasteries in the Middle Ages, when it was in demand everywhere for the preservation of food. At the time of Richard III, the Bay of Bourgneuf supplied 80 per cent of salt used in London. Today it is still made, on a smaller scale, with the same techniques in the salt marshes of Guérande, Noirmoutier, St-Hilaire and Olonne, and makes interesting, and comparatively cheap, presents for foodie friends back home. Also grown in the same marshes is the red, fleshy-leaved samphire (*salicorne*) that turns green when cooked and is sold, pickled, as a condiment, or fresh for brief cooking and use as a vegetable or in a salad.

The island of Noirmoutier enjoys a microclimate that enables it to produce the first French new potatoes of the year - rather like Jersey Royals for the British - as early as February. The delicious, fresh taste in early spring compensates for the slightly sorry sight of the island's fields under plastic wraps through the winter.

14

Poultry and meat

One of the region's most important agricultural products today is poultry. Chicken and duck are familiar enough; guinea-fowl (*pintade*) can be cooked like chicken; quail (*caille*) - of which you need one or two per person - may be roasted or casseroled for about 20 minutes, and needs extra flavour from added bits of bacon, Muscadet, Pineau, grapes etc. Beautiful, speckled quail's eggs make an attractive starter when hard-boiled (bring to the boil, simmer for about four minutes, and then cool rapidly under cold water) and served with salt or mayonnaise. You can also barbecue quail: split the birds down the backbone, open them out and then marinate them for a few hours in a tasty combination of herbs, oil, onions and other flavourings.

Meat is often sold in boned and rolled joints that make carving a real pleasure - just indicate to the butcher the length you want, or tell him how many people it's for. If you have a barbecue with a battery-operated spit, try doing a piece of beef (*rôti de boeuf*), studded with a few cloves of garlic if you like. It doesn't take long to cook - about 20 to 30 minutes, depending on thickness - and, though it is not cheap, there is no waste. In the unlikely event of any being left over, it is even better cold.

Cheese and butter

Many craftsman-made cheeses can be found in the market-halls of Vendean towns and villages; even if you don't usually like goat's cheese it's worth trying one of the very mild fresh white ones, whose characteristic flavour is less pronounced. Among local cow's-milk cheeses are Halbran, fairly hard and tasty, and the slightly blander Mizotte. Look out in markets for dairy stalls selling butter cut from huge yellow mountains - you buy it by the pound (*une livre* is the equivalent of 500g) or kilogram, and can choose from unsalted (*doux*), slightly salted (*demi-sel*) or salty (*salé*).

Desserts

For the sweet-toothed, there is quite a choice. The Vendée is known for its loaves of impossibly light, fluffy brioche (a sweet bread made of eggs, flour, sugar, yeast, salt, butter and milk, plus a dash of rum or orange-flower water). Traditionally an Easter speciality, it is still served at midnight, with coffee, at local weddings. Every baker has his own version, though it is said to originate in Vendrennes, near Les Herbiers. Other treats include *flan maraîchin* (a pastry case holding an egg custard), *tourteau au fromage* (a zingy, black-domed cheesecake made from goat's cheese, nestling in a pastry case and tasting rather better than it looks), *fouace* or *fouasse* (a cross between cake and bread, firmer in texture than brioche), and "*R'tournez'y*" - a delicious vanilla, hazelnut and wild strawberry ice-cream confection sold by the best pâtisseries, bearing the Vendée's hearts-and-crown logo.

GOLF

Vendée Golf Pass

A season ticket is available, valid for one month, covering the Vendée's five 18-hole, par-72 courses: 1 July-31 August, 1,000F; 1 September-30 June, 800F. This entitles you to one round on each, plus a discount on further green fees. Golf clubs may be hired on the spot. Information and reservations: Club des Golfs de Vendée, Golf des Fontenelles, 85220 L'Aiguillon-sur-Vie (tel: 02 51 54 57 57; fax: 02 51 55 45 77). The courses are at St-Jean-de-Monts, L'Aiguillon-sur-Vie (near Coëx), Nesmy (near La Roche-sur-Yon), Olonne-sur-Mer (near Les Sables-d'Olonne), and Port-Bourgenay (near Talmont-St-Hilaire). A handicap of 36 or less is normally required. Between May and September it is best to book in advance for the more popular courses like St-Jean and Port-Bourgenay.

Swin-Golf

This is not a misprint but a family golfing game over a special nine- or 18-hole course, using just one club with three different faces in place of a normal bagful.

Mini-Golf

Great fun for all ages, these nine- or 18-hole circuits with jokey hazards built into them will entertain everyone from six-year-olds to grandparents.

HOTELS AND RESTAURANTS

Good reference books are the Michelin red guide or the Logis de France book for both hotels and restaurants - Michelin awards up to three rosettes for gastronomic excellence. Those who read French will find the *Guide du Routard* series a reliable source of information on where to eat and sleep; its chatty style is guaranteed to brush up your grasp of current colloquialisms. The Gîtes de France brochure (see page 9) lists B&Bs (*chambres d'hôte*), graded with *épis*, or ears of wheat; *Bienvenue au Château*, free from the French Tourist Office in London, gives details of stylish private accommodation, often in historic settings.

Restaurant guides include the upmarket *Gault-Millau* (which accords marks out of 20), and the *Guide des Relais Routiers* for good-value meals. Some of the top places to eat in the Vendée feature in *Les Tables de la Vendée Gourmande* and *Les Toques Vendéennes*, both booklets available free from tourist offices and quality food shops. From Monday to Friday, even the top restaurants offer good-value fixed-price menus at lunchtimes, so this is a good opportunity to sample gastronomic output at affordable rates. You can often eat well and cheaply at small, family-run establishments - look around a market-square, for example, or ask the locals for advice - and most hypermarkets have good, reasonably-priced self-service restaurants.

For true local flavour, it's worth trying a *ferme-auberge*. These are real restaurants, rather than farmhouse kitchens, where at least half the produce served has to be home-produced - so you're guaranteed fresh duck, lamb, *foie gras*, vegetables, or whatever is the farm's speciality.

MAPS

You need good maps to get the most out of a holiday. The familiar, yellow-backed Michelin series at 1:200,000 (1cm=2km) is excellent and, at around 12F, good value. Most useful of these will be No 67 (Nantes/Les Sables-d'Olonne) and No 71 (La Rochelle/Royan/Bordeaux). Even better - though more expensive - are the IGN (Institut Géographique National) green series on the scale of 1:100,000 (1cm=1km) - either No 32 (Nantes/Les Sables-d'Olonne) or No 33 (Cholet/Niort), depending on where you are based. For even more detail on an area you want to walk or explore in depth nothing beats the 1:25,000 IGN blue series where 4cm=1km. The IGN also produces a red series at 1:250,000 (1cm=2.5km), of which No 107 covers Poitou-Charentes from St-Nazaire to Royan and Tours to Limoges, its scope making it handy if you are touring by car over a wide area.

All are widely available in the Vendée. Michelin and IGN green series can also be found in good UK bookshops, while maps in the blue and red IGN series may be purchased from Stanfords, 12-14 Long Acre, London WC2E 9LP.

MARKETS

Markets are normally morning-only events, finishing around noon. Below is a day-by-day guide; check out the main entries for the respective towns and villages, however, as some markets are summer only, and others may be held on alternate weeks:

Monday: Aizenay; Benet; L'Herbaudière; Jard; Longeville; Merlin-Plage; La Roche; Les Sables; St-Michel-Mont-Mercure; Touvois.

Tuesday: L'Aiguillon-sur-Mer; Le Boupère; Brem; La Chaize-le-Vicomte; Challans; Chantonnay; Mortagne; Noirmoutier; Port-Joinville (Ile d'Yeu); La Roche; Les Sables; St-Gilles; Sion; La Tranche.

Wednesday: Champagné; Chavagnes-en-Paillers; La Chevrolière; Commequiers; Croix-de-Vie; Les Essarts; Foussais-Payré; L'Hermenault; Luçon; Machecoul; Merlin-Plage; Rocheservière; Les Sables; St-Jean-de-Monts; Soullans; La Grière (La Tranche).
Thursday: Beauvoir; Brétignolles; Chaillé-les-Marais; Chantonnay; La Faute; La Garnache; La Guérinière (Noirmoutier); Les Herbiers; Mareuil; La Mothe-Achard; Le Poiré-sur-Vie; Pouzauges; La Roche; Les Sables; St-Gilles; St-Hilaire-de-Riez; St-Michel-en-l'Herm.
Friday: L'Aiguillon-sur-Mer; Brem; Challans; Clisson; Coulon; Longeville; La Mothe-Achard; Moutiers-les-Mauxfaits; Noirmoutier; Les Sables; Ste-Hermine; Sion; Soullans.
Saturday: La Barre; Bouin; Bourgneuf; Challans; Chantonnay; Chavagnes-en-Paillers; Cholet; Coëx; Coulon; Croix-de-Vie; Les Essarts; La Faute; Fontenay; Les Herbiers; Luçon; Merlin-Plage; Montaigu; Le Poiré-sur-Vie; Port-Joinville; La Roche; Les Sables; St-Jean-de-Monts; Talmont; La Tranche.
Sunday: Beauvoir; Brétignolles; La Faute; La Guérinière (Noirmoutier); Maillé; Noirmoutier; Notre-Dame-de-Monts; Notre-Dame-de-Riez; Olonne; Les Sables; St-Florent-des-Bois; St-Gilles; St-Hilaire-de-Riez; St-Philbert-de-Grand-Lieu; Soullans.

MEASUREMENTS
All indications of distance, area and weight in this guide are metric.
    1kg = 2.2lb
    500g = 1.1lb (also often called *une livre*)
    1litre = 1.75pt (1 gallon = 4.54litres)
    1km = 0.6 miles (1 mile = 1.6km)
    1 hectare = 2.47 acres (260 hectares = 1 square mile)

MEDICAL TREATMENT
Obviously it is best to take out comprehensive travel insurance for your annual holiday, but if you hold a form E111 (obtainable free from UK post offices on quotation of your National Insurance number), you can claim some reimbursement of medical expenses under the reciprocal arrangement between Britain and France. After consulting and paying the doctor or dentist (around 150F), take the *feuille de soins* (medical treatment form) that you are given and hand it to the chemist with your *ordonnance* (prescription) form. The chemist dispenses the drugs (it is most important to keep any sticky labels from the boxes), and adds their details to the form.

Take or send the form and sticky labels, with your E111 and the passport (or a photocopy of its important pages, if you are posting it) relating to the person in whose name the E111 is issued, to the nearest Caisse Primaire Assurance Maladie (CPAM). These are located at La Roche-sur-Yon, Challans, Fontenay-le-Comte, Les Herbiers, and Les Sables-d'Olonne. You should get quite a large percentage of your costs reimbursed. The offices at La Roche and Les Sables can arrange to hand over the cash, or at least a cheque you can cash locally; otherwise the system operates by sending a cheque to your home in around six weeks.

Chemists are often consulted about minor ailments and discuss them with doctor-like gravity, binding up sprained ankles and dishing out reasonably strong medicines without the need for getting into the intricacies of the French health system. You do not, however, get reimbursed for this treatment.

There are casualty departments (*urgences*) at the *département's* main hospitals: Challans (Boulevard de l'Est, on the north-east corner of the inner ring road); La Roche-sur-Yon (signposted "CHD" on the Cholet road at Les Oudairies, on the north-east side of town); Fontenay-le-Comte (Rue Rabelais, the La Roche road, west of Place Viète); Les Sables-d'Olonne (Route de Talmont); and also at Nantes, Niort and Cholet.

MONEY

France embraced the euro well ahead of Britain: since 1999 prices everywhere have been shown in both euros and francs. The new currency comes into circulation in January 2002; from June of that year the familiar French notes and coins will be gradually be withdrawn. 1 euro (€), made up of 100 cents, is the equivalent of 6 francs 56 centimes in French francs, or roughly 70 UK pence.

In towns and large villages banks usually open from Tuesday to Saturday, between 9am and noon, and 2pm till 6pm. When cashing travellers' cheques or changing money in a bank you are often asked for your passport, so it is as well to carry it with you. Banks close for public holidays (see below) from lunch-time the previous day. This can catch you unawares, as also can the fact that if the holiday falls on a Tuesday or a Thursday there is a tendency to join the day up to the nearest weekend (*faire le pont*) and close for several days at a stretch.

However, if you have the sort of bank card that extracts cash from a hole in the wall in Britain, the chances are that it will work in France, as long as it bears a similar logo to one of those displayed on the French cashpoint machine, or *guichet automatique*; on-screen instructions are usually given in English as well as French.

Credit cards like MasterCard, Visa, American Express and Diner's Club are widely accepted (particularly the first two, which are known as *cartes bancaires*) at petrol stations, supermarkets, hotels, restaurants and stores (except, of course, small village shops, restaurants and cafés). The microchip incorporated into French credit cards allows the cardholder to tap a secret authorisation code onto a special little keyboard. If you use a British card, you will still have to sign for the goods you buy, and you may need to remind the shopkeeper of this if he/she offers you the keyboard to punch. Cards without the microchip (i.e. most UK-issued ones at the time of writing) will *not* operate unmanned petrol pumps marked "24/24", so never let the fuel tank run low at lunchtimes, late at night, or on Sundays.

MOTORING

You should always have the car's documents - original of log-book (plus letter of authorisation from the owner if the vehicle is not registered in your name), green card or insurance certificate - and your driving licence and passport in the vehicle when you are on the road. You can be stopped at any time for spot checks, and it is an offence to be without them. (Major roads are particularly heavily policed around 5pm each day and on Sunday afternoons.) On-the-spot fines are common; speeding penalties start at around 1,100F/167.64€ (approximately £110).

Drink/drive limits are actually lower than those operating in England, and random breath tests can be carried out. You should carry a warning triangle for use if your car breaks down, and a spare set of bulbs for your lights. (It is an offence to drive with any light out of order.)

Seat belts must be worn by all front- and rear-seat passengers. No child under 10 may travel in the front seat. Motorists are not allowed to stop on the open road without pulling right off it onto a verge or into a layby.

Although the old *priorité à droite* rule by which any vehicle arriving from your right-hand side had the right of way has faded, there can still be some instances when it applies - particularly in towns - so if you are not sure from the road signs and markings whether the priority is yours, it's wise to give way. Note that if a French driver flashes headlights at you he is not giving you the right of way - he is announcing that he is taking it for himself.

Speed limits
130kph/81mph on motorways (110kph/68mph in bad weather conditions).
110kph/68mph on dual carriageways (100kph/62mph in bad weather conditions).
90kph/56mph on other roads (80kph/50mph in bad weather conditions).
(Where visibility is reduced to 50 metres, limits on all open roads are 50kph/31mph.)
50kph/31mph in towns and villages, unless marked otherwise, from the moment you have passed the village's name-board, until you pass the crossed-out name on the way out - even if no speed limit is marked.
30kph/19mph in some town centres.

Parking
Meters do not need much explanation, except to say look closely at the times and days. A free period often covers protracted French lunchtimes in inland towns; while, at seaside resorts, even Sundays and public holidays still require payment. In streets and car parks the system is often one of pay-and-display (*horodateur* or *distributeur*) - again, look carefully to see exactly what hours and days require payment. The third, and oldest-established, method of parking regulation is by cardboard parking disc in areas designated as *zones bleues* by street signs or by painted blue marks on the road. If you do not already own a parking disc (*disque de contrôle de stationnement*), you can usually pick one up at the nearest tourist office for about 10F/1.52€.

NATURISM
Nudism is permitted on certain secluded beaches: Luzeronde on Noirmoutier island, south-east of L'Herbaudière; Les Lays, at La Barre-de-Monts; Merlin-Plage, at St-Jean; Petit Pont Jaunay, south of St-Gilles; Sauveterre, north of Les Sables; between Les Conches and La Terrière, near La Tranche; and Pointe d'Arçay beach at La Faute.

NEWSPAPERS
One-day-old English newspapers are available - though without their magazine sections - throughout the holiday season in good newsagents/bookshops like Maisons de la Presse. Local daily newspapers are *Ouest-France* (with the larger circulation) and *Vendée-Matin*. As well as international and national news, each carries invaluable pages of local snippets to interest the French-reading holidaymaker, such as cinema and exhibition listings, weather maps, details of local fêtes, scandals, accidents and other indispensable trivia. Both produce useful supplements in July and August listing events and places to visit - you can usually pick up free copies in tourist offices.

POST OFFICES
Main offices are open Monday to Friday 8am-7pm; Saturday 8am until noon. However, outside La Roche-sur-Yon and large cities like Nantes they close from noon until 2pm for lunch. You can send faxes (*télécopies*) from the larger post offices (and, indeed, from coin-operated machines in some supermarkets), and consult phone books or Minitel machines (computerised telephone directories). Letter-rate postage to the UK is the same as that within France, so you might want to buy a book of 10 stamps (*un carnet de timbres*) at post office or tobacconist for your postcards.

PUBLIC HOLIDAYS
Public holidays (*jours fériés*) are: 1 January, Easter Monday (*lundi de Pâques*), 1 May, 8 May (Armistice 1945, or VE Day), Ascension Day, Whit Monday (*lundi de Pentecôte*), 14 July (*Fête Nationale*), 15 August (*l'Assomption*), 1 November (*la Toussaint*), 11 November (Armistice 1918), and 25 December.

RIDING

There are many equestrian centres (*centres équestres*) in the region - enquire through local tourist offices. Style is often a bit more casual and "wild western" that the British are used to and not all establishments seem to provide hard hats (*bombes*), so it is as well to check this point first if you have not brought your own.

SAFETY

Safety norms are improving, though not always as stringently adhered to as they are in Britain. You will probably notice a scarcity of lifejackets, riding-hats and safety barriers, and that amusement park rides seem a bit more perilous than you are accustomed to.

SHOPPING

Markets usually operate mornings only, up to about noon. The lunch hour is sacrosanct in France, and most shops - apart from large supermarkets and hyper-markets - close between noon and 2pm. Consequently, the lie-a-bed holidaymaker will find the mornings extremely short for shopping but, in contrast, the afternoons deliciously long as shops generally stay open until around 7pm. Local food shops are usually open on Sunday mornings - as are some of the supermarkets in holiday areas - though almost everything is closed on Sunday afternoons. Factory shops, or *magasins d'usine*, are becoming more popular; some of the best are included in entries for the relevant towns and villages.

STAR-GAZING

If you are staying somewhere far from street-lighting, under night skies that are really dark, the planets and the constellations stand out wonderfully - especially under the wide skies of open marshland areas. In mid-August you may also spot shooting-stars.

TELEPHONING

As in the UK, telephone cabins come in two varieties - those that take cash and those that take cards - and *télécartes* can be purchased from post offices and tobacconists (*tabacs*). If you want to make a transfer-charge call (*une communication en PCV*) or to have somebody call you back in a call-box, look around first to find the number, which should be printed somewhere on the wall inside the cabin. (French numbers are quoted in pairs - 01 23 45 67 89 would be "*zéro-un, vingt-trois, quarante-cinq, soixante-sept, quatre-vingt-neuf*", so you need to practise that first before telling the operator.) To make a transfer-charge call to the UK you should dial 0800 99 0044 for an English-speaking operator.

To call within France, you simply dial the 10 figures of the number. To call a number in Britain direct, dial 00 44, followed by the British number you require but omitting its initial zero. Cheap-rate time for calls to England is Monday to Friday from 7pm to 8am, Saturdays from 2pm, Sundays and French public holidays all day.

Although all Vendée telephone subscribers' numbers fit into a single telephone directory, you have to know which town or village someone lives in before looking them up, as entries are listed under localities. This can be a problem if the person you are calling lives in an isolated country house or a small hamlet, as you need the name of the *commune* (the larger village under which it falls administratively) to be able to find the entry.

Mobile phones

If you are intending to use your mobile phone in France, check with your service provider whether you need to pay any extra for foreign use. Once in France, to call a French number you just dial the 10 figures; however, anyone dialling you from within France must treat yours as a foreign number, doing the 00 44 first and dropping the initial zero. If you want to dial a UK number (including UK-based mobiles), you must treat it as a foreign one, i.e. dial 00 44 followed by the UK number without the initial zero; anyone calling your mobile from the UK just dials your normal mobile number as if you were in the UK.

Emergency numbers:
The EC-wide number, covering all three emergency services   112
The individual French ones are:

Fire (*pompiers*)	18
Police (*police* in towns; *gendarmerie* in rural areas)	17
Ambulance (paramedics, known as *SAMU*)	15
Operator (*opérateur*)	13
Directory enquiries (*renseignements*)	12
(for overseas directory enquiries dial 00 33 12 + country identification number - i.e. 44 for UK)	

TENNIS
Most villages have a municipal tennis court or two, which can be booked by the hour, for a modest fee, a day or so in advance. Ask at tourist office or *mairie*.

TIPPING
Strictly speaking, service is now included in the bill for bars, hotels and restaurants, and indicated by the words *prix nets*. However, people often leave something extra - even if it is just the bits of loose change on the plate - if service was particularly good or if they are likely to return. It is customary to tip usherettes in a theatre about 10F if they show you to your seat; hairdressers and taxi-drivers about 10 per cent of the bill; and a few francs to a guide after an interesting tour.

WALKING
Long-distance walks
The IGN map 903 shows all the Grande-Randonnée (long-distance footpath) routes in France; *topo-guides* (special large-scale maps) describing each walk in detail are obtainable from good bookshops. Grande-Randonnée footpaths in the Vendée, marked with red-and-yellow signs, include GR36, GR364, GR Pays Entre Vie et Yon and GR Pays de la Côte de Lumière.
Local walks
You can, of course, walk shorter sections of the Grande-Randonnée routes. In addition, almost every village has a network of signposted footpaths leading to its main beauty spots and places of interest. Maps are usually given on large panels in village car parks, or may be obtained from local tourist offices or *mairies*.

WEATHER
The Vendée claims a summer sunshine record similar to that of the South of France - though obviously there can be exceptions. If you're staying in a house, you'll find it a great help to close curtains or shutters before the sun gets too strong; if you're in a tent or a mobile home, then the best advice when the temperature climbs is to head for somewhere air-conditioned - the latest museums, hypermarkets or shopping malls. Coolest museums to date are the Musée Milcendeau at Soullans, the Mémorial building at Les Lucs, the Chabotterie (exhibition area) at St-Sulpice-le-Verdon, and the Écomusée in the Puy-du-Fou château; or you can chill out at Les Flâneries - the large shopping centre on the north side of La Roche. The same advice holds good for rainy weather, too, when those in tents or caravans would be well advised to head inland to museums, junk shops, restaurants and shopping centres less overwhelmed with other dripping campers.

WILDLIFE

Among bird-life, hoopoes and buzzards are not uncommon (see also Birdwatching, page 10). Swallowtail butterflies are a far more usual sight than they are in Britain, and at twilight you may sense the occasional bat swooping overhead or, once darkness falls, spy glow-worms as pinpricks of bright neon in the hedgerows and grass verges. In certain weather conditions mosquitoes may be a problem (you can buy *citronelle* oil from chemists, to rub on the skin at night; supermarkets sell various plug-in insect repellants if you are in a house with power points); other insects are not particularly troublesome, though the wasp-like *frelons* (hornets) can give a nasty sting. As in Britain, the only poisonous snake is the *vipère* or adder, a shy creature that might bask on sunny heathland but will beat a rapid retreat if it senses you coming.

WINES

Besides the celebrated dry white Muscadet made from a Burgundy grape variety called Melon, and the even drier white Gros-Plant derived from the Folle-Blanche grape - both of which are grown on the northern limits of the *département* - the Vendée has four wine-growing areas producing a series of unpretentious reds, whites and rosés which have earned VDQS status (see below). These wines, produced at Brem-sur-Mer, Mareuil-sur-Lay, Vix, and Pissotte and marketed under the Fiefs Vendéens label, have a long history. Known to the Romans, they were quaffed by the 16th-century writer Rabelais and served at the table of Cardinal Richelieu when he was bishop of Luçon. There is a museum of wine-making techniques at Brem, and welcoming vineyards in each area at which you can taste the output. The small village of Rosnay, near Mareuil, has 44 producers among a population of just over 450 - a proportion said to be a record, even for France.

The main categories of wine quality, in descending order, are: AOC (*Appellation d'Origine Contrôlée*), bestowed on the region's three types of Muscadet - Muscadet de Sèvre-et-Maine, Muscadet des Coteaux de la Loire, and the standard Muscadet; VDQS (*Vin Délimité de Qualité Supérieure*), accorded to Gros-Plant and Fiefs Vendéens wines, and also to the reds, rosés and whites produced in the Coteaux d'Ancenis area alongside the Loire to the west of Nantes; *Vin de Pays*, denoting a rougher table wine; and *Vin de Table*, covering the rest.

The finest of the local wines is Muscadet de Sèvre-et-Maine (produced to the east of Nantes), particularly that which is bottled *sur lie* - left for longer in the barrel on the lees, or sediment, to acquire a near-sparkling quality. In the heart of the Muscadet area, south-east of Nantes, you will find museums of wine at Le Pallet and at La Haye-Fouassière.

Stronger local specialities include: Pineau des Charentes - a delicious fortified wine made from Charente grape-juice blended with cognac, that comes in white or rosé versions and is drunk, chilled, as an apéritif; Troussepinette, a red apéritif flavoured with hedgerow fruits; Kamok, a coffee-based liqueur made since 1812 in Luçon; and Séguin, a brandy-type drink, distilled at Machecoul from wines of the Loire.

A LITTLE FRENCH HISTORY

You will probably decide that the last thing you want on holiday is a history lesson. Nevertheless, there may come a moment when you want to understand more of the Vendée Wars, for example, or to work out which British historical periods coincided with which French ones. Here are some historical landmarks, with a few notes about architectural styles, plus a potted history of events in the Vendée.

Date	French history	Corresponding British history
7500-2500BC	Neolithic period (*dolmens, menhirs*).	Neolithic period.
4th century AD	Christianity reaches Poitou.	Christianity reaches Britain.
MIDDLE AGES		
AD486	Beginning of Merovingian period.	Anglo-Saxon.
751	Beginning of Carolingian period.	Saxon kingdoms.
987	Beginning of Capetian period.	Ethelred II (Saxon),
	(*Romanesque architecture,*	then Danes, Saxons
	10th-12th century - pilgrims.)	and Normans.
1152	Henri Plantagenêt (Henry II of	From 1154
	England) marries Eleanor of Aquitaine.	Henry II (Plantagenet).
	(*Gothic architecture,*	
	12th-15th centuries.)	
1189-1199		Richard Cœur-de-Lion.
1337-1453	Hundred Years War between	Edward III
	France and England.	(Plantagenet).
1431	Death of Joan of Arc.	Henry VI (Lancaster).
MODERN TIMES		
1515	Accession of François I (d 1547).	Henry VIII (Tudor).
	(*Renaissance architecture.*)	
1562-98	Wars of Religion in France -	Elizabeth I (Tudor).
	destruction of many churches.	
1589	Accession of Henri IV of France	Elizabeth I.
	(d 1610).	
	(*Classical architecture 1589-1789.*)	
1598	Edict of Nantes allowing Protestants	Elizabeth I.
	freedom to worship.	
1610	Accession of Louis XIII (d 1643)	James I (Stuart).
	(1622, king fights	
	Protestants near St-Gilles).	

Date	French history	Corresponding British history
1624-42	Richelieu prime minister (1627-28 siege of La Rochelle).	Charles I (Stuart).
1643	Louis XIV - "the Sun King" (d 1715).	Charles I.
1685	Revocation of Edict of Nantes by Louis XIV - 400,000 Huguenots (French Protestants) flee abroad, many to England.	James II (Stuart).
1774	Accession of Louis XVI.	George III (Hanover).
1789	**FRENCH REVOLUTION**	George III.
1792-1804	First Republic.	George III.
1793	Louis XVI guillotined 21 January.	George III.
1793-96	**WARS OF THE VENDÉE**	George III
1804-14	First Empire - Napoleon I (Bonaparte), exiled in 1814 to Elba. *(Delicate, Classical-style architecture and furniture, resembling Britain's Regency style.)*	George III.
1814-15	First Restoration - Louis XVIII.	George III.
1815	Napoleon returns for 100 days (April-June), then banished to St Helena.	George III.
	Louis de la Rochejaquelein leads royalist invasion against the emperor Napoleon.	George III.
1815	Second Restoration - Louis XVIII (d 1824).	
1824	Charles X (exiled 1830).	George IV (Hanover).
1830	Louis-Philippe I (abdicates 1848 in favour of his grandson, the Comte de Paris).	William IV (Hanover).
1832	The Duchesse de Berry, daughter-in-law of Charles X, attempts a rebellion in the Vendée to place her son on the French throne.	William IV.
1848-52	Second Republic.	Victoria (Hanover).
1852-70	Second Empire Napoleon III (Louis-Napoleon). *(Opulent architecture with wrought-iron features; heavy, Victorian-style furniture.)*	Victoria.
1870-1940	Third Republic.	Victoria.
1940-44	Occupation of France (including Vendée) by Germany.	George VI (Windsor).
1947-59	Fourth Republic.	George VI/ Elizabeth II (Windsor).
1959-date	Fifth Republic.	Elizabeth II.

GENERAL HISTORY RELEVANT TO THE VENDÉE

The region was inhabited from prehistoric times - evidence in the shape of menhirs and dolmens dating from 2500BC and earlier is scattered all around, particularly in the Avrillé and Le Bernard areas in the south. From the end of the 10th century AD, after the collapse of Charlemagne's empire, feudal castles began to appear in the Vendée at St-Mesmin, Ardelay, Noirmoutier, Tiffauges and Talmont. From the 11th century much of France, including the area now known as the Vendée, saw the passage of pilgrims making their way from northern countries towards the shrine of

St James the Elder at Santiago de Compostela, in north-west Spain. During the next 200 years abbeys, churches, convents, almshouses and hospitals sprang up along the most popular routes through western France to welcome and protect the 500,000 people who made the long journey, though in the Vendée these fine Romanesque buildings received heavy damage during the succession of wars over the following centuries.

The marriage, in 1152, of Eleanor of Aquitaine to Henri Plantagenêt, Duke of Normandy (who, two years later, became King Henry II of England) combined her dowry of western France with his existing lands in the north to bring half of France into English hands. Their son Richard the Lionheart - Richard I of England - enjoyed hunting, and often stayed in the region, notably at Talmont, where he provided funds for a number of buildings including the abbeys of Lieu-Dieu and St-Jean-d'Orbestier. More than a century later, after his accession to the throne of England in 1327, Edward III made a claim through his mother's line to the crown of France. The resulting Hundred Years War betwen the two countries - sustained by Richard II, Henry IV and Henry V - made much of northern and western France into a battleground until 1453 when the French succeeded in winning back everything but the town of Calais (which they recovered only in 1558).

Since the Vendée held a considerable number of influential Protestants (*les Réformés*) the 36-year-long Wars of Religion that broke out in 1562 between Catholics and Protestants raged fiercely throughout the region and had much the same effect on the Vendée's monasteries and other religious buildings, as had the Hundred Years War a century earlier. Eventually Henri IV, who had been brought up a Protestant and converted to Catholicism on his accession, granted freedom of worship to the Protestants in 1598, through the Edict of Nantes, and the conflict came to an end. (The Edict was revoked a century later by Louis XIV.) Cardinal Richelieu, one-time bishop of Luçon, and chief minister to Louis XIII between 1624 and 1642, saw the need to unite the whole of France - Catholic and Protestant - under one crown. To prevent strategic strongholds falling into Protestant hands, and to reduce the power of provincial dukes and princes, he ordered the destruction of many castles, including those of La Garnache, Les Essarts and Apremont.

THE REVOLUTION AND THE WARS OF THE VENDÉE

After the Storming of the Bastille in 1789 and the Declaration of the First Republic in 1792 the new régime in France was total. The nobility was abolished. Priests who refused to swear allegience to the Republican government (rather than to the king, who had been the previous head of the Church) were deported and replaced with "loyal" ones. The names of towns and villages were changed from any with religious overtones (St-Gilles-sur-Vie becoming Port-Fidèle, for example). Years, months, weeks and days were altered, with Year I starting on 22 September 1793, the 12 months (composed of three 10-day weeks) being renamed Vendémiaire, Frimaire, Brumaire..." etc, and the days themselves being re-baptised "Primidi, Duodi, Tridi, Quartidi ..." and so on. Even the then-familiar measurements of *pieds* and *pouces* (feet and inches) were replaced by the brand-new metric system.

After having endured the absolute power of the king, many of the urban middle-classes embraced the new philosophies and the idea of a world of greater justice that they believed lay ahead. The downtrodden labouring classes, too, welcomed the Declaration of the Rights of Man, and looked forward to the abolition of the taxes that they had to pay to the crown.

New ideas permeated only slowly to the Vendée - then known as Bas-Poitou - more than 350km from Paris. In this rural region there was less social inequality than elsewhere: aristocrats were not as rich, tenant farmers were less poor, and priests more revered in a religion that mixed orthodox Catholicism with local superstition.

The Vendean peasants were appalled to find that the Revolution removed their king (Louis XVI was executed in January 1793), forced on them the unpopular new priests loyal to the changed order, and called for the payment to the Republican government of even higher taxes than had been due under the monarchy. Worse, the confiscated goods of the old Church and deported clergy were thought to be lining the pockets of the *bourgeoisie*, or middle classes, who had engineered for themselves top administrative posts. Ignoring the new priests who had been assigned to their churches, the Vendeans continued to worship clandestinely, protected by armed look-outs, at open-air Masses said by rebellious, pre-Revolutionary clergy.

The culmination, the spark that ignited three years of horrific civil warfare, was the Republican government's decision in February 1793 to raise a 300,000-strong army for the defence of France's borders against threatened invasion by Germany and other neighbouring countries opposed to the overthrow of the French monarchy. The people of Bas-Poitou and neighbouring *départements* refused to submit to formal conscription so Republican soldiers were sent in to draw names at random. Riots ensued. In March the town of Machecoul saw the massacre of its Republican sympathisers; other villages followed suit.

But the event generally considered the start of the wars was the mass refusal of conscription on 11 March 1793 by the people of St-Florent-le-Vieil on the river Loire, midway between Nantes and Angers, in the *département* of Maine-et-Loire. The populace routed the "*Bleus*" ("Blues", or Republican troops, sometimes referred to as *patriots*), and captured their cannon. The villagers called upon a humble carter, Jacques Cathelineau, to lead them and the others who joined the cause. He and former gamekeeper Jean-Nicolas Stofflet were working-class generals; for the rest, the Vendean peasantry prevailed on trusted members of the local aristocracy to take command - François Athanase Charette de la Contrie, Louis de Lescure, Henri de la Rochejaquelein, the Duc d'Elbée - whose names have passed into local folklore.

After some spectacular Vendean victories in the early days at Bressuire, Thouars, Fontenay-le-Comte and Saumur, and then at Angers in June 1793 the "*Blancs*" ("Whites" or royalist Vendeans, also sometimes referred to by their opponents as *brigands*) seemed invincible. Part of their success was due to the fact that they would disperse to their homes or hide in the countryside immediately after a battle, leaving no "army" for the Blues to seek out and destroy. (This autonomy also proved a problem - troops would often act on impulse, without awaiting orders.) However, the initially ill-prepared Republicans were soon reinforced by General Kléber's crack troops known as the "Mayençais" who had been fighting on the German front, and victory turned to defeat at Nantes (where Cathelineau was mortally wounded after four months as general). The Whites lost Cholet, where Lescure was severely wounded, and then, in search of hoped-for reinforcements from England (to which many of the French nobility had fled), the Vendean army made a seemingly-impossible dash north across the river Loire. Before his death - from wounds also sustained at Cholet - another leader, the Marquis de Bonchamps, earned his place in history by refusing to allow his Vendean forces to massacre their 4,000-5,000 Republican prisoners, and insisting they be turned free.

This exodus, known as the "Virée de Galerne" has, ever since, evoked a kind of Dunkirk spirit in the region. Harried by the Blues, on 18 October 1793 the Vendeans ferried between 60,000 and 100,000 men, women and children north across the wide and treacherous river - the wounded Lescure among them. Their aim was to capture a suitable port - Granville, on the Cherbourg peninsula, or St-Malo - ready to receive the expected English aid. During the epic journey the hungry, cold Vendeans marched some 200km north where they were joined by Breton guerrillas known as "Chouans" and, in November, laid siege unsuccessfully to Granville. After a fruitless wait for help from England (William Pitt eventually sent forces in 1795, who were cut down during an attempt to land on the Quiberon peninsula on the south coast of Brittany), the Vendeans set off back towards the Loire. At Le Mans, 10,000 of them were slain by the town's heavily-armed Republicans. Tens of thousands more died, either in combat or from sickness or hunger. In December 1793 a few thousand managed to re-cross the Loire; many others, prevented from doing the same, fled west where 6,000 fell victim to Republican troops in the forest of Savenay, west of Nantes; the few who escaped hid out in impenetrable countryside, or in the marsh-land around Guérande.

Determined that such insurrection should never happen again, the Republican General Turreau gave orders that *colonnes infernales* ("fiery columns" of troops) should lay waste every village and kill every remaining person in the *département* of Bas-Poitou - that would henceforth be renamed "Vendée". From early 1794 these death squads passed from village to village burning, pillaging and massacring. At Les Lucs-sur-Boulogne 563 people - women, children and old men - were shot as they knelt in church. At Les Sables-d'Olonne, blood from the guillotine ran thickly on to the town's golden sands; at Nantes even the 1½ minutes required for this method of execution proved too slow and General Carrier, in charge of the city, instituted a more efficient method by drowning boatloads of prisoners in the river Loire.

The few surviving Vendeans returned home to ruined houses, murdered families, and a reign of terror. Hidden among the gorse and bracken of the *bocage*, they continued a guerrilla warfare for many months. Charette and Stofflet signed peace treaties with the Republicans in 1795, though Charette continued to lead skirmishes and ambushes against the Blues until his capture at La Chabotterie in March 1796 and subsequent execution. (Stofflet had been taken, and shot, a few weeks earlier.)

Under a treaty drawn up by the Republican General Hoche in 1799, freedom of worship returned to France. Napoleon Bonaparte made supervision of the unruly region less difficult by transferring the capital from Fontenay-le-Comte to La

Roche-sur-Yon, in the geographical heart of the Vendée. Here, he created a new town of straight, broad avenues, allowing rapid deployment of troops to quell future uprisings.

Although, with Charette's death, the wars reached an end, some further attempts were made to rekindle them. During Napoleon's brief return to power in 1815, Louis de la Rochejaquelein (brother of Henri) carried out an unsuccessful invasion near Croix-de-Vie. Seventeen years later the Duchesse de Berry tried to seize the French throne for her son, the Duke of Bordeaux - grandson of Charles X.

Debate still rages as to whether the uprising that cost so many lives was truly spontaneous or was engineered by landowners and priests reluctant to lose their power and fortunes. Atrocities were, no doubt, perpetrated by both Vendean and Republican forces but, in the area where the memories live on, a certain amount of bias in the retelling of the stories is inevitable.

INTERESTING VENDÉE WAR SITES AND MUSEUMS

Logis de la Chabotterie. Country house where General Charette was captured and interrogated. Atmospheric 18th-century-style interior and garden; exhibition on Vendée themes; indoor, multi-media Charette trail (see page 109).

Les Lucs-sur-Boulogne. Scene of a terrible massacre (see above). Memorial chapel built on the site; modern Chemin de la Mémoire building; story told in stained-glass windows in main village church (see page 104).

Noirmoutier Castle. The island was won by the Republicans in 1794. Bullet-ridden chair on display in which injured Vendean general d'Elbée was shot on the square outside; also the painting of this scene, and other souvenirs (see page 38).

Mont des Alouettes. Sails of windmills on this ridge passed coded messages to Vendean guerrillas. Three mills remain, one restored to working order (see page 103).

Museum of Puy-du-Fou. Historical museum in ruined Renaissance château. Uprising is illustrated with a mini *son-et-lumière* show (see page 100).

Grasla Forest. Woodland where 2,500 Vendeans hid out in 1794. Reconstruction of encampment; video giving excellent explanation of Vendée Wars (see page 96).

Musée d'Art et d'Histoire, Cholet. Modern museum, with portraits of Vendean leaders, and a good English explanation of uprising (see page 98).

Panthéon de la Vendée. Cemetery where many combattants are buried (see page 102).

"Sur les Pas de Charette". A signposted route around 13 places associated with the Vendean general; leaflet from tourist offices and from the Logis de la Chabotterie.

For further reading:

IN ENGLISH:

La Vendée, by Anthony Trollope. Historical novel, based closely on the memoirs of Madame de la Rochejaquelein, which first appeared in 1850. It paints a vivid picture of the early part of the war and of some of its principal characters. (Penguin, 1993.)

Citizens, by Simon Schama. Highly readable history of the French Revolution, with a substantial section on the Wars of the Vendée. (Viking, 1989.)

IN FRENCH:

Blancs et Bleus dans la Vendée Déchirée, by Jean-Clément Martin. Pocket-sized, information-packed book, alive with evocative paintings and drawings. (Découvertes Gallimard, 1987.)

Plein Ciel sur les Châteaux de Vendée, by Joseph Rouillé. Aerial views and history of Vendean castles and their fates during the wars. (Ed. du Vieux Chouan, 1989.)

L'Accent de ma Mère, by Michel Ragon. Autobiography of a present-day writer and critic whose memories of his Vendean childhood are interwoven with accounts of the wars 150 years earlier. (Livre de Poche, Albin Michel, 1980.)

Les Mouchoirs Rouges de Cholet by Michel Ragon (see above). Historical novel about the Vendée Wars. (Livre de Poche, Albin Michel, 1984.)

RECENT TIMES

Vast areas of pine and *chêne vert* (holm oak) were planted from the mid-19th century to anchor the shifting sands along the coast around St-Jean-de-Monts and north of Les Sables-d'Olonne. The coming of the railways in the 1860s helped to develop tourism around the ports of Les Sables and Croix-de-Vie where you can still see some fine examples of Victorian-period seaside architecture. Railways also provided a means of escape for many of the inhabitants of marshland farms, leading to a rural exodus around the turn of the century as young people found more lucrative work in towns. From the late 18th until the mid-20th century there were coal-mining and glass-making industries at Faymoreau-les-Mines, north-east of Fontenay-le-Comte.

The brooding silhouette of the occasional blockhouse reminds you that for more than four years of World War II the Vendée was occupied by German forces, who fortified the coastline and denied access to many of the villages along it. A Commonwealth War Graves Commission sign on the wall of a country cemetery usually indicates that it contains the graves of an Allied aircrew shot down over the Vendée or - particularly around the Loire estuary - of some of the 3,000 people who drowned when the merchant ship *Lancastria* was sunk by enemy action in 1940 while evacuating Allied servicemen at the fall of France.

After tourism, the wealth of the *département* today is based on agriculture (beef and dairy cattle, pigs and poultry in the *bocage*, cereal-growing in the plain, sheep and cattle in the marshes, and early vegetables on the island of Noirmoutier), fishing (sardines, tuna, sole, langoustines, oysters and mussels), manufacture of clothes and shoes, boat-building (Jeanneau, and the world-famous Bénéteau yacht company), food-canning, and construction of agricultural machinery.

Typical architecture of the region includes *bourrines* - low thatched cottages with whitewashed, mud-built walls (remaining examples dotted about the Marais Breton, between La Barre-de-Monts and St-Hilaire-de-Riez); and *logis*, much grander, stone houses with tiled roofs, such as the Logis de la Chabotterie at St-Sulpice-le-Verdon.

FAMOUS AND INFAMOUS VENDEANS

Memorable names connected with the Vendée include *Gilles de Rais* (1404-40), companion-in-arms of Joan of Arc and notorious in legend as the murderous "Bluebeard"; *Pierre Garcie-Ferrande* (c1430-c1520), intrepid navigator from St-Gilles-sur-Vie, praised by King François I for his charting of Europe's coastline; *François Rabelais* (c1494-1553), Renaissance humorist, writer, monk, and father of good living, who spent time at Fontenay-le-Comte and Maillezais; *François Viète* (1540-1603), inventor of modern algebra, born at Fontenay-le-Comte; *Cardinal Richelieu* (1585-1642), prime minister to Louis XIII and bishop of Luçon from 1606 to 1622; *Nau l'Olonnois* (c1630-71), bloodthirsty pirate from Olonne-sur-Mer who was chopped up and eaten by cannibals; painter *Paul Baudry* (1824-86), commissioned to decorate the foyer of the Paris Opéra; statesman *Georges Clemenceau* (1841-1929) who drew up the Treaty of Versailles after World War I, born at Mouilleron-en-Pareds; artist *Benjamin Rabier* (1864-1939) of La Roche-sur-Yon, creator of the cheery logo for Vache-qui-Rit (Laughing Cow) cheese; distinguished soldier *Jean de Lattre de Tassigny* (1889-1952), born and buried at Mouilleron-en-Pareds; and a present-day hero, yachtsman *Philippe Jeantot* of Les Sables-d'Olonne, mastermind of the notorious Vendée-Globe sailing race.

1. CHALLANS, ST-GILLES-CROIX-DE-VIE AND THE ISLANDS

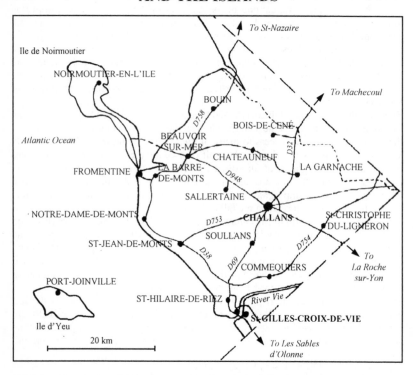

The busy Tuesday market in the marshland capital of Challans is a weekly highlight throughout the year. In summer the town steps back a hundred years for four extra, activity-packed traditional fair days. Just inland from the popular coastal resorts is the chequerboard landscape of the Marais Breton, a peaceful fenland crisscrossed with tamarisk-lined canals and dotted with small farmsteads as well as quaint little cottages known as *bourrines*. Rather more sophisticated 19th-century villas overlook the sea at Sion and at St-Gilles-Croix-de-Vie, while across the water, a couple of attractive islands wait to be explored: the rugged Ile d'Yeu may be reached by boat; the balmier island of Noirmoutier is accessible by bridge or, more romantically, by a 4km causeway across the bed of the sea - at low tide, of course.

LA BARRE-DE-MONTS   **i** tel: 02 51 68 51 83/fax: 02 51 93 83 26
Forest walks wind through the perfumed pine woods that hold the shifting sands in place around this village on the mainland side of the Noirmoutier bridge, 16km north-west of Challans. Look out around here for the last of the *bourrines*, the once-commonplace thatched houses that were homes for farm labourers, and for wooden *pêcheries* - spindly canalside cabins on stilts, with dangling square nets that are let down to catch fish as the tide rises.
Market: Saturday.
Centre de Découverte du Marais Breton-Vendéen. An ultra-modern entrance building welcomes you to this open-air museum 2km east of La Barre where methods of fenland agriculture are demonstrated in the context of a late-19th-century farm. To

take in the whole of the 12-hectare site requires a good couple of hours - and a fair amount of walking. After an introductory video with headset translation for English-speakers - a development soon to be extended to other areas of the farm - you follow paths to furnished reed-thatched *bourrines* (see above), and earth-and-straw-walled outbuildings full of poultry, spotted Bayeux pigs and old farm machinery, and read interesting descriptions of the region's salt industry alongside working salt-pans. There are occasional demonstrations of clog-making, basket-weaving and other crafts, and in one of the farthest buildings is a hide from which you can watch herons and other marshland birds. On summer Sundays you may catch other traditional local activities such as folk-dancing, punting in flat-bottomed craft known as *yoles* (a century ago, the only form of transport through the flooded marshland in winter), canal-vaulting (*saut à la ningle*) using punting poles, and ploughing with oxen or with sturdy Breton draught horses. There's not much shade, so take protective clothing in hot weather. ▲ *1 Feb-15 Nov, Tues-Sun 2-6pm (1 May-30 Sept, Tues-Sat 10am-noon & 2-6pm, Sun & public holidays 3-7pm; 1 July-31 Aug, Mon 10am-7pm, Tues 10am-9pm, Wed-Sat 10am-7pm, Sun & public holidays 3-7pm); Christmas holidays, Tues-Sun 2-5.30pm; closed 25 Dec & 1 Jan. Le Daviaud (tel: 02 51 68 57 03). 26F/3.96€, children 8F/1.22€.*

Pey de la Blet. You can eyeball passing birds from a wooden platform, level with the tops of the pine trees, 2km south of La Barre, which gives a magnificent view towards the Ile d'Yeu and across the marshes. Take the road towards Noirmoutier bridge and immediately go left at a roundabout, where Le Pey is signposted along a lane skirting the forest. After about 1km, stop opposite the Camping de la Bergère, cross the cycle track in the woods and you'll see a flight of 122 steps leading to the treetops. ●

Parcours sportif. At the same spot, look out for a sports trail, offering a series of solid wooden constructions to jump on or off or jog between, and rejoicing in the name of CRAPA (Circuit Rustique d'Activité Physique Aménagé, in case you were wondering). ●

BEAUVOIR-SUR-MER   **i tel: 02 51 68 71 13**

Despite its name, this appealing little town 16km north-west of Challans is no longer on the coast but stranded 3km inland. Large signs on the west side give times of low tide, when you can safely enjoy the unforgettable experience of driving your car across the Passage du Gois - the causeway 5km beyond Beauvoir that links the mainland with the island of Noirmoutier (see page 37). Take a moment to visit the 12th- to 14th-century church of St Philbert - indeed, if you come from Challans by car the D948 practically thrusts you in through the north door on a tight double bend. A statue of the saint, who founded the abbey at Noirmoutier, can be seen in a little square nearby.

Market: Thursday and Sunday.

Festival: Les Foulées du Gois (spectacular running event on the causeway, with 1,500 competitors; the best of them, in the final class, have to race the incoming tide), June. Foire aux Moules (mussel festival), August.

Specialities: Oysters. Clams. Mussels.

Chapel of Bourdevert. An enchanting little church stands at a country crossroads on the D59, 4km east of Beauvoir. Dating from the 12th or 13th century, it is said to have been built by two sailors in gratitude for surviving a shipwreck in the days when the sea still lapped against this spot. Push open the gnarled wooden door (the key may be obtained from a nearby address if locked) and step inside. Light streams through two simple arched windows, a model ship is suspended from the painted rafters, and on either side of the ornate altar hangs a collection of babies' shoes - placed there by parents who come and pray to the Virgin to guide their children's first steps. Mass is said at 3pm on the second Sunday of the month, and a pilgrimage takes place in early September. ●

Maison de l'Ane. You probably wouldn't believe there could be 25 different types of donkey! At this farm 1km west of Beauvoir you will see many of them on show, from the small, grey Provençal variety to the large, shaggy Baudet de Poitou - not forgetting the Egyptian white and the Berry black. You can also take donkey rides and, in summer, visit a working salt-pan nearby. ▲ *Easter-1 Nov, Tues-Sun 2-7pm (1 July-31 Aug, daily 10am-7.30pm). Route du Gois (tel: 02 51 93 85 70). 20F/3.04€, children 15F/2.29€; family (2+2) 60F/9.14€.*

Port du Bec. The rickety-looking wooden jetties either side of the canal leading to the sea have earned this picturesque little fishing hamlet, 5.5km north-west of Beauvoir, its nickname of "the Chinese port". Lobster-pots litter the quays, and brightly-painted boats lie alongside with coloured flags fluttering. High tide provides the scene of greatest activity as the fishermen return from their expeditions into Bourgneuf bay. Parallel to the vast dyke that holds the sea back from the neighbouring marshes is a road lined for 4km with oyster-producing enterprises, so it is not surprising to find that the port is part of the *Route de l'Huître*, or oyster route (leaflet from tourist offices). A Maison des Cultures Marines is planned, to explain the development of these molluscs; in the meantime if you want to sample some, drop in at lunchtime to the Mord'eau café and you can down a dozen for 25F/3.81€. ●

BOIS-DE-CÉNÉ

A few ancient houses dating from Renaissance times add to the attraction of this village 10km north of Challans. Standing in a leafy churchyard, the restored 14th-century church contains Romanesque pillars with interesting stone carvings on the top - including some of the Seven Deadly Sins (you may wish to cover the children's eyes for the saucier ones!).

L'Abbaye de l'Ile Chauvet. The site of this ancient abbey, just to the west of the village, was indeed once a small island. To reach it, take the Châteauneuf road, and then turn right across marshes drained by 12th-century monks, whose monasteries became prosperous from the resulting salt trade. A driveway leads through woods to a 19th-century mansion, behind which lie the romantic ruins of the church, founded by Benedictines in 1130, much damaged by the English in 1381, and finally abandoned following its destruction by the Republicans after the French Revolution. The guided tour leads through a handsome Romanesque doorway to the roofless chancel. Part of the refectory building still stands, and a museum showing models of the landscape in earlier times has been arranged beneath the magnificent oak beams of the former dormitory on the first floor. ✳ *1 July-mid Sept, Sun-Fri 2-6pm. Ile Chauvet (tel: 02 51 68 13 19). 25F/3.81€, children under 10 free.*

PINTA: la Route du Sel. This organisation - the intials stand for Pistes Nouvelles et Traces Anciennes (new trails along old routes) - offers some entrancing ways to discover the wide-open spaces of the marshes, using ancient salt routes. You can take guided trips from the well-signposted PINTA farm in the heart of the Ile Chauvet marshland (to the left of the abbey driveway - see above) or rent canoes independently from about 30F/4.57€ per person per hour. It can be scorching on a hot summer day, so take hats and suitable clothing. Guided tours by canoe include: magical dawn outings to see buzzards, lapwing, water rats and other wildlife (190F/28.96€ including breakfast); day-long trips along the salt routes (255F/38.86€ per person including picnic lunch); and late afternoon journeys enabling you to view marshland fauna as dusk falls and enjoy a convivial evening meal (295F/44.96€ including dinner and wine). ✳ *Route du Sel farm, Ile Chauvet; booking through local tourist offices, or direct with PINTA (tel: 02 51 93 03 40).*

Observatoire. The small, thatched wooden observatory overlooking the marshland near Ile Chauvet Abbey has good explanatory panels in several languages describing the migrating species of bird that you might see nearby. Just a field away is a platform installed to encourage storks to nest. If you've brought binoculars, you might catch a glimpse of them during spring or summer. ● *Signposted off D28 Châteauneuf road.*

BOUIN

Oysters reign today as the most important product of this pretty village (once an island), 20km north-west of Challans, full of ancient houses, low-built cottages and narrow lanes. However, Bouin originally made its fortune from salt-making - in the 15th century 80 per cent of that used in London came from the area. The riches from this precious commodity endowed the impressive church with three handsome altarpieces; in July and August you can take a guided tour up the tower for a panoramic view across the oyster beds, the Bay of Bourgneuf, and the 14km of dykes that protect the village from the sea. The oyster fishermen work at the nearby Port du Bec (see page 32), Port des Champs and Port des Brochets - the leaflet *La Route de l'Huître*, available from tourist offices, tells you where you can taste their produce.
Market: Saturday.
Festival: Les Gobeurs d'Huîtres (oyster-eating festival - competitors have to swallow three dozen in the shortest possible time), August.
Antiques: La Madeleine. *Sat, Sun & school holiday periods 10am-7pm (1 June-30 Sept daily 10am-7pm). Route de Nantes (tel: 02 51 49 08 99).*
Specialities: Oysters.
Champ des Fusillés. A sombre monument on the D21, some 2km south-east of Bouin, marks the place where 33 of the inhabitants looked their last across the marshland one January day in 1794, before being shot by Republicans. ●
Port la Roche. This picturesque spot at the junction of the river Falleron and the main *étier* (canal) is the hydraulic hub of the tranquil Machecoul marshes. North of the D59 at a point midway between Bouin and Machecoul, the hamlet has three locks that control the water levels. Reeds taller than the marshland cottages line the narrow canals, and the fields are still enclosed by rough slip-rails instead of gates, supported on their traditional stone posts. ●

CHALLANS   **i tel: 02 51 93 19 75/fax: 02 51 49 76 04**

As the "*capitale du canard*" this charming market town 16km from the coast was once to France what Aylesbury was to England, and you will find many duck-related dishes on local menus. Formerly reared in enormous numbers in the surrounding marshes, these birds have now been overtaken by free-range black chickens (*poulet noir*) and guinea-fowl (*pintade*). Challans is renowned for its terrific market-day on Tuesdays, when people come from all around to stock up on fresh fish, vegetables, cheese (particularly delicious goat's cheeses from a farm at nearby La Garnache) and other produce in the covered food hall, and to look over the hundreds of stalls outside, filling the streets and squares with local colour and offering clothes, farm equipment, gadgets and even live poultry. The town bristles with restaurants and smart shops - stroll along the pedestrianised Rue Gobin, or try home-made chocolates and pâtisseries from Billet on Place Aristide-Briand, alongside the market-hall.
The town's imposing 19th-century church - strangely, divorced from its bell-tower, which stands across the way in a leafy square where the previous church once stood - contains two magnificent rose windows and a *chemin de la croix*, or Stations of the Cross, composed of snowy-white life-sized statues.
You'll find more sculpture behind the *mairie*, where the twin Vendean artists Jan and Joel Martel (1896-1966) created a memorial to their friend, local painter Charles

Milcendeau (see page 44), full of aspects of marshland life. Another Martel sculpture decorates the façade of the cinema in Rue Carnot.

Market: Tuesday (throughout the town). Friday and Saturday (food hall only).

Specialities: Duck of Challans (often cooked in Muscadet). Free-range chicken. Black-domed *tourteau au fromage* (a sort of cheesecake). *Flan maraîchin* (pastry case filled with egg custard).

Brocante: Toutoccas, huge warehouse full of furniture and bric-à-brac. *Tues-Sat 9.30am-12.30pm & 2.30-7pm, Sun 3-7pm. 3km east of Challans on D948 La Roche-sur-Yon road (tel: 02 51 68 29 41).*

Festivals: Autrefois Challans (see below), July and August. Foire des Minées (agricultural and trade fair), September.

Autrefois Challans...la foire. On four occasions in July and August the clock is turned back, and more than 1,000 local people dress up in turn-of-the-(last)-century costume. The men sport blue denim smocks and heavy clogs or traditional marshland garb of black close-fitting trousers and short, matador-style jacket with jaunty small-brimmed hats; the women wear pretty lace *coiffes* or the face-shading white bonnets known as *quichenottes* (supposedly a corruption of the English "Kiss not" from the time of English occupation during the Hundred Years War) that were a common sight until about 20 years ago. Horse-drawn carts clatter through the streets, farmers trade ducks and chickens, children re-enact schoolroom scenes, and old folk spin, weave, strip kernels from corncobs and indulge in old-fashioned diversions like *l'aluette* (a boisterous card game) or *palets* (a riotous contest involving metal discs thrown at a board). ✳ *Two Thursdays in July and two Thursdays in August, 10am-7pm. Tel: 02 51 68 19 10. Free.*

Auberge Louis XIII. Just beyond the post office, on Rue Carnot, stands one of the oldest buildings in Challans, a 16th-century inn under whose ancient beams you can still take refreshment. Across the street, and slightly nearer the town centre, is another venerable house, the Maison Louis XIII, where the French king is said to have spent the night of 14 April 1622 before his victory over Protestant forces in the marshland of St-Hilaire-de-Riez. ●

CHATEAUNEUF

Hanging in the small church of this village 8km north of Challans, is one of the oldest bells in the Vendée, dating from 1487. Even more ancient is the *motte féodale*, or feudal mound, signposted at the side of the Bois-de-Céné road. Try climbing its steep sides to appreciate what a good vantage point it must have made. The surrounding meadows and marshland are a haven for a variety of birds including, in spring and summer, the occasional pair of storks.

Brocante: Occamat, an enormous building-reclamation yard selling all manner of things, from doorknobs to parts of factory assembly lines. *Mon, Tues, Thurs-Sat, 9am-noon & 2-6pm. Route des Ribottées, signposted off the D28 2km west of the village (tel: 02 51 49 10 20).*

Le Petit Moulin. The sails of this windmill, built in 1703, still provide the power to grind corn - though now essentially for animal feed. Monsieur Vrignaud, third-generation miller, explains the process animatedly (ask for an English information sheet to help you keep up) as he demonstrates the engaging of the wooden gears and adjusting of the slatted sails. Keep an eye on children among the clanking machinery and on the spiral stairs, which are potentially perilous even for a nimble adult. There's a *crêperie*, and a mill shop selling wheat, buckwheat and millet flour; a farm shop next door offers poultry, eggs, preserves, jams and the widely-enjoyed *mogettes*. ▲ *1 Mar-31 Oct, daily 2-7pm (1 July-31 Aug, daily 10am-noon & 2-7pm). Signposted from village centre (tel: 02 51 49 31 07). 16F/2.44€, children 8F/1.22€.*

COMMEQUIERS   **i tel: 02 51 55 33 66**

The bustling village on the edge of the *bocage*, 9km south-east of Challans was a centre of considerable feudal power until the end of the Middle Ages, as testified by the remains of its imposing castle. Have a look inside the village church for some colourful modern stained glass and for an interesting baptismal font, set in the centre of a sunken seating area.

Market: Wednesday and Saturday.

Festivals: Fête Médiévale (medieval day) around castle, August.

Château. The eight handsome - though crumbling - round towers of the stone castle lying off the D754, north of the village, give these ancient ruins the appearance of the best kind of sandcastle. Take a wooden footbridge across the water-filled moat to explore the inner secrets of a fortress that was demolished in 1628 on orders from Cardinal Richelieu. ●

Vélo-Rail. With two people to do the pedalling and a couple of others travelling on a deck-chair arrangement in between them, an afternoon on one of these flat-bed wagons, known as *draisines*, that run on a stretch of disused railway line makes a brilliant outing. The 10km route takes in a viaduct over the river Vie and level-crossings across the D82 (be careful!). It's as well to take some food and drink as you'll need to keep up your strength - the wagons are heavy, though everyone joins forces to lift one off the rails when you meet another coming towards you. The weight of the wagon also means you need to allow extra braking distance if the track is wet. ▲ *Easter-mid June, Wed, Sat, Sun & public holidays 2-7pm; mid June-mid Sept, daily 10am-7pm; advance booking essential in summer. Tel: 02 51 54 79 99. From 100F/15.24€ per wagon for two hours (120F/3.04€ in July & Aug).*

Tannerie. The strong of stomach will be fascinated to follow the carefully-labelled self-guided trail laid out at Monsieur Bocquier's tannery, 1km south of the village, to show how he soaks, stirs, washes, mashes and cures hides to transform horrible-looking skins into fluffy rugs and other products. It's a bit of a smelly process, so queasier folk would be better advised just to browse around the shop for goatskin rugs and soft lambskin slippers - though even here you'll find some strange items made out of horses' hooves, ducks' feet and so on. ● *Mon-Sat 8am-noon & 2-7pm; closed public holidays. Route de St-Gilles (tel: 02 51 55 93 42). Free.*

Pierres-Folles. In a copse along the lane opposite the tannery (see above) is concealed one of the region's many neolithic monuments. Turn left at the edge of the wood and then take a footpath towards the interior for a short distance. In a clearing you come across the huge dolmen, a table-like structure - now partially collapsed - of giant stones, all the more mysterious and impressive for being hidden in this out-of-the-way spot. ●

FROMENTINE

Sprucely-kept village some 16km west of Challans, on the edge of La Barre-de-Monts, with a gloriously sandy beach set against the elegant backdrop of the Noirmoutier bridge and, to the south, wild, empty dunes gradually blending with a forest of pines.

In styles ranging from Art Deco to frankly fake Arabian, some unusual villas of the 1920s and 30s still line the promenade, though sadly others were sacrificed during the last war to make way for lookout posts and gun emplacements.

Ile d'Yeu trips. Fromentine is the departure point for excursions to the Ile d'Yeu, 25km off shore (see page 45); boats or fast *vedettes* convey foot-passengers across from around 135F/20.58€ for a day return. If you're hoping to park for the day while you visit the island, make sure you arrive in good time. Meters in the village are designed for short-term parking only, so it is essential to sort out a space in one of the long-stay garages (about 40F/6.10€ per day); the more distant ones offer a shuttle service to the boat. *Information on crossings from Compagnie Yeu-Continent (tel: 02 51 39 00 00).*

Route de l'Huître. Fromentine is the southernmost point of the Oyster Route - a link-up between producers of the prized molluscs between here and La Bernerie-en-Retz who give tours of their establishments and usually a chance to sample the precious shellfish, too. Brochures are available from most tourist offices, who will help you ring and book a time to visit.

LA GARNACHE

Large village 6km north-east of Challans, clustered around the ruins of its feudal castle (see below). In the church are some colourful Stations of the Cross in 19th-century mosaics, and a wooden figure of Christ carved in 1938 by Vendean sculptor Arthur Guéniot.

Market: Thursday.

Specialities: "Le Garnachoix" goat's cheese.

Château Féodal. Excellent guided tours (in English as well as French) of the ruined 13th-to-15th-century stronghold built by the lords of La Garnache, partially destroyed in 1622 at the behest of Louis XIII and further still under the Revolution, leaving just the 12th-century keep and two vertical slices of the castle's original round stone towers. Rooms in the keep contain medieval-style draperies, examples of weapons (which you can sometimes handle), a chilly provisions store, and a model of the château in its former glory. Outside, the ramparts and the remains of the defences conjure up more of the castle's history; elegant gardens have been planted in the former moat, and colourful birds flutter in an outdoor aviary. Atmospheric guided tours by candlelight on Wednesday evenings in July and August. ▲ *Mid June-mid Sept, Mon-Fri 10am-7pm, Sun 2.30-7pm (1 July-31 Aug, daily 10am-7pm; late-night, Wed in July 10.15-11pm, in Aug 9.30-11pm). Route de Nantes (tel: 02 51 35 03 05). 30F/4.57€, children 18F/2.74€; under-10s free.*

Musée Passé et Traditions. Located in a small, turn-of-the-century *borderie*, or farmworker's cottage, is a comprehensive and well-explained collection of furniture, farm implements and local costume (including *coiffes*, or lace head-dresses). ▲ *15 June-15 Sept, daily 2.30-7.30pm. La Borderie, Route de St-Christophe (tel: 02 51 68 12 81). 15F/2.29€, children free.*

ILE DE NOIRMOUTIER   **i** tel: 02 51 39 80 71/fax: 02 51 39 53 16

Barely 1km off the coast, this long, thin island 20km north-west of Challans is connected to the mainland by a toll bridge from Fromentine and, at low tide, by "Le Gois", a 4.5km causeway that is one of the wonders of France.

Thanks to its micro-climate, Noirmoutier produces the first yellow pompoms of mimosa in the dark depths of February, delectable early potatoes served at the smartest tables in France, and a tremendous harvest of seafood - particulary conger eel, sole and squid. The island's economy once depended to a great extent on salt production, and you can still see the rectangular drying-pans (especially north of the road from Noirmoutier-en-l'Ile to L'Epine) where sea water is allowed to evaporate, leaving crystals to be raked up into little white pyramids. A blue-signposted *Route de l'Ile* leads motorists and cyclists around the lanes and past low, whitewashed houses to such pretty villages as Le Vieil, La Blanche and Bois de la Chaise.

The colourful, animated port of L'Herbaudière on the north coast of the island is a centre for fishing and yachting. At Bois de la Chaise, a wooded area on the north-east coast where elegant turn-of-the-century villas line sandy tracks among forests of holm oaks, the air in February is heavy with the perfume of mimosa; the sheltered beach - distinctly Breton in atmosphere - is so poular in high summer that parking is impossible (better to go by bike or on foot). La Guérinière, on the south coast (now by-passed by the super-highway that connects the bridge with the island's capital), is an attractive village strung out along the old main road of the island and full of shops selling beach-balls, shrimping nets and other traditional holiday equipment; the late film director Jacques Démy (who made the 1963 film *Les Parapluies de Cherbourg*) owned one of the nearby windmills as a holiday home.

The island's capital is Noirmoutier-en-l'Ile, a trim, pretty place with smart shops and restaurants along its quayside and surrounding the stalwart 12th-century castle. The street on the south side of St Philbert's church leads you into the Banzeau district, one of the most attractive parts of town, its narrow lanes lined with whitewashed houses that were formerly homes of fishermen but are now chic retreats for Parisians. On the other side of the harbour channel you can walk along to the end of the track for the sad sight of a boat "graveyard", full of abandoned craft half sunk in the mud.

One word of warning: the island's shape and road system makes Noirmoutier town something of a traffic bottleneck. In July and August the number of vehicles attempting to enter it - especially when low tide has lured thousands of extra visitors across the causeway and along the fast dual-carriageway - can create impossible hold-ups on the town's main approach road. On such days, it is better to investigate the sleepy charms of Barbâtre on the south shore, the excellent museum of La Guérinière (see below) nearby, or to visit L'Epine, and Port du Morin to the north-west; if you are good enough at navigating the byways, you can skirt the west side of Noirmoutier town and explore the smart north-coast village of Le Vieil.

Markets: Monday at L'Herbaudière; Tuesday, Friday and Sunday at Noirmoutier-en-l'Ile; Thursday and Sunday at La Guérinière.

Festivals: Mimosa weekends, Bois de la Chaise, January/February. Festival de la Peinture (art festival), July. Foire aux Antiquaires (two-day antiques fair), July and August. Foire à la Brocante (flea market), July and August. Festival de Noirmoutier-en-l'Ile (open-air theatre performances in castle courtyard), August. Régates du Bois de la Chaise (vintage-yacht racing), August.

Specialities: Salt. Fish. Potatoes (especially the Bonnotte). The marshland plant *salicorne* (samphire). Crunchy "St Philbert" biscuits from Giraudet in Noirmoutier's pedestrianised Grande Rue.

Passage du Gois. A drive either to or from the island along this submersible roadway edged with bladderwrack and still glistening with seawater is an unforgettable experience - particularly on a moonlit night. Until 1971 the 4.5km causeway, passable just twice a day either side of low water, was the only access to Noirmoutier, except for a passenger ferry from Pornic. Its dog-leg route is studded with sturdy poles or platforms that provide windswept sanctuary for anyone caught out by the rising waters; if you return for a look at high tide you can see why they might be necessary!

Nature and tides are merciless, and you should treat this phenomenon with the greatest respect. Tide-tables (*horaires des marées*) are available from tourist offices in the area to indicate safe crossing times, which vary each day. Times are also published in local papers and shown on huge roadside panels around Beauvoir-sur-Mer and on the Noirmoutier side of the causeway, supplemented with flashing signals of warning once the tide begins rising.

Cross only within 60 minutes either side of low water (*basse mer*), and never park on the causeway itself, which is wide enough for just one lane of traffic in each direction - you'll probably notice the locals parking on the occasional hard area of sea-bed to take advantage of extra-low tides (indicated by the highest figures in the column of the tide-tables marked "*coëfficient*"), scrabbling in the extensive mudflats for cockles and other shellfish.

Allow plenty of time to cross at peak periods (summer Sunday afternoons, and throughout July and August); it can be a bit worrying to find yourself stuck in a traffic jam, beginning to fret about the tide. The handsome bridge from near Fromentine now provides alternative - if less exciting - road access. For the return to the mainland, follow signposts to the quaintly-termed "*continent*" - either *par le pont* (by bridge) or *par Le Gois* (by causeway). ●

Château of Noirmoutier-en-l'Ile. The imposing, dry-moated castle in the centre of the island's capital is visible from afar across the flat landscape. During its turbulent, 800-year history the building served as a prison for insurgents of the Paris Commune in 1871, as a centre for internees in World War I, as a victualling centre for the Germans during the World War II Occupation, and then held German prisoners after the Liberation. Steep stone steps lead to rooms displaying stuffed birds, navigational equipment, maritime maps, archaeological remains and local history - anyone of gory disposition will appreciate the bullet-ridden chair in which the Vendéen general the Duc d'Elbée was shot, in January 1794, by Republican troops in the elegant square outside the castle gates (also the subject of one of the paintings on view). On the top floor is a proudly-displayed but rather gaudy collection of lustre-ware from Jersey, the type of souvenir cherished by 18th- and 19th-century sailors and fishermen. ▲ *1 Feb-15 Nov, Wed-Mon 10am-12.30pm & 2.30-6pm (15 June-15 Sept, daily 10am-7pm). Place d'Armes (tel: 02 51 39 10 42). 22F/3.34€, children 13F/1.98€. Joint ticket with Naval Construction Museum (see below) 32F/4.87€ & 18F/2.74€.*

Église St-Philbert. Beneath the church that lies to the north of the castle and accessible from near the side of the main altar, is a beautiful 11th-century crypt that holds the empty tomb of St Philbert, who founded a monastery on the island in AD674. Because of repeated Viking invasions, the saint's remains were removed by his followers to St Philbert-de-Grand-Lieu (see page 123), and later to Tournus in Burgundy. Press the button for a taped explanation of the church's history, with musical accompaniment. ●

Naval Construction Museum. The different stages in the building of wooden boats are explained in a reconstructed 19th-century workshop, where the graceful curves of the ships' timbers echo those of the solid roof rafters above. ▲ *1 Apr-2 Nov, Tues-Sun 10am-12.30pm & 2.30-6pm (15 June-15 Sept, daily 10am-7pm). Rue de l'Ecluse, Noirmoutier-en-l'Ile (tel: 02 51 39 24 00). 20F/3.04€, children 10F/1.52€. Joint ticket with castle (see above).*

Sealand. All the names on the fishmonger's slab come to life in the huge tanks that line the walls of this excellent aquarium: turbots swim with elegant wave-like movements of their bodies, langoustes and crabs stalk haughtily across the gravel floor, small sharks cruise nonchalantly through the water, octopuses pulsate in the depths, the sinister *murène* (moray eel) lurks in rocky crevices, and sealions splash in a semi-open-air pool - you can go down steps to watch their underwater antics from behind 60mm-thick glass. A rather poor video purporting to tell you about the sea life concentrates mostly on describing how good the different species are to eat. Some jewel-coloured tropical fish are on view, with useful explanations for anyone who is contemplating keeping them at home. If you are thinking of this as a wet-weather outing in summer, be warned - you won't be the only ones! ▲ *7 Feb-14 Nov, daily 10am-12.30pm & 2-7pm (1 July-31 Aug, daily 10am-8pm). Rue de l'Ecluse, Noirmoutier-en-l'Ile (tel: 02 51 39 08 11). 45F/6.86€, children 30F/4.57€.*

Maison du Sel. Just beyond the aquarium is a huge tarred wooden shed, its characteristically sloping sides proclaiming it to be a *salorge*, or salt warehouse, in which you can learn about the harvesting of sea salt, formerly one of the island's main industries. Today, interest has been rekindled and local *sauniers*, or salt-makers, have increased production to more than 3,500 tonnes a year. A good video is on show (in French), plus various tools and a mountain of very salty crystalline salt. ✻ *1 July-mid Sept, daily 10am-12.30pm & 3.30-7pm. Rue de l'Ecluse, Noirmoutier-en-l'Ile (tel: 02 51 39 08 30). Admission charge.*

Océanile. Stylishly-designed aqua park on the southern outskirts of Noirmoutier town, its silhouette resembling a huge wrecked ship. It offers several different pools, indoors and out, including jacuzzi, chutes, wave machine and paddling pool. Some of the water features may be a bit dramatic for very small children, but bigger ones love it. It's best to take a picnic to eat on the lawns, as the queues for the café can be tedious. ▲ *Mid June-mid Sept, daily 10am-7pm. Noirmoutier-en-l'Ile (tel: 02 51 35 91 35). 85F/12.95€, children 64F/9.76€; half-day (from 3pm) 67F/10.21€ & 51F/ 7.77€.*

Musée des Traditions de l'Ile. A charming museum showing the islanders' activities and way of life linked to fishing, salt production, farming and the manufacture of linen at the turn of the century. Collections of tools are on display, and a series of rooms shows typical interiors of island homes. ▲ *Easter holidays, then 1 May-30 Sept, daily 2.30-5pm (1 July-31 Aug, daily 10am-7pm). Place de l'Église, La Guérinière (tel: 02 51 39 41 39). 20F/3.04€, children 10F/1.52€.*

Bird reserves. To see ducks, geese and small waders in winter, and plenty of avocets, egrets and redshanks in spring and summer, plus panoramic views across the salt-marshes, follow the jetty south-east from Noirmoutier town quay towards the Marais de Mullembourg and Fort Larron. Another good place for birdwatchers is the Polder de Sebastopol, just north of the causeway entrance. ● *Mon-Fri 9am-6pm (1 July-31 Aug, daily 9am-7pm). Fort Larron Visitor Centre (tel: 02 51 35 81 16). 30F/4.57€, children 20F/3.04€.*

Route de l'Ile. Some 40km of signposted lanes around the island's prettiest spots. Maps and cycle-hire details from the island's tourist offices - the main one is on the dual carriageway at Barbâtre, at the junction of the roads from bridge and causeway (tel: 02 51 39 80 71). ●

NOTRE-DAME-DE-MONTS **i tel: 02 51 58 84 97/fax: 02 51 58 15 56**
Seaside village 6km south of the Noirmoutier toll bridge and just north of the huge resort of St-Jean-de-Monts, with the finest-textured sand on the Vendée coast. Notre-Dame is firmly orientated towards "windy" sports: dinghy-sailing, windsurfing, speedsailing, sand-yachting, kite-flying and frisbee-throwing. In keeping with this theme, one of the two windmills in the village centre is to become a Jardin du Vent (garden of the wind), offering a stylish blend of information and entertainment controlled by the sea breezes.
Market: Sunday.
Festival: 48 Heures du Cerf-Volant (two-day kite festival), July.
Salle Panoramique. Choose a clear day to take the lift up the 70m *château d'eau*, or water tower, 3km east of the village on the D82, for a bird's-eye view of the marshes, the coast, the Ile d'Yeu and the island of Noirmoutier. Headphones give commentary in French, English, German - and the local dialect, or patois. Pack a map and binoculars, if you've got them. ▲ *1 Feb-31 Oct (& Nov half-term), Sun & public holidays 2-6pm (1 May-30 Sept, Tues-Sat 10am-noon & 2-6pm, Sun & public holidays 3-7pm; 1 July-31 Aug, Mon-Sat 10am-7pm, Sun 3-7pm). La Croix (tel: 02 51 58 86 09). 20F/3.04€, children 6F/0.91€.*
Maison de la Dune et de la Forêt. Inside this cheerily-painted building on the coastal cycleway, just north of the village centre, you can read (in French) about the history of the forest, planted in 1850 to fix the shifting dunes - a hurricane buried part of the original village in 1741 - and learn about its flora and fauna, from orchids to wild boar. ✻ *1 July-31 Aug, daily 10am-12.30pm & 7.30-9.30pm. Avenue de l'Abbé Thibaud (tel: 02 51 58 84 97).*
Pont d'Yeu. Not, alas, a bridge to the Ile d'Yeu, this natural phenomenon is just a rocky spit of land 50 metres wide and several kilometres long, heading in that direction. Lying to the south of Notre-Dame's main beach, it is uncovered only at the

lowest low tides. (If you have the current tidetables, look for the days with the highest figures in the *coëfficients* column.) Legend says that St Martin wanted to evangelise the people of the Ile d'Yeu but could find no boat to take him there. In exchange for the soul of the first Christian to use it, the Devil offered to build him a path across, and the saint accepted - on condition it was completed before cockcrow. Satan's crew set to work, plying the local cockerel with alcohol to buy extra time - but the confused bird crowed even earlier than usual, so the route was never finished.
● *A small signpost off the D38 indicates the lane leading to it.*

ST-CHRISTOPHE-DU-LIGNERON

A restored 17th-century castle - visited in 1828 by the Duchesse de Berry (see page 28), but now offering bed-&-breakfast to a more varied clientele - stands on the D178 on the edge of this village 9km south-east of Challans. Besides this landmark, St-Christophe has another outstanding feature: its enormous annual flea markets (see below) that draw *brocante*-hunters from far and wide.
Festivals: Fête des Battages (old-time harvest), July.
Brocante: Les Puces Ligneronnaises (see below), July and August.
Les Puces Ligneronnaises. This vast open-air flea market is held twice a year on the sports ground at the northern end of the village. Some 150 stalls offer many happy hours of treasure-hunting among chests of huge, monogrammed linen sheets, racks of old picture-postcards, and displays of furniture, glass and bric-à-brac. ✳ *Mid-July & mid-Aug, Sun 10am-5pm. Tel: 02 51 35 27 27. 2F, in aid of charity.*

ST-GILLES-CROIX-DE-VIE   **ℹ tel: 02 51 55 03 66/fax: 02 51 55 69 60**

A pair of attractive towns on opposite sides of the river Vie, with Croix-de-Vie on the north bank, where the railway line from Paris terminates at the buffers alongside both the fishing harbour and the main street. To the west of the level-crossing, some elegant 19th-century villas line the seafront near Boisvinet beach. Croix-de-Vie is renowned for sardines and anchovies, and for a large canning industry (trade name "Les Dieux") for these, and for other products like fish soup and tuna. Connoisseurs should look in local shops, or ask at the tourist office, for cans of *sardines millésimées* - vintage sardines, to be laid down and lovingly turned from time to time over the years so that the fish are evenly imbued with oil. The sea is also the background to the towns' other claim to fame as the headquarters of Bénéteau, one of the world's biggest manufacturers of mass-production yachts. Many of the company's products can be seen among the 800 craft moored in the Croix-de-Vie marina.
You can take a ferry from here for the 65-min crossing to the Ile d'Yeu (Garcie Ferrande, tel: 02 51 55 45 42); and the 45-min Navijet (tel: 02 51 54 15 15). Half-day and whole-day cruises are also possible on a *vieux gréement* (an old, sail-powered fishing boat), or sea-fishing trips on more conventional craft.
Across the river, at St Gilles-sur-Vie, stands an attractive old church (in the tower of which one of Napoleon's generals was killed in 1815, during the second Vendean uprising). A selection of fairground rides is in more or less permanent residence on the quayside; farther on is the Grande Plage, a lovely stretch of beach - choose your time carefully, though, as it can become impossibly crowded in high summer when the incoming tide compresses sunbathers onto an ever-narrower ribbon of sand. Some charming French domestic seaside architecture along the roads leading to the beach is a reminder of St-Gilles' heyday as a seaside resort in the 1860s. If you find parking round here a problem in July and August, you can also reach the quieter northern end of the Grande Plage by taking the *passeur*, a little ferry from the north side of the river, that plies across the harbour entrance from the quay just across the railway line from Croix-de-Vie's *mairie*, and deposits you a minute later a short walk from the emptier end of the beach.

Monuments to look out for in St-Gilles include the bust of local navigator Pierre Garcie-Ferrande (on the south side of the main bridge) and a war memorial by the Martel brothers in the form of a grieving Vendean woman, a short distance along Rue du Maréchal Leclerc, which runs off the quay.

Markets: Tuesday, Thursday and Sunday, St-Gilles-sur-Vie; Wednesday and Saturday, Croix-de-Vie.

Festivals: International jazz festival, Whitsuntide (May/June); Fête de la Mer (festival of the sea), July; Festival des Vins de Loire (Loire wine festival), July; Fête du Mouton (sheep festival) at Givrand, 3km south of St-Gilles, July; Fête du Port, August; Foire aux Oignons (two-day onion festival), August.

Specialities: Sardines, fresh or canned.

Brocante: Gilles Occase. *Daily 2.30-6.30pm (school holiday periods, daily 10am-noon & 2.30-6.30pm). Zone Industrielle on south side of the D6, just to the east of the St-Gilles bypass, behind Evinrude factory (tel: 02 51 55 83 37).*

Maison du Pêcheur. A tiny, whitewashed, fisherman's house in one of Croix-de-Vie's oldest streets, just across from the tourist office, is furnished with items typical of a Vendean interior in the 1920s. As the whole place measures only about 35 square metres, it doesn't take long to visit its two rooms and backyard; don't miss the intricately laundered *coiffes*, or starched head-dresses, and the sepia photographs of sail-powered sardine-fishing boats. ▲ *Easter & May holiday periods, then 1 June-15 Sept, Wed-Sat & Mon 2.30-6pm (1 July-31 Aug, Wed-Sat & Mon 10am-noon & 2.30-6.30pm). 22 Rue du Maroc, Croix-de-Vie (tel: 02 51 54 08 09). 10F/1.52€, children 5F/0.76€.*

Les P'tits Mousses. Children over nine, and parents, can have a great time manoeuvring miniature ferries, tugs, tankers and fishing boats on the quiet waters of the Jaunay river, a stone's throw from St Gilles' Grande Plage. Lifejackets provided. To drive unaccompanied, children must be aged at least 13. ▲ *Easter-mid Sept, Sat, Sun, public holidays & school holidays 10.30am-1pm & 2.30-7pm (1-30 June, daily 10.30am-1pm & 2.30-7pm; 1 July-31 Aug, daily 10.30am-1pm & 2.30-11pm). Port Miniature, Avenue de la Cour St-Laud, St-Gilles (tel: 06 61 16 08 59). 30F/4.57€ for 15 mins.*

Aquarium Marin. Intriguing collection of live fish and shellfish in a series of tanks, located on the promenade of the Grande Plage. All are local to these waters, so you get a scuba diver's view of turbot, squid, octopus, bass, and gigantic conger eel - creatures you would expect to see only motionless in the fishmonger's window - without getting your feet wet. Ask for descriptive sheet in English. ▲ *15 April-15 Oct, daily 2-6pm (15 June-15 Sept, daily 10am-6.30pm). Grande Plage, St-Gilles (tel: 02 51 55 56 95). 25F/3.81€, children 15F/2.29€.*

Nécropole Mérovingienne. Each summer in Givrand, 5km south-east of St-Gilles, the village council puts on display a small collection of jewellery and other items discovered during archaeological excavations in a graveyard dating from around AD500. In a basement area beneath the building is a subtly-lit group of coffins carved out of stone from quarries near Saumur, more than 150km away. ✳ *1 July-31 Aug, Mon 3-7pm; Tues-Sun 10am-noon & 3-7pm. Maison de la Cour, near church (tel: 02 51 55 13 31). Free.*

ST-HILAIRE-DE-RIEZ   **i tel: 02 51 54 31 97/fax: 02 51 55 27 13**

Well endowed with dunes, pine trees and a huge sandy beach, this little town 5km north of St-Gilles-Croix-de-Vie was one of the Vendée's earliest coastal resorts. Today, St-Hilaire embraces the holiday area of Merlin-Plage, the marshland village of Notre-Dame-de-Riez and the dramatically-sited clifftop resort of Sion-sur-l'Océan, and sees its population swell in summer to 150,000.

Look out for some attractive seaside villas dating from the 1880s, and the 17th-century church containing several religious paintings by well-known local artist Henry Simon (1910-87).

Markets: Monday morning and Wednesday and Saturday afternoons at Merlin-Plage (July and August only), 7km north-west. Tuesday and Friday at Sion, 2km west. Thursday and Sunday, St Hilaire-de-Riez. Sunday at Notre-Dame-de-Riez (mid June-mid September only), 5km north-east.

Festivals: Vintage car rally, Easter.

Brocante: Chez Pierrot. *Mon-Wed & Fri-Sat 2.30-6.30pm. On the D83 at Notre-Dame-de-Riez, 4km north-east of St-Hilaire (tel: 02 51 54 45 50).*

Corniche Vendéenne. As an antidote to the endless sandy beaches, the shoreline at Sion rises, 2km west of St-Hilaire centre, to provide the northernmost cliffs of the Vendée, and some breakaway rock-stacks known as the *Cinq Pineaux* (Five Pine Cones). In a bid to slow coastal erosion caused by wind, mountain-bikers and human feet, clifftop cycling is banned and gravel paths have been set out for walkers. The small beaches among the cliffs between Sion and Croix-de-Vie are crowded in summer but provide a series of sheltered coves to protect out-of-season visitors - and, above the aptly-named *Trou du Diable* (Devil's Hole), some dramatic effects of wind and water for those who brave the autumn gales. ●

Atlantic Toboggan. Only the bravest should embark on the Kamikaze water chute (*toboggan*, in French, means slide) at this family aqua-park, located 7km north-west of St-Hilaire. It has a total of five 15m water slides, plus pools, playgrounds and picnic-spots. ▲ *Late May-mid Sept, daily 10am-7pm. Les Becs, Merlin-Plage, on the D123 (tel: 02 51 58 05 37). 75F/11.43€, children 65F/9.91€, under-threes free; from 4pm, 50F/7.62€ for all.*

L'Isle aux Jeux. Cheerful family play park, with swimming pools, rowing boats, slides, giant chess, archery, trampolining, skittles, mini-golf and pony rides in a grassy, landscaped enclosure on the dual carriageway, just south of St-Hilaire's cemetery. ✳ *Late June-early Sept, daily 10.30am-8pm. 127 Avenue de l'Isle-de-Riez (tel: 02 51 54 41 40). 45F/6.86€ includes all activities, children 40F/6.10€.*

Bourrine du Bois-Juquaud. Snappily-entitled "Unité Agro-Pastorale du Bois-Juquaud", this pretty limewashed cottage and its outbuildings 4km north of St-Hilaire are thatched with reeds in local style and are the subjects of countless picture-postcards. A clock ticks softly in the traditionally-furnished living-room; outside, the primitive building materials and neat vegetable garden give an insight into the self-sufficient life of the marshland peasants. Good visitor centre, with changing exhibitions. ▲ *1 Feb-31 Oct (plus Nov & Christmas holiday periods), Sun & public holidays 2-6pm (1 May-30 Sept, Tues-Sat 10am-noon & 2-6pm, Sun & public holidays 3-7pm; 1 July-31 Aug, Mon-Sat 10am-7pm; Sun 3-7pm). Le Pissot (tel: 02 51 49 27 37). 14F/2.14€, children free.*

Louis de la Rochejaquelein Memorial. A simple stone cross in a cluster of trees at Les Mattes, 6km north-west of St-Hilaire off the D59, marks the place where the Vendean general Louis de la Rochejaquelein fell, rallying his troops, on 4 June 1815. Brother of the Vendean leader Henri de la Rochejaquelein (see page 26), he had landed from England a few days earlier and embarked on a short-lived attempt to revive the royalist cause and drive Napoleon's forces from the marshes. A thousand soldiers from each side faced one another on this sandy terrain, at that time the only practicable route between St-Gilles and Soullans. ●

Église de Notre-Dame-de-Riez. The church of this little village 4km north-east of St-Hilaire is proud of a gilded *ostensoir*, or monstrance, donated in 1622 by King Louis XIII after his victory nearby over the Protestants. Although the treasure itself is not on display, you can see it depicted in a painting by local artist Henry Simon. If you should pass this way in January, be sure to drop in for a look at the church's Vendean-style Christmas crib. ●

ST-JEAN-DE-MONTS   **i tel: 02 51 59 60 61/fax: 02 51 59 62 28**

Large, colourful objects - banana, fish, ball, house etc - erected on tall posts help families to keep their bearings on the huge sandy beach of this popular seaside resort, 17km west of Challans. It's not surprising to see that St-Jean calls itself a "Station Kid", since there is plenty going on for children. Teenagers scoot along the seafront on four-seater *quadricycles*, while younger children can enjoy sessions on some of the beach swings and slides, and pedal one of the little metal pony-carts on the beach or some more sophisticated vehicles at the Boobaloo circuit on Avenue de la Forêt.

Anyone looking to expend more energy will find sand-yachting at the northern end of the beach, plus golf (see below), tennis, riding and archery, and a heated seawater swimming pool at the resort's "thalassotherapy" (sea-water treatment) spa. Details of all these from the tourist office in the Palais des Congrès, where you will also find regular art exhibitions.

The 7km of sand and the modern esplanade are, of course, the resort's main attractions. However, the old fishing village, now half a mile inland, contains an attractively restored church with a 17th-century bell-tower, its pointed spire roofed with wooden tiles. Diagonally across from the church is a wonderful fish shop - though watch that no tiny fingers come too close to the lobsters' claws!

Markets: Wednesday and Saturday, near the church in the old village (daily in summer). Daily, Rue du Marché, near the beach (summer only).

Festival: Fête Maraîchine (marshland games, including cowpat-throwing and canal-jumping) at Le Perrier, 6km north-east, August.

Golf: Golf de St-Jean-de-Monts. On north-west side of town, an 18-hole course - nine holes among pine trees, nine alongside the sea (see page 15 for Vendée Golf Pass). *Avenue des Pays-de-la-Loire (tel: 02 51 58 82 73).*

Ferme des Pommettes. A great welcome for all the family at this marshland farm just north of the town, on the D82, where you are given supplies of barley to feed to a series of friendly animals - from rabbits to donkeys. Interesting 15-minute video about life on the farm (also in English), though the explicit scenes of birth, artificial insemination etc may need a bit of explanation! Also a nine-hole "swin-golf" course. ▲ *1 Apr-15 June, Sat, Sun, public holidays and school holidays 2-7pm; 16 June-30 Sept, daily 2-7pm (1 July-15 Sept, daily 10am-7pm). Le Vieux Cerne (tel: 02 51 59 02 26). 18F/2.74€, children 15F/2.29€.*

Promenade en Yole. Guided trip through the open marshland in a *yole*, a traditional flat-bottomed boat, 6km north-east of St-Jean. ✳ *1 July-31 Aug. Mon-Sat, departures from 2pm to 6pm. Meet at information point, Route de Challans, Le Perrier (tel: 06 86 06 01 52). 25F/3.81€, children 20F/3.04€, under-sixes free.*

SALLERTAINE   **i tel: 02 51 35 51 81**

A delightful village on what was once an island, overlooking the flat landscape of the Marais Breton, 8km west of Challans. Formerly a bustling centre to which farming families would travel by flat-bottomed boat on Sundays to attend Mass, Sallertaine now attracts artists and craftspeople in the summer months, when some of the older buildings are transformed into temporary shops. These sell everything from toys to weather-vanes, while the (permanent) village baker turns out tasty *flans maraichins* (egg custard in pastry cases) and brioches. Signposted walks into the countryside lead you in the footsteps of "Jean Nesmy", the fictional hero of a 19th-century novel, and you can also circumnavigate the "island" by canoe.

Festivals: Fête à la Bourrine à Rosalie (see below; traditional dancing, skills and crafts), 5km west of Sallertaine, 15 August.

Chêne Vert café. For an unusual experience, take a look at the taxidermy displays both in the bar and in one of the adjoining rooms of this village café. More bizarre items include a gigantic boar's head, a cat and mouse, a rat, and the bust of a cockerel

- the handiwork of the eccentric *patronne* (owner's wife), who has also planted up an attractive garden at the back (though don't venture in without ordering a drink!). ●

Vieille Église. A wonderful 12th-century church, saved in the nick of time from total destruction in 1915 by René Bazin (the writer whose 1899 novel *La Terre qui Meurt* conjures up for French-readers an unforgettable picture of the drift from the land and of the pressures of farming life in the marshes 100 years ago). Beneath the flaking whitewash you can just make out vestiges of some ancient frescoes, and where once the congregation sat is a series of tableaux showing showing aspects of marshland life. As the costumed figures are "retired" shop-window dummies, it does tend to suggest (falsely) that the local peasantry was composed entirely of doe-eyed young men and skinny, over-made-up damsels, but the setting more than makes up for this shortcoming. ▲ *Mid June-mid Sept, daily 2.30-7pm (1 July-31 Aug, daily 10.30am-12.30pm & 2.30-7pm). Tel: 02 51 35 51 81. Free.*

Randonnées PINTA. These one-hour guided canoe trips around the former island of Sallertaine make an excellent introduction to the Marais Breton (see page 32). ✳ *1 July-31 Aug, hourly. PINTA office (tel: 02 51 93 03 40). 75F/11.43€, children free.*

Moulin de Rairé. The miller takes visitors up rickety wooden staircases to visit three floors of his working windmill - built in 1560, 3km north-west of Sallertaine, and claimed to have been in continuous use since. The view across the marshes from the top-floor window, regularly interrupted by the wood-slatted sails creaking past, is breath-taking. Anybody with small children in tow will need to watch out for the flailing machinery and narrow, open stairs. English leaflets are available to clarify Monsieur Burgaud's enthusiastic explanations and demonstrations. Downstairs, organic bread flour is on sale, and in a barn nearby is an interesting display of photographs and milling equipment. ▲ *1 Feb-31 May, school holiday periods daily 2-6pm; 1 June-30 Sept, daily 2-6pm (1 July-31 Aug, daily 10am-noon & 2-6.30pm). Off the D103 St-Urbain road (tel: 02 51 35 51 82). 18F/2.74€, children 8F/1.22€.*

Bourrine à Rosalie. A reed-thatched, two-roomed cottage, inhabited until recently by the doughty old lady whose photograph hangs on the wall, nestles in the marshes 5km west of Sallertaine. The simple, whitewashed interior gives an (albeit slightly sanitised) image of the hard life in one of these isolated marshland farms, where beds needed long legs to stay above winter flood-waters. Neat labels explain the origins and purposes of items on display. Outside are an orchard, ducks and a donkey. ▲ *Easter-30 Sept, Sat, Sun & public holidays 3-7pm (15 June-15 Sept, daily 2.30-6.30pm; 1 July-31 Aug, daily 10.30am-12.30pm & 2-7pm). On C116, between Sallertaine and St-Jean-de-Monts (tel: 02 51 49 43 60). 10F/1.52€, children 5F/0.76€.*

SOULLANS   ℹ **tel: 02 51 35 28 68**

This large village on the frontier of the marshes and the hillier bocage, 6km south of Challans, was the birthplace of one of the Vendée's best-known artists, Charles Milcendeau, whose father kept a café on the market square.

Market: Friday.

Festivals: Foire à la Brocante (antique fair), April.

Musée Milcendeau-Jean Yole. Charming museum, created from two *bourrines*, or traditional whitewashed cottages, in the heart of the countryside 3km south of Soullans. It is devoted to two of the village's most celebrated inhabitants: the painter Charles Milcendeau (1872-1919), whose home this was, and his contemporary - a doctor and, later, writer and politician - Léopold Robert (1878-1956) who under the pseudonym "Jean Yole" published many books in praise of the Vendée and who is commemorated here by a small collection of photographs and objects.

In the first building, transformed into an airy, state-of-the-art gallery, hang dozens of portraits of Milcendeau's family and neighbours - exactly the sort of ruddy-cheeked country folk you see in the markets today - as well as some dramatic, wintry views of the scenes that surrounded his marshland home. (If you have driven across parched August pastures to reach the museum, you may feel he went a bit over the top in some of these, but February's rains can - and do - produce the same effect today.) Seen through cleverly-shaped windows, the landscapes outside are framed almost like those within. A good audio-visual presentation explains the artist's life and his travels in Spain, which influenced much of his other work (Soullans is twinned with Ledesma, the village near Salamanca that provided so much of his inspiration).

When you enter the painter's bedroom-cum-studio in the second house, you are guaranteed to gasp. In place of whitewash, Milcendeau covered the walls with stylised birds, cats and flowers in vivid blues and yellows, arranged stuffed pigeons at the windows and reshaped the doorways in Moorish style - all in an attempt to imbue his damp cottage with the sunshine and colour of his beloved Spain. ▲ *1 Feb-31 Oct (plus Nov & Christmas holiday periods), Sun & public holidays 2-6pm (1 May-30 Sept, Tues-Sat 10am-noon & 2-6pm, Sun 3-7pm; 1 July-31 Aug, daily 10am-7pm). Le Bois-Durand (tel: 02 51 35 03 84). 20F/3.04€, children 6F/0.91€.*

ILE D'YEU   **i tel: 02 51 58 32 58**

Time seems to have stood still on this picturesque island of 23sq km that lies an hour-and-a-half's boat-ride off the coast (45 minutes by hydrojet) to the west of St-Gilles-Croix-de-Vie. Few cars travel the gorse-lined lanes, and the island's houses, often topped with pretty weathervanes, seem bleached by the 4,500 hours of sun that beats down on them each year.

Various ports on the mainland offer trips to Port-Joinville, the island's capital - though, at a minimum of around 165F/9.91€ per adult for a day return (and 114F/17.37€ for a 5- to 17-year-old), it can be an expensive proposition for a family. You need to book ahead in the peak season. On arrival, it is a good idea to hire bicycles (at about 50F/7.62€ a day) to explore the island - perfectly feasible in a day. (It is not worth taking your own as the ferry companies charge more than that to transport each one.) If you contemplate a day exploring the island, consider buying sandwiches and drinks in Port-Joinville, or on the mainland before you set off, as there is a severe lack of places for snacks on the way.

The north-east side of the island is full of sheltered, sandy coves for swimming and picnicking. More dramatic features will be found on the rocky south coast: the 40-metre-high Grand Phare, or lighthouse, built in the 1950s between Port-Joinville and the aerodrome; the caves on the Sables Rouis beach; the ghostly ruins of a feudal fortress (the Vieux Château), due south of Port-Joinville; the pretty fishing harbour of Port de la Meule overlooked by the tiny, whitewashed chapel of Notre-Dame-de-Bonne-Nouvelle, to the east; a Toytown-sized harbour on the western edge of the sandy Plage des Vieilles; and, in the village of St-Sauveur at the centre of the island, an attractive Romanesque church. Among several neolithic monuments is an enormous, rat-shaped stone, the *pierre tremblante*, balanced above a cliff to the east of Port de la Meule that will move if pressed firmly in a particular spot.

In 1945 the 90-year-old Marshal Pétain, who headed the Vichy government during World War II, was incarcerated in the gloomy Pierre-Levée fort (see below) after his death sentence for treason was commuted to life imprisonment. He died six years later, and is buried in the island's cemetery.

Travel there by fast VIIV hydrojets from La Fosse (Noirmoutier) or Fromentine (tel: 02 51 39 00 00), from St-Gilles-Croix-de-Vie (tel: 02 51 54 15 15) or, shortly, from Les Sables-d'Olonne. Aeroplane service from Bouin and La Roche-sur-Yon (tel: 02 51 62 31 65); helicopter from Fromentine (Oya Hélicoptères, tel: 02 51 59 22 22).

Market: Daily at Port-Joinville. Daily (July and August only) at St-Sauveur.

Specialities: Patagos, or *palourdes* (clams), with cream sauce. Tuna. *Tarte aux pruneaux* (prune tart). *Min-Min* - prune-and-butter sweets.

Musée de la Pêche. Fascinating glimpse of the fishing industry on which the island's economy has depended for so long. An excellent 20-minute video - very visual, even if you don't understand much of the commentary - explains the rigours of the fishing trade; there are also displays of boatbuilder's tools and navigational equipment, plus maps of wrecks and models of different types of craft. ✳ *1 July-31 Aug, Mon-Fri 10am-12.30pm & 4-7pm. Abri du Marin, 7 Quai de la Chapelle, Port-Joinville (tel: 02 51 59 31 00). 20F/3.04€, children 12F/1.83€.*

Monument de la Norvège. A granite monument on the waterfront at Port-Joinville commemorates a terrible tragedy. In January 1917 the Ile d'Yeu lifeboat went to the aid of an open boat carrying seven survivors from a torpedoed Norwegian ship. Having picked up the starving sailors, the lifeboat crew found the tide against them. They anchored to wait for it to turn, but the rope broke and the helpless craft was blown north-west by freezing winds. After three days without food or water the boat reached the coast of Finistère, in Brittany, but five Norwegians and six of the 12 islanders had died of cold and hunger. ● *Quai de la Norvège.*

Fort de Pierre-Levée/La Citadelle. Head south or south-west from Port-Joinville and follow signposts uphill to this dismal fortress in which Marshal Pétain was held after World War II. A bridge leads over the dry moat into the huge courtyard. Pétain is buried in the island's cemetery a little farther east; his grave backs onto the roadside wall and faces in the opposite direction to all the others. ●

Musée Historial. Guided tours explaining the history of the Ile d'Yeu in the house where Marshal Pétain's wife lived during her husband's imprisonment. ✳ *1 July-31 Aug, daily 9am-noon & 2-6pm. Hotel des Voyageurs, Port-Joinville (tel: 02 51 58 36 88). 20F/3.04€, children 12F/1.83€.*

Vieux Château. The remains of the 14th-century fortress, 1km north-west of Port de la Meule, seem to grow from the rocks themselves. Built during the Hundred Years War, it changed hands several times between the French and the English. ● *Exterior only;* ✳ *Mid June-mid Sept, guided tours daily every half-hour 10am-5pm; 14F/2.14€, children 7F/1.07€. Tel: 02 51 59 45 45.*

2. LES SABLES-D'OLONNE, LA ROCHE-SUR-YON AND THE BAS-BOCAGE

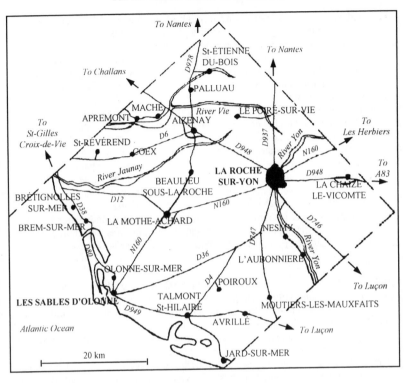

Richard the Lionheart was probably the first Briton to appreciate holidaying in this popular area - though he came for the hunting rather than the beaches. Endless golden sands, broken only by the cliffs at Château-d'Olonne and Jard, stretch along this part of the coastline, with the Vendée's smartest resort of Les Sables-d'Olonne providing bustle and entertainment even for out-of-season visitors. Among the inland villages, picturesque Apremont with its lake, castle and steep narrow streets is a summer favourite with families.

AIZENAY
i tel: 02 51 94 62 72

Situated on the edge of a 228-hectare forest 16km north-west of La Roche-sur-Yon, this pleasant little town is easily pinpointed on any map of France as it usually sits on the centre fold. The woodland, criss-crossed with signposted walks, is home to roe deer and wild boar and is a favourite hunting-ground for autumn mushroom-collectors. Those with a sweeter tooth should look, opposite the enormous early-20th-century church, for the Angélus pâtisserie that sells the most irresistible cakes, hand-made chocolates and home-made ice-cream.

Market: First and third Mondays of the month.
Festivals: Fête du Millet, August.
Specialities: Millet. Goat's cheese.
Crafts: Poterie Ismail et Marie-Claire. Easily visible by its old tree, hung with pots of all sizes. *Mon-Sat 9am-noon & 3-7pm. Route de La Roche (tel: 02 51 48 32 08).*

Factory shops: Comme Mode (men's clothing); *Wed-Sat 10am-12.30pm & 2-7pm; Route de Nantes (tel: 02 51 34 77 39).* Tuileries Gauvrit (hand-made terracotta bricks and tiles); *Mon-Sat 9am-noon & 2-6pm; La Gombretière, 2km south-east (tel: 02 51 94 60 90).*

Forest walks. Marked footpaths wind through glades inhabited by deer and squirrels, past a pond full of frogs and a children's play area. You may also come across a field of millet - connected in most people's minds with budgies, but which represents here an attempt to revive the taste for a cereal that once featured in the local diet. (No less an authority that Dr John Kellogg declared millet to be the only grain capable of sustaining human life, on its own.) ● *Access via D6 Le Poiré road and by Le Sentier du Souvenir (see below).*

Sentier du Souvenir. On the eastern fringe of the forest, a memorial commemorates five members of a US bomber crew who died when their Flying Fortress crashed into a field (gradually encroached on since by the woodland) in March 1944. Among the trees, modern aluminium shards have been artfully placed bearing on them the tale (in French) of the survivors - five in all, of whom two escaped to Spain. You can still see the crater where part of the fuselage hit the ground. ● *From the D948 La Roche-sur-Yon road, turn off north on to the D101A towards La Genétouze; car park is on left in 100m - sometimes with US and French flags flying.*

Stèle de la Brionnière. A granite monument beside a country lane, 6km south-west of Aizenay, marks the spot where a consignment of arms was parachuted to local Resistance workers on 11 August 1943. ● *Signposted from the D6 (St-Gilles-Croix-de-Vie road).*

APREMONT   **i tel: 02 51 55 70 54/fax: 02 51 55 42 41**

Extremely picturesque village, clinging to the rocky sides of the Vie valley 26km north-west of La Roche-sur-Yon, dominated by a tall water-tower and by the romantic remains of a Renaissance castle. Around Rue des Bretons, to the south of the river, a few imposing mansions line the narrow streets; on the north side, smaller houses stagger up a steep slope alongside the church.

A dam, or *barrage*, signposted just east of the bridge, has created a 170-hectare lake - the largest in the Vendée - that attracts to its sandy beach and shady banks lovers of fishing, swimming and water-sports from miles around - including a large number of British visitors. Just before the dam you can also hire boats and paddle down the placid river below the imposing castle towers; if you take a canoe, which can be dragged ashore to get around the occasional obstacle, you can ultimately reach the hamlet of Dolbeau, 4km to the west.

Festivals: Fête des Battages (threshing and old-time rural crafts), July.

Specialities: Traditionally-cured Jambon de Vendée (ham) by G. Petitgas, available in most supermarkets.

Château d'Apremont. Two towers and a chapel remain of the fine castle built in 1534 by Admiral Philippe Chabot de Brion, a childhood friend of François I who had accompanied the French king at the Field of the Cloth of Gold 14 years earlier. The young King Louis XIII is said to have slept in a first-floor room on 17 April 1622, after defeating the Protestants at Riez. Constructed on the site of an earlier 13th-century stronghold (parts of which still surround the outer courtyard), the castle later fell into disrepair and was partially demolished in 1733 - some of the stone being used to build the present-day Pirmil bridge at Nantes.

You can climb its east tower via a series of empty rooms, looking out over the increasingly small rooftops of Apremont, until you reach the magnificent tracery of wooden beams that support the pointed roof. Back at ground level, follow the signs to the 16th-century *voûte cavalière*, a steep indoor ramp hewn into the rock, that could take horsemen from the courtyard level to the water-meadow below. The other interesting feature, half-buried beneath a corner of the garden, is an ice-house, or *glacière*, where winter ice would have been stored to preserve food in hotter months, or even to create chilled desserts - it still provides some welcome cool air in the height of summer. A descriptive leaflet is available in English. The more recent buildings that surround the inner courtyard contain the *mairie*, the local fire station, and occasional art exhibitions. Sometimes, on summer nights, you may catch an open-air theatrical or other performance. ▲ *Late March-mid Sept, daily 2-6pm (1 June-31 Aug, daily 10.30am-6.30pm). Tel: 02 51 55 27 18. 20F/3.04€, children 15F/2.29€ (1 July-31 Aug, 25F/3.81€, children 20F/3.04€; includes the water tower - see below).*

Salle Panoramique. Let yourself be whisked up by lift up the 80m-high *château d'eau*, or water tower, for a stupendous view westward to the sea and islands and eastward towards plain and *haut-bocage*. Choose a clear day, and take binoculars and a map for an interesting exercise in orientation. ✳ *1 July-31 Aug, daily 10.30am-6.30pm. Route de Maché (tel: 02 51 55 27 18). Admission charge, see above.*

L'AUBONNIERE

For some unexpectedly dramatic scenery along the valley of the river Yon, follow signs to a "*gîte d'étape*" (hostel for hikers), leading east off the narrow lane between Chaillé-sous-les-Ormeaux and Le Champ-St-Père (some 14km south-east of La Roche-sur-Yon). At the end you reach a carefully renovated set of honey-coloured buildings that have been turned into accommodation and a small museum.

Écomusée de l'Aubonnière. Good explanations are given about the geology of this beautiful spot and about how the rapid current caused by the steep descent of the Yon between here and Luçon was harnessed to provide energy for tanning, paper-making and other industries. ● *Sat, Sun 2.30-5.30pm. Tel: 02 51 34 90 66. 10F/1.52€, children 8F/1.22€.*

Le Grand Rochereau. Wander down the path to a magical spot where the fast-flowing Yon tumbles over weirs and swirls around alder trees and granite boulders, and look for the ruins of little watermills (see above) beneath thick shrouds of ivy. Some parts of the bank are pretty steep, particularly if you walk to the right, so hold securely on to any small children. ●

Guinguette de Piquet. Amid rampant greenery, you can sip drinks or eat a simple barbecue meal at this quaint open-air bar high above the gurgling river Yon, and dance to live accordion music on summer weekends. Though it's not far from l'Aubonnière as the crow flies, to get there by road you have to back-track to Chaillé and turn south-east towards Rosnay, on the D50. After the pretty village of Le Tablier, turn right by the Maison de l'Abeille, and continue about 2km to the Piquet car park. ▲ *April-Oct (in good weather), Sat, Sun from 11am (1 June-30 Sept, daily from 11am; dancing Sat from 8.30pm; Sun from 4pm). Tel: 02 51 46 73 52.*

AVRILLÉ   **i tel: 02 51 22 30 70/fax: 02 51 22 31 31**

Its huge amount of prehistoric remains have earned the area around Avrillé, 23km east of Les Sables-d'Olonne, the nickname of "the Carnac of the Vendée" (after the megalith-rich site in Brittany). Among 23 dolmens and 100 menhirs scattered around the village, and that of nearby Le Bernard, you can see one of the largest standing-stones in France - the 7-metre-high Menhir du Camp de César in the garden behind the *mairie*.

The tourist office provides maps enabling you to find the rest, and organises guided visits to some sites; CAIRN (see below) also produces a free leaflet on the location of the megaliths.

Château de la Guignardière. Such a well-preserved Renaissance stately home is a rare sight in the Vendée. La Guignardière, about 1km west of the village, was built in

1555 by Jean Girard, who held an important post in the court of the French king Henri II. Having been occupied during the Wars of the Vendée by Republicans, the château escaped destruction in the post-Revolutionary conflicts. Guided tours (in English as well as French) take you from vaulted cellars to beamed attics, by way of dining-room, kitchens and a granite staircase pierced with occasional holes through which defenders could shoot at any enemy coming up. You can picnic in the castle's grounds, which contain no fewer than 14 menhirs of varying sizes among the trees; archaeologists have recently raised some of the fallen ones and are still trying to work out what these alignments signified. One of the outbuildings contains a small museum of prehistoric discoveries. ▲ *1 May-30 Sept, daily 2-6pm (1 June-31 Aug, daily 10am-6pm). Route de Talmont (tel: 02 51 22 33 06). 35F/5.34€ (grounds only, 19F/2.90€), students 27F/4.11€, children over 10 years 12F/1.83€.*

Fontaine St-Gré. Miraculous properties are ascribed to the holy spring trickling from a granite stone, signposted along a footpath off the D105 Longeville road about 2km south-west of Avrillé. A tranquil pond holds water that was collected on St Peter and St Paul's Day (29 June) and treasured for its effectiveness against asthma, heart disease, paralysis and rheumatism. ●

CAIRN. If you want to try lighting fires with two sticks, making jewellery from shells, polishing stone axes, making a little pottery, or weaving in the style of our ancestors, visit this archaeological neolithic research centre 3.5km south-west of Avrillé.

On July and August afternoons, visitors are given the opportunity to try one or two such crafts, or to help with erecting a standing-stone, constructing a cairn, or daubing mud on the walls of a neolithic-style thatched longhouse. With two exhibition rooms to take in first - fortunately one is usually enlivened by an archaeologist knapping flints inside a giant glass case - and the screening of a fairly plodding video, the tour does get off to a slightly heavy start. However, it comes to life outside with the hands-on experiences that are both fun and enlightening (though a few concessions to non-French speaking visitors would be welcome). ▲ *Easter-30 Sept, Sun-Fri 3-6pm (1 July-31 Aug, Mon-Fri 10am-1pm & 3-7pm; Sat, Sun 3-7pm; neolithic techniques demonstrated daily 3.30-6.30pm). St-Hilaire-la-Forêt (tel: 02 51 33 38 38). 36F/5.49€, students 26F/3.96€, children 12F/1.83€.*

Dolmen de la Frébouchère. Follow the signs into the countryside from the village of Le Bernard, 6km south-east of Avrillé, to the Vendée's largest prehistoric burial-chamber. In spite of the rather incongruous pink gravel that has been spread around to prettify the area, the huge dolmen - its top slab weighing 100 tonnes - remains a stirring sight. ●

BEAULIEU-SOUS-LA-ROCHE

This picturesque village, clustered around a tree-shaded square 19km west of La Roche-sur-Yon, has become a focus for cultural and arts-orientated events. High-quality exhibitions are mounted in the Maison des Arts (see below); across the road, the welcoming Café des Arts holds shows of contemporary art in an upstairs room; the village shops include a friendly antique dealer and, in the courtyard behind, an interesting antiquarian bookshop.

Festivals: Foere a Bialu (old-time street market), July; Foire à la Brocante (antiques fair), August; Marché de Noël (Christmas market), December.

Crafts: Marie-Christine Grangiens (glazed stoneware pottery). *Wed-Sat 3-7pm. La Cantardière, 3km north of the village (tel: 02 51 98 88 22).*

Maison des Arts. Interesting changing exhibitions of arts and handicrafts, and, in December, of some enchanting Christmas cribs. ● *During exhibitions: Daily 3-7pm. Place de l'Église (tel: 02 51 98 23 80). Admission charge varies.*

Landeronde. The squat little 11th-century church of this small village 4km south-east of Beaulieu is known for its exquisitely-decorated altar-pieces and painted wooden sculptures (look out for plague-sufferer St Roch, accompanied by the faithful dog that brought him food during his self-imposed isolation). ●

BREM-SUR-MER   ℹ tel: 02 51 90 92 33

Though now a kilometre from the sea, this pretty village 15km north of Les Sables-d'Olonne was formerly, as its name implies, a seaside port. Strange as it seems to think of salt-breezes wafting over vineyards, Brem is a centre of wine production. No fewer than 13 growers produce reds, whites and rosés - served, it is said, at the table of Cardinal Richelieu, and today marketed under the Fiefs Vendéens label.

If you're trying to find some seaside that's off the beaten track, try the miraculously unspoilt Havre de la Gachère, an area of sand dunes and beach about 3km south of Brem. After the bridge over the Auzance, take the side road to La Gachère village rather than the main D80 towards Les Sables, and turn right at Les Granges, following the sign to the Plage des Dunes.

Market: Tuesday and Friday (July and August only).

Specialities: Oysters. Fiefs Vendéens wines.

Festivals: Broc-à-Brem (brocante market), July.

Crafts: Christian and Chantal Bourcereau (earthenware, porcelain and raku pottery). *1 June-30 Sept, daily 9am-8pm. La Corde, 2km east of Brem, off D54 (tel: 02 51 90 50 77).*

Musée du Vin. A small wine museum on the south-east edge of the village tells the history of the local vineyards through displays of old tools and equipment, and offers tastings and sales of local wines. You can also read the curious tale of a discovery at nearby Brétignolles in 1908. On finding a large barrel washed up on the beach, the villagers bored a hole in it and tasted the contents - a delicious amber-coloured liquid. Keen to take it home, they began to load the barrel onto a cart when it fell and broke open - revealing a pickled orang-utan that had been en route for a museum! ▲ *Easter-14 June, Mon-Sat 2.30-7.30pm; 15 June-15 Sept, Mon-Sat 10am-12.30pm & 3-7pm. Moulin de Bellevue, Route des Sables-d'Olonne (tel: 02 51 90 56 28). Free.*

Parc d'Attractions des Dunes. Roundabouts and ball ponds for younger children and a large range of karts, bobsleighs and other rides for slightly older ones at this excellent little amusement park on the north-west side of Brem, on the D38. ▲ *Easter-15 Sept, Sat, Sun 2-8pm (15-30 June, daily 2-7pm; 1 July-31 Aug, daily 10.30am-7.30pm). Rue de l'Ecours (tel: 02 51 90 54 29). 38F/5.79€, children under four free.*

Église St-Nicolas-de-Brem. A few hundred metres north-west of Brem you come across a real delight, the remains of a Romanesque church built by monks from St Martin's monastery near Tours in 1020. Of its original three naves, just the central one survived destruction by Protestants during the Wars of Religion. The triangular carving above the west door is thought to show St Nicholas - he is surrounded by sculpted acrobats and other figures; on the south wall, two fire-breathing serpents intertwine above a small window. You can enter through the low north doorway to admire the simple, whitewashed interior where some 12th-century frescoes were revealed in the early 1980s beneath layers of paint: on the left, a crucifixion and on the right, a scene of three women at Christ's tomb after the Resurrection. Occasional concerts are held in the church. ●

Dolmens and menhirs. Neolithic man was busy raising stones and building tombs here 5,000 years ago. North-west of Brem and to the west of the roundabout on the D38 is a somewhat collapsed dolmen on the track that runs parallel to the coast, leading to La Normandelière beach. Other prehistoric stones are the Menhir de la Crulière (down a track to the north of the D54 about 2km east of Brem), and the Menhir de la Conche Verte (which you can find if you follow the GR364 footpath into the pine forest of Olonne, to the south of Brem). ●

BRÉTIGNOLLES-SUR-MER   **i tel: 02 51 90 12 78/fax: 02 51 22 40 72**

A cheerful seaside atmosphere pervades this village 19km north-west of Les Sables, with a bazaar selling buckets, spades, bodyboards and other holiday paraphernalia. The beach really has something for everyone: as well as being sandy enough for digging and sunbathing, it is covered with interesting-shaped pebbles and, at low tide, offers good rockpools. There is also an enjoyable crazy golf along Avenue de la Plage. Surfers often find good waves at La Sauzaie, to the north; to the south, at La Normandelière, is a beach with seaside bars and a sailing school, plus rocks at low tide and a shallow inland seawater pool where small swimmers and sailors can safely try new skills.

Market: Thursday and Sunday.

Labyrinthe. An amazing maze, in a field of - what else? - maize, on the D38 just south of Brétignolles. Layouts change each year, sometimes taking the form of a treasure hunt, with clues in English and French. Wandering among the dead-ends and the thick "walls" of vegetation hearing voices of other, unseen visitors makes for a strangely disorientating experience. ▲ *Mid July-31 Aug, daily 1-7pm; 1 Sept-31 Oct, Sun 1-7pm. Tel: 06 68 41 67 99. 25F/3.81€, children 20F/3.04€.*

Église de la Chaize-Giraud. Although the interior of this Romanesque church 5km north-east of Brétignolles has been heavily restored after damage during the Revolution, it retains much of its original atmosphere. The west façade is all that remains of the 12th-century construction; you can make out, on the right, the Adoration of the Kings and, on the left, Gabriel making his momentous announcement to the Virgin Mary. Some delightfully-carved stone faces adorn the roof-line and the imposing doorway. ●

LA CHAIZE-LE-VICOMTE

It's worth turning off the D948 to explore the back streets and rural lanes of this pleasant village 8.5km east of La Roche-sur-Yon. Don't miss the Vendée's largest

Romanesque church, an austere building with decorated columns inside, and, above the *mairie*, an amazing collection of taxidermy (see below).
Market: Third Tuesday of the month.
Festivals: Fête des Chasseurs (game fair), August.
Musée Ornithologique Charles Payraudeau. Hundreds of stuffed birds, left to the town by a 19th-century naturalist. Restored, perky and impeccably displayed against a black background, they are neatly labelled and given coloured codes showing which can legally be shot! The museum is located on the first floor of the *mairie*, on the western fringe of the village. ● *Mon-Fri 9am-noon & 2-5pm. Mairie (tel: 02 51 05 70 21). 10F/1.52€, students 5F/0.76€, children free.*

COËX   i tel: 02 51 54 28 80

A busy, flower-filled village 25km west of La Roche-sur-Yon, renowned for its scented garden. Coëx - the locals pronouce the name "kwex" - lies at the far end of the Vélo-Rail line from Commequiers (see page 35), and on the cycleway that will shortly link La Roche-sur-Yon to the coast along the route of the old railway line.
Market: Saturday.
Festivals: Carnaval de mi-Carême (mid-Lent carnival, with huge floats), March. Foire à la brocante (antiques fair), April. Village gaulois (a real Astérix atmosphere) at L'Aiguillon-sur-Vie, 6km south-west of Coëx, July. Foire aux Pinceaux (open-air painting day) at L'Aiguillon-sur-Vie, August. Fête de la Confiture (jam festival), September.
Golf: Golf des Fontenelles. A 6,185-metre course, 3km west of Coëx (see page 15 for Vendée Golf Pass). *Tel: 02 51 54 13 94.*
Les Olfacties. Behind the church is a large, unexpectedly colourful garden laid out with all kinds of plants - every one endowed with intense fragrance. The scents of geraniums and roses mingle with more unusual aromas of aniseed, chocolate and even tar; there are herb and woodland gardens, waterside walks, exotic plants, a breath-takingly colourful bank of wild flowers, and a delightful children's play area around a Japanese-style hut. Indoors are descriptions of perfume-making and a few hands-on activities for children, such as creating bird calls. ▲ *Early June-late Sept, daily 10.30am-7pm. Entrance behind church (tel: 02 51 55 53 41). 30F/4.57€, students 20F/3.04€, children 5F/0.76€.*
Lac du Jaunay. Picturesque 125-hectare lake 2km south of Coëx, that is strangely invisible from the surrounding road network. One of the prettiest places on its tree-lined shores is La Baudrière, about 5km south of Coëx, which has the atmosphere of a seaside fishing hamlet and where, in summer, you can rent canoes, pedaloes and mountain-bikes. A footpath has been created around the whole lake; you can pick up the more picturesque (and rather easier) half by setting off anticlockwise from La Baudrière and then returning there via the nearby road bridge that crosses the lake. ●

JARD-SUR-MER   i tel: 02 51 33 40 47/fax: 02 51 33 96 42

A charming seaside village 20km south-east of Les Sables-d'Olonne, with a pretty harbour providing moorings for up to 450 boats, plus three sandy beaches, and many attractive villas half hidden among pine woods. By the port stands the Moulin de Conchette. With the neighbouring Moulin de Bellevue, it is the last of nine windmills that ground corn in the area a century ago.
Among some delightful walks is the Circuit du Payré, starting just beyond the turning to the Abbey of Lieu-Dieu (see below), which leads along clifftops and past gnarled holm oaks to the Pointe du Payré.
Market: Monday.

Église Ste-Radegonde. Ancient Romanesque church dedicated to a one-time queen of France (see page 59). Fortified in the Middle Ages, and sacked by Protestants in 1568, it has a roof that has been much reworked, and a Renaissance-style chapel added in 1573 - look for the central pillar, famous for its "palm leaf" decoration. ✳ *Guided tours in summer (tel: 02 51 33 40 47).*

L'Abbaye de Lieu-Dieu. A couple of kilometres to the west of the village and towering over the unspoilt agricultural buildings around, stands an imposing abbey built more than 800 years ago by Richard Coeur-de-Lion, King of England and Duke of Aquitaine. After a long period of prosperity, it suffered greatly in the Hundred Years War and was further ruined by Protestants during the Wars of Religion. Though the interior is not currently open for visits, you can sneak a look from the farmyard in front at its unusual architecture, embellished by a couple of slate-roofed octagonal turrets. ●

Maison de Clemenceau. As soon as you see this enchanting low-built cottage on the sands, 2km south-east of Jard, you can understand why Georges Clemenceau (see pages 89 and 107) chose it for his retirement home. After his momentous work on the Treaty of Versailles that brought an end to World War I, the fiery politician withdrew here to write his memoirs from his study overlooking the sea. The interior is full of books, clothes, furniture and objects, as if the "Tiger" (as he was affectionately known) had just left it to go out for a stroll round his beloved garden with his friend the Impressionist painter Claude Monet or with visiting dignitaries like the young Hirohito. Monet gave him a hand with the garden design, though you wouldn't guess it now. A 20-minute video precedes the guided tour; English notes available. ● *Wed-Mon 10am-12.30pm & 2-5.30pm (1 Apr-30 Sept, daily 9.30am-7pm). St-Vincent-sur-Jard (tel: 02 51 33 40 32). 25F/3.81€, students 15F/2.29€, children under 12 free.*

MACHÉ

The casual passer-by would hardly suspect this small lakeside village off the D948, 24km north-west of La Roche-sur-Yon, to be one of the world's leading quail-rearing centres, yet its three local enterprises sell 10 million of the tiny table-ready birds each year to shops and restaurants as far away as Japan. (To try them at their best, drop into the friendly Fougerais restaurant, just off the D948 Challans road.) A couple of pleasant spots to make for are the bridge on Rue du Lac, where a Parc de Loisirs offers pedaloes, mini-golf and a shady children's playground, and the bottom of Rue du Moulin-à-Eau, where you can fish in the 170-hectare lake and walk - or, in places, scramble - along an occasionally precipitous waterside path.

Festivals: Fête de la Caille (quail festival), July. Fête du Lac (lakeside games), 15 August.

Specialities: Quail. Ostrich.

Crafts: Clogmaking (see below).

Sabotier. Until the arrival of rubber boots, each country man, woman and child clumped through three pairs of clogs a year. During the summer Monsieur Thénard, head of what is now a large souvenir-making enterprise, demonstrates how to turn log into clog with techniques he used until the 1960s. The workshop equipment is amazingly unprotected, so keep children's fingers (and your own) away from the spinning lathes and routers. ✳ *1 July-31 Aug, Wed 10.30am. Free, but shopping opportunity provided. Route d'Apremont (tel: 02 51 55 70 48).*

Eurotruche. A forward-looking local poultry farmer has moved into ostrich-breeding, so if you're keen on these birds (*autruches* in French) this is for you. After watching a 10-minute video on raising ostriches, you can wander around the enclosures to observe them and their near relatives, emus and rheas. There is also a collection of ducks, guineafowl, donkeys, goats and other farmyard animals, plus a shop selling decorated eggs and a restaurant (open lunchtime in July and August) where you can sample ostrich steaks. ▲ *Easter to 30 June, Sat, Sun & public holidays 2-6pm; 1 July-31 Aug daily 10am-7pm. La Logerie, on D948 2.5km to the north-west of the village (tel: 02 51 55 63 74). 30F/4.57€, children 15F/2.29€.*

LA MOTHE-ACHARD   **i tel: 02 51 05 90 49**

Large village midway between La Roche-sur-Yon and Les Sables-d'Olonne with a picturesque 1920s iron and glass market-hall. Among curiosities in the area are Château-Gaillard, an eccentrically-battlemented former presbytery in the village of Le Girouard, 6km south-east of La Mothe, and a couple of stone wolves that - appropriately - stand guard outside the *mairie* of Ste-Flaive-des-Loups (St Flavia of the Wolves), 5km to the east.

Market: Friday (except after the first Thursday of month, when a larger market is held).

Festival: Fête de la Citrouille (pumpkin festival), October.

Le Potager Extraordinaire. Every curcubitaceous plant (marrow, pumpkin, squash, gourd etc) you could imagine - more than 300 different types, including rare varieties, and the bizarrely-shaped Devil's Claws and Turban Squash - is grown here, 2km north of La Mothe. The area is laid out in a series of gardens on different themes - poisonous, flowering, organic, tropical and giant plants; during the 45-minute tours (leaflet available in English) staff give enthusiastic instructions on how to cook their favourite vegetables - you can buy whatever's in season, and try for yourself. ▲ *Mid July-31 Aug, daily 10.30am-12.30pm & 2.30-7pm; 1 Sept-mid Oct, Tues-Sun 10.30am-12.30pm & 2.30-7pm. Les Mares, on La Roche road (tel: 02 51 46 67 83). 20F/3.04€, children 10F/1.52€.*

Musée La Roue Tourne. Within the slightly unprepossessing exterior is an idiosyncratic collection - based initially on old perambulators and pushchairs, but extended to embrace early radio-sets and bikes, plus domestic paraphernalia in room-settings. British visitors will appreciate the upright, no-nonsense Raleigh bicycle and the graceful Silver Cross pram; other baby-transporters are elegant in wickerwork, low and chunky like a small 1940s' car, or streamlined in space-age plastic. ▲ *Easter to 31 Oct, Sun & public holidays 2-6pm (1 July-31 Aug, daily 2-6pm). Rue de la Gare (tel: 02 51 38 65 85). 15F/2.29€, children 5F/0.76€.*

Katsika. Like shaggy poodles, the frisky, curly-coated angora goats, skip around this farm 5km south of La Mothe. Vividly-coloured wool, sweaters and delectably fluffy rugs, plus goat's cheese and other produce, are for sale in the barn; photographs show the process of transforming fleece into knittable wool. Children will love stroking the cuddly kids from the milking herd. ▲ *1 Apr-15 Nov, Sun 3-7pm (1 July-31 Aug, daily 3-7pm). Le Moulin du Puy-Gaudin, off D21 Talmont road (tel: 02 51 46 61 79). 15F/2.29€, children 5F/0.76€.*

Mémoires du Pey. A fascinating collection of agricultural implements fills two large barns on a farm 8km south of La Mothe. The owner has amassed a huge number of tools - from dairy equipment and bread-making materials to a fork for fending off wolves and some examples of the vicious-looking weapons the Vendeans managed to conjure from their everyday tools during the 18th-century civil war. ▲ *1 June-30 Sept, daily 2-6pm. Le Puy Babin, signposted off the D87, 1km east of St-Mathurin (tel: 02 51 22 74 11). 15F/2.29€, children free.*

MOUTIERS-LES-MAUXFAITS   **i tel: 02 51 98 94 13**

The pride of this ancient village 21km south of La Roche-sur-Yon, on the road to La Tranche-sur-Mer, is its unusual 18th-century market hall, whose roman-tiled roof rests on an intricate structure of solid oak beams and 41 stalwart stone columns. A harmonious collection of old houses is clustered around the market alongside the well-preserved Romanesque church of St-Jacques, familiar to pilgrims en route to Santiago de Compostela. At the Lac du Graon, 5km north-east of Moutiers, summer visitors can sail, fish or rent boats.

Market: Friday.

Festival: Puces (flea market), August. Concours d'Equitation (national one-day riding event combining dressage, cross-country and showjumping) at Bois-Lambert, 2km south, August. Folklore and wild boar festival at St-Avaugourd-des-Landes, 5km north-west, August.

Arborétum. If you call ahead to make an appointment, you can visit this private, 2-hectare garden 5km north-west of Moutiers, crammed with an unbelievable number of trees and shrubs, including conifers, maples and many variegated plants. ▲ *1 Mar-1 Nov, by appointment only. St-Avaugourd-des-Landes (tel: 02 51 98 90 11). 15F/2.29€, children under nine, free.*

Pépinières Boutin & Fils. Take a present home for your garden from these vast nurseries 6km west of Moutiers. As well as exhibition gardens and enormous glasshouses full of olive trees and tender shrubs, you will find plenty of good-value plants in superb condition over a huge outdoor area. ● *Mon-Sat 8am-12.30pm & 2-7pm (1 Oct-20 Dec & 1 March-31 May, Mon-Sat 8am-12.30pm & 2-7pm, Sun & public holidays 9am-1pm). Belle-Fontaine, on D45 to west of St-Avaugourd-des-Landes (tel: 02 51 98 94 44). Free.*

NESMY

Since the 13th century, local clay deposits have sustained the pottery industry (see below) of this village 6km south of La Roche-sur-Yon. A couple of murals decorate some shop walls near the church - large-scale reproductions of Jean-François Millet's *The Angelus* and *The Gleaners*.

Festivals: Fête des Vieux Métiers (weaving, rope-making and 80 other old crafts) at Aubigny, 4km west, August. Fête des Vendanges (festival of new wine), October.

Golf:. Golf de la Domangère. An 18-hole course designed around a 15th-century mansion that is now a hotel and clubhouse. The seventh hole is the longest in France (see page 15 for Vendée Golf Pass). *On D85, 3km north of the village (tel: 02 51 07 60 15).*

Factory shop: Pottery (see below).

Vieille Poterie. Monsieur Charpentreau's family has been working this pottery since 1890. Inside the rickety buildings, you can look into the clay-spattered workshops that are a hive of industry on weekdays. A pleasantly chaotic shop sells the hand-turned and hand-painted products that range from pretty, flower-decorated plates, candlesticks, jugs and dishes to traditional 60-litre salt-glazed storage jars suitable for a lifetime's supply of gherkins. Descriptive leaflet available in English. ● *Shop: Mon-Sat 10am-noon & 2-6.30pm, Sun 2.30-6.30pm. Rue Georges-Clemenceau (tel: 02 51 07 62 57).*

Moulin de Rambourg. Restored watermill in a verdant spot beside a ford across the river Yon, signposted off the D85 some 2km north-east of Nesmy. The mill ceased commercial activity in 1981, but panels have been installed to explain how the machinery worked to produce the extremely fine flour for which it was known. Outside there are picnic places and waterside footpaths plus, in summer, canoe hire on the river. ✳ *1 July-31 Aug, Tues-Sun 10am-12.30pm & 2-6pm (tel: 02 51 07 62 64). 15F/2.29€, children free.*

OLONNE-SUR-MER   **i tel: 02 51 90 75 45**

In the area globally known as the Pays des Olonnes, you could be forgiven for finding the names of the villages misleading. Ile-d'Olonne, at the north-west tip of the group, is no longer an island; Olonne-sur-Mer, lying diagonally south-east, is now stranded 2km from the sea; and at Château-d'Olonne, farther south-east, there is no sign of a château. (Les Sables-d'Olonne, on the other hand, spreading out to the south and west of these three, has no shortage of *sable*.) Of the first three, Olonne-sur-Mer has the largest tourist office, so this entry will embrace the first three (for Les Sables, see page 61).

Festivals: Fête des Vieux Métiers (more than 100 old crafts demonstrated), Ile-d'Olonne, July. Scénographie (*son-et-lumière*) at Château de Pierre-Levée, Olonne, August (see below). Fête du vin nouveau (festival of new wine), Olonne, September.

Golf: Golf des Olonnes. Plenty of water features on this 6,127-metre course (see page 15 for Vendée Golf Pass). *2km east of Olonne, near the large roundabout on the N160 (tel: 02 51 33 16 16).*

Mémoire des Olonnes. Museum of local costume, customs and way of life in a converted school building near the village cemetery. It includes a reconstructed bar and kitchen setting, plus a good collection of agricultural and woodworking tools and some lovely local *coiffes*, or head-dresses. Guided tour (in French) by friendly local ladies. ▲ *15 June-15 Sept, Thurs-Sat 4-7pm (1 July-31 Aug, Mon-Sat 3-6.30pm). Rue de la Fontaine, 500m west of main crossroads (tel: 02 51 90 75 85). 10F/1.52€, children free.*

Château de Pierre-Levée. Although this lovely stone house modelled on the Trianon at Versailles is not generally open to the public, you can get a good view of it from the road that leads to the golf club, 2km east of Olonne. In August some 200 local residents take part in an excellent *son-et-lumière* presentation in the grounds, telling the history of the house and of the surrounding area. ✱ *Scénographie: usually five days in August. Just east of the N160 (booking tel: 02 51 90 75 45). Tickets approximately 80F/12.19€, children 40F/6.10€.*

Observatoire d'oiseaux. Wood-built birdwatching post 2km north of Olonne, overlooking the old salt marshes that are home to France's second-largest colony of avocets. Telescopes are provided and help is given in identifying the stilts and other wading birds that take up temporary residence in this wetland: huge migrating flocks pass by in March/April and August/September. In summer you can enjoy a bird's-eye view from the tower of Ile-d'Olonne church - easily recognisable from its witch's-hat-shaped spire - though try and avoid a time when the clock might strike! ▲ *Observatory: Easter-mid Sept, daily during school holiday periods 10am-5pm (1 July-31 Aug, daily 9am-7.30pm). Champclou, nr Ile-d'Olonne, signposted off D38 (tel: 02 51 33 12 97). 12F/1.83€, children 5F/0.76€.*

Musée de la Gare. A former railway station at Ile-d'Olonne, some 50m north-west of the church, is being transformed into a museum of local life, with displays of *coiffes*, or head-dresses, plus pictures and old tools relating to the farming, wine and salt-making industries. ▲ *Opens summer 2000. Chemin de la Ceinture, Ile-d'Olonne (tel: 02 51 33 11 72). Admission details not fixed at time of writing.*

Puits d'Enfer. About 2km south-east of Les Sables, and 3km south of Château-d'Olonne, the coastline turns to water-eroded cliffs and gulleys, where spray is driven up like geysers on stormy days, earning the site its name of "Hell's Well". (Be careful not to stray near the edge in fierce weather conditions.) This was the site of a gruesome discovery referred to as "*la malle sanglante*" in February 1949, when a bloodstained laundry basket containing the body of an elderly Parisian, murdered by his housekeeper, was found at the bottom of the cliff. ●

Abbaye St-Jean-d'Orbestier. The solid remnants of a 12th-century abbey, said to have been built by Richard the Lionheart, stand just back from the sea 3km south of Château-d'Olonne. Half-hidden by some institutional buildings, the partially-restored church now provides a venue for summer films and concerts (you might be lucky enough to see the "Musée du Sable" - more than 6,000 different samples of sand from all over the world amassed by children from a Château-d'Olonne school - which has been presenting short summer and autumn exhibitions here each year, while awaiting permanent premises). ✳ *1 July-31 Aug, guided tours of the abbey on Sat, Sun (tel: 02 51 23 88 02). Admission charges vary.*

PALLUAU
i tel: 02 51 98 60 24/fax: 02 51 98 60 83

An air of faded gentility pervades this village 22km north-west of La Roche-sur-Yon, its main street lined with *maisons bourgeoises*, or grand, slate-roofed houses. In the Middle Ages thousands of pilgrims from Britain and Scandinavia passed through en route to northern Spain and the shrine of St James the Elder at Santiago de Compostela (see page 24), having disembarked from boats that came over to collect cargoes of salt from centres on the coast. After much research on the routes, a lengthy "pilgrims' way" has been signposted with roadside bollards leading from Bois-de-Cené, 27km to the north-west, to Apremont, 13km to the south-west.

Relais St-Jacques de Compostelle. As well as housing the village tourist office, this former barn contains an exhibition about the investigations into the pilgrim routes. Names of fields, churches, hamlets and villages are vital clues - those containing James or Jacques, *abbaye* (abbey) or *maladrerie* (hospital) hint at sites of monastic settlements that sprung up between the 10th and 12th centuries to care for the physical and spiritual needs of pilgrims. ▲ *15 June-30 Sept, daily 10am-12.30pm & 3-6pm. Free.*

Château de Palluau. If you are intrigued by the naked brick chimneys among the trees opposite the *relais*, above, you can walk down a track on the other side of the road (follow it straight on, rather than bearing left at the fork) for a closer view of a once-proud medieval building, ruined in 1794 by the ravages of the Vendée Wars. Although some restoration work is planned, its stone walls are still in dangerous condition, so do not be tempted to enter. ●

LE POIRÉ-SUR-VIE
i tel: 02 51 31 61 38/fax: 02 51 31 89 12

The picturesque village perched on a rocky outcrop 13km north-west of La Roche-sur-Yon is clustered around a central market place overlooked by one or two fine Renaissance houses. Among artistic features are a wonderfully baroque altar-piece in the church and, across the square, a wall decorated with a huge painting of a wedding, by well-known contemporary "naïve" artist Raphaël Toussaint. Le Poiré is the hub of a large network of footpaths (maps available from the Le Poiré tourist office in the Moulin à Elise watermill. Any strange piles of vegetation you may see during your autumn rambles, stacked to dry around single poles in the fields, will be the ubiquitous *mogettes*, the small white haricot beans that appear on many menus - often accompanying local gammon. In July and August new season's beans are on sale still in their pods. Known as *demi-secs*, these can be cooked without the usual preliminary soaking.

Market: Thursday, Saturday, Sunday.

Festivals: Nuit de la Mogette (white bean festival), 14 August. Fête du Blé Noir (buckwheat festival), September.

Specialities: Mogettes (haricot beans).

Factory shop: Aux P'tites Puces (see below).

Moulin à Elise. The large wheel of this restored 19th-century watermill creaks and splashes around while the miller gives a 15-minute explanation of the process, with the aid of a complex diagram showing the to-ings and fro-ings the wheat undergoes before emerging as bags of flour. You can climb the stairs for a look at the hopper feeding the millstones with grain, and buy little bags of both ordinary and *blé noir* (buckwheat) flour in the shop below. Nearby are picnic tables, footpaths and a *crêperie*. ▲ *1 Apr-31 Oct, Sun & public holidays 3-7pm (1 July-31 Aug, Fri-Sun & public holidays 3-7pm). Tel: 02 51 31 61 38. 12F/1.83€, children free.*

Aux P'tites Puces. Not, strictly speaking, on the tourist circuit, but a visit to these two huge warehouses, selling every conceivable type of fabric by the *kilogram*, is an unmissable experience for anyone who can sew. If you have ever needed material to make mackintoshes, or those odd bits to repair dungaree or bra straps, this self-service Aladdin's cave is the answer. It also offers bedspreads, *bleus de travail* (blue workman's overalls), cast-iron firebacks and even wire-netting. Stock changes fast, as much of it is end-of-range stuff. ● *Thurs-Sat 9.30am-12.30pm & 2.30-6.45pm. Route d'Aizenay (tel: 02 51 06 49 50).*

Piscine Odelis. Swishing and splashing are very much to the fore in this entertaining indoor swimming-pool complex, with slides, swings and other delights. ● *Mon-Sat 3-6.30pm; Sun 9am-12.15pm. Rue du Petit-Bois (tel: 02 51 31 63 54). 20F/3.05€, children 15F/2.29€.*

Pierre des Farfadets. The neolithic "goblins' stone" - sometimes called also the Pierre de la Merlière - is located about 4km west of Le Poiré on a footpath known as the Sentier des Farfadets. This 12-tonne block of granite bears more than 300 mysterious signs, engraved on it by prehistoric or, some say, fairy hands - though others claim that they are the fingermarks of Gargantua, Rabelais' legendary giant (see page 85), who used it for playing marbles. ●

Chapelle Ste-Radégonde. In the depths of the countryside, 3km south of Le Poiré and signposted off the road north of the village of La Genétouze, stands a small chapel, rebuilt in 1863 on the site of an earlier one, dedicated to a 6th-century saint who was once a queen of France. According to legend, Radégonde was fleeing from her cruel husband when she came across a peasant sowing oats and besought him not to tell anybody that she had passed that way. He agreed, whereupon the seeds he had sown grew instantly, high enough to hide the fugitive. Her pursuing husband, witnessing this miracle, recognised the hand of God, and abandoned his chase. The door of the chapel is generally locked, but the setting is picturesquely wooded, and you can walk down a sunken lane to the stream that runs below. ●

POIROUX

Small village on the edge of a wooded valley, 20km east of Les Sables, notable for its trees, vines and woodland park - and for a derelict six-storey industrial mill that rather blights the centre.

La Folie de Finfarine. Signposted opposite the abandoned mill, and altogether easier on the eye, is the visitor centre of a forest park designed to give a feeling for woods and their flora and fauna. With true Gallic flair, the presentation is great: wild flowers are artfully framed through a window; a romantic video shows the changing seasons; blocks of wood have handles so you can test their relative weight; and litmus paper is ready to be dipped into various tree essences so you can sniff the difference. (Slightly confusingly, the French word *essence* in connection with trees means "species".) Outside, you can wander round and look at the different groups of trees; the paths are somewhat overgrown and the map is a bit sketchy, but it's a pleasantly shady place in hot weather, and there's a great children's playground - made of wood, of course. ▲ *1 April-31 Oct, Wed, Thurs, Sat, Sun 2-6pm (1 July-31 Aug, daily 11am-6.30pm). Tel: 02 51 96 22 50. 20F/3.04€, children 10F/1.52€.*

LA ROCHE-SUR-YON   **i tel: 02 51 36 00 85/fax: 02 51 47 46 57**

After the Wars of the Vendée, Napoleon Bonaparte wished to create a new capital for the unruly *département* (having decided that the existing one of Fontenay-le-Comte was too far away from the centre) and in 1804 picked on the small village of La Roche-sur-Yon. Demolishing much of the old part (though a corner of it can still be seen around Place de la Vieille Horloge), he created a "new town" of Classical-style buildings and die-straight streets around the central parade-ground, from which radiated avenues designed to give 20,000 soldiers instant access to any trouble-spots. Modestly, he called it "Napoléon". With the fluctuating status of France over the next 66 years the town's name was changed no fewer than seven times, reverting finally to that of the original village in 1870. ("Napoléon-Vendée" - the name the town bore under Napoléon III at the time the railway arrived in the 1860s - is still etched indelibly into the stone above one of the station platforms.)

The lack of interesting nooks and crannies that the grid layout imposed helped earn La Roche the unenviable description of "about the dullest town in France" from the 19th-century travel writer John Murray. However, efforts have been made since to liven up its image. Excellent art exhibitions are held in the Conseil Général's Hôtel du Département, or county hall. A witty fountain of oil drums now makes a splash in front of the theatre; the few old buildings around Place de la Vieille Horloge have been restored; and on summer weekends you can sip evening drinks at the café in the Jardin de la Mairie to the accompaniment of jazz and other entertainment.

Famous past residents include artist Paul Baudry (1824-86), who decorated the foyer of the Paris Opéra and was born in the street that now bears his name; and if you ever eat Vache-qui-Rit (Laughing Cow) cheese, you have probably stared at the work of another La Roche citizen, Benjamin Rabier (1864-1939) - known throughout France as the creator of Gédéon, a sort of Gallic Donald Duck, whose cartoon exploits gripped the nation in the 1920s and 30s.

There are two principal shopping areas: Rue Georges-Clemenceau and its offshoots; and the market area behind the large Classical-style church on Place Napoléon, with smart shops on Rue des Halles and other pedestrianised streets. Junk-shop fantatics should not miss Emmaüs (see below).

A signposted Circuit Napoléon leads you on a 2.5km perambulation around some of the most obvious sights. Horse-drawn carriage rides cover much the same route during the summer. Farther afield you can embark on some of the Sentiers de la Fragonnette (a series of walks around beauty spots on the town's perimeter), or the 70km GR circuit Entre Vie et Yon. Maps of all these are available from the La Roche tourist office on Rue Georges-Clemenceau, opposite the town's beautiful, art deco post office building.

A few words of warning to drivers: remember the very low (30kph) speed limit in the centre, and avoid the town's many bus lanes (particularly tricky around Place Napoléon). Also, if you should plunge into the network of small side roads, beware of the occasional *priorité à droite* - this means that traffic approaching you at a junction from your right-hand side may have right of way. So, unless there is a definite stop sign for them - give way!

Market: Tuesday, Thursday and Saturday (busiest day), market hall. Second Monday of the month, large, open-air market, Place Napoléon.

Brocante: Emmaüs (three floors filled with furniture, books and objects, part of a network of shops set up by Abbé Pierre, an elderly French priest, to sell donated goods and to be run by, and for the benefit of, down-and-outs); *Tues, Wed, Fri 2.30-6pm, Sat 9am-noon & 2.30-6pm; 34 Rue Paul Doumer, off Place Napoléon.* La Trocante (huge junk emporium just north of the town); *Mon & Wed-Sat 10am-noon & 2-7pm; Sun 2-7pm; Route de Nantes (tel: 02 51 08 83 61).*

Haras National. This stud - one of the largest in France - was founded by Napoleon in 1842 to breed horses for his army. Today its roomy boxes are home to around 65 stallions of various breeds - from draught horses to elegant riding horses, and from Connemara ponies to thoroughbred trotters. The guide on the hour-long tour of this impeccably-kept city farm explains how the animals are exercised, shod, and generally cared for - and lets you stroke a few, too. ▲ *1 July-31 Aug, Mon-Sat 10.30am-noon & 2.30-6pm (closed public holidays); 1-30 Sept, Mon-Fri guided tour 3pm. Boulevard des Etats-Unis (tel: 02 51 46 14 47). 25F/3.81€, children 15F/2.29€.*

Maison des Métiers. Attractively-restored 18th-century house in the heart of the old town. Upstairs and down, it is filled with high-quality products made by local craftspeople - textiles, baskets, lamps, furniture, pottery and leather goods, all for sale. ● *Tues-Thurs & Sat 9.15am-noon & 2.15-6.30pm, Fri 9.15am-6.30pm. Place de la Vieille Horloge (tel: 02 51 62 51 33). Free.*

Maison Renaissance. Across the square from the Maison des Métiers is an elegant Italianate house dating from 1566, which contains summer exhibitions on different aspects of local history. ✳ *1 July-31 Aug. Tues-Sat 2-6pm (closed on public holidays). Place de la Vieille Horloge (tel: 02 51 47 90 86). Admission charges vary.*

Les Flâneries. Large shopping mall 7km north of La Roche which, as well as providing retail therapy, offers a haven for holidaymakers in wet weather (for shelter) and on hot days (for its air-conditioning). Shops - mostly open at lunchtime - include a pet shop, DIY, electrical, clothes and furniture stores; there are also fast food outlets (including McDonalds) and is soon to be a multiplex cinema. ● *Mon-Sat 9am-7pm. Route de Nantes.*

Lac de Moulin-Papon. You'll need a good map in order to work your way to the edge of this 5km-long lake just north of La Roche. It's best to start exploring from the D37, which runs north towards the village of Dompierre-sur-Yon and parallel with the D937 Nantes road (turn east near McDonald's, then north towards Dompierre). You can cross the lake at Moulin-Neuf for a look at the rural scenery on the other side. Although no swimming is permitted, you can sail or fish, and there is a lengthy footpath that makes almost a complete circuit, with information panels giving details - even in Braille - of local flora. On the edge of Dompierre, beside a stream and away from the lake, is a pretty spot for picnics: turn west alongside the church and you'll find it by the newly-restored Chapelle de Margerie. ●

Abbaye des Fontenelles. The proud remains of a Romanesque abbey, built in 1210 and partially destroyed by the English during the 100 Years War, loom half-hidden among outbuildings and trees at a farm 3km west of La Roche. Inside is the tomb of Béatrice de Machecoul, an ogress reputed to have eaten the hearts of small children. After repenting, she did penance by walking 25km barefoot from Talmont on a route strewn with brambles. Today, the interior is accessible only to pigeons, but you are allowed to wander around the outside to glimpse the tracery of its vaulting through the high, glassless windows and study the grimacing, carved faces high up beneath the eaves. ● *Signposted to the north of the N160. Follow the lane for a couple of kilometres, park outside farm entrance and walk up the drive.*

LES SABLES-D'OLONNE   **i** tel: 02 51 96 85 85/fax: 02 51 96 85 71

By far the most ritzy seaside resort in the Vendée, Les Sables offers a vast, gently-shelving beach of ultra-manicured sand and, on the other side of the same spit of land, a busy fishing port lined with good restaurants, and narrow, often hilly, streets full of interesting shops. Among the town's quirkiest features is the series of shell murals created by the residents of a little street just behind the seafront promenade. Walk a little way north along Rue Travot, then take Rue d'Assas on the right. In front of you is a splendid representation of Neptune and, along the same street, other decorations of mussel, scallop and limpet shells.

Parking can be a problem - meters function relentlessly, even on Sundays and public holidays. Alternatives are to find a car park, make for one of the residential streets behind the eastern end of the beach, or drive around to La Chaume (see below) and then take the inexpensive little passenger ferry across the harbour mouth - cheaper still if you buy a book of 10 tickets (*un carnet de tickets pour le bac*) at the *tabac* opposite the gangway in La Chaume. The dazzling glass building on the Les Sables seafront houses the tourist office, and also a theatre, disco, restaurant and one of the town's two casinos. From about 8.30pm on summer evenings the whole beachfront promenade is full of lively street performers entertaining passers-by in front of the pavement cafés.

Shoppers will enjoy the pedestrianised streets to the east and north of the church, while small children would probably prefer the little roundabouts in Place de la Liberté, the gardens near the *hôtel de ville*, or town hall.

If you fancy a trip out to sea - for either a simple jaunt round the bay, an opportunity to fish for mackerel to take home for supper, or a few hours on board a working trawler - various possibilities are available through the tourist office. For those who like things a little speedier, between Easter and September a 30-knot craft can take you in an hour to the Ile d'Yeu where you can spend an enjoyable day cycling around this attractive island (see page 45).

Markets: Tuesday-Sunday, Halles Centrales (see below). Daily, plus open-air stalls on Tuesday, Friday, Sunday & public holidays, Boulevard Arago (south-east of Musée Ste-Croix). Wednesday and Saturday, Cours Dupont (south-east of the station). Monday-Saturday 8.30am-12.30pm & 4-7pm (closed public holidays) Fish market, Quai Franqueville.

Festivals: Fête de la Mer (festival of the sea), August. Régates de la Ch'nou (old-style fishing boats and traditions), August.

Specialities: Tuna. Langoustines. Sole.

Brocante: Marché aux Puces (weekly flea market), Fridays in July and August, Place de la Liberté.

Halles Centrales. If you enter the lovely central market-hall from Rue du Palais, on the seaward side of the church, you can look down from the peppermint-green and cream painted first-floor level on to a colourful mosaic of traders selling heaps of golden *mirabelle* plums, gleaming mountains of butter, and bunches of fresh, but out-of-the-ordinary, herbs like basil and coriander. ● *Tues-Sun 8am-1pm (15 June-15 Sept, daily 8am-1pm).*

Rue de l'Enfer. This street, off the south side of Rue des Halles and several blocks west of the central market, is reputed to be the narrowest in France. You'll need to breathe in to squeeze along it - at the bottom, the walls on either side hardly allow for the breadth of an average person's shoulders. ●

Musée de l'Abbaye de Ste-Croix. Delightful museum and gallery of modern art in one wing of a 17th-century building that was formerly a Benedictine convent. Temporary exhibitions are held throughout the year; the permanent collection, which is often shifted around to different parts of the building, includes a couple of charming pictures of Les Sables in the 1920s by Albert Marquet (1875-1947), a large selection of colourful collages and paintings by Gaston Chaissac (1910-64), and a collection of mixed-media Surrealist works by Romanian artist Victor Brauner (1903-66) - some of the latter are a bit explicit, so you might want to preview it before finding yourself compelled to give the children an impromptu sex-education lesson! Under a network of beams in the attic is a lovely collection of local costumes, model ships and items relating to the fishing industry, including some wonderful naïve paintings of boats by fisherman-turned-artist Paul-Emile Pajot (1873-1929) and his son Gilbert. ● *Tues-Sun 2.30-5.30pm (15 June-30 Sept, daily 10am-noon & 2.30-6.30pm); closed on public holidays. Rue de Verdun (tel: 02 51 32 01 16). 30F/4.57€, students and children 10F/1.52€ (free on Sun).*

Musée des Guerres de Vendée. You need at least some knowledge of the personalities and events of the Wars of the Vendée (see page 25) to get the most out of this museum in an attractive 18th-century house between the casino and the fishing port. Most of its displays consist of costumed waxworks portraying the wars' principal characters (a descriptive sheet in English identifies the significant figures). The basement holds Republican generals such as Kléber (leader of the fearsome Mayençais troops), Carrier (who instituted the horrific drownings in the Loire), Boulard (commander of the garrison stationed at Les Sables), and Hoche, who finally succeeded in drawing up a peace treaty. A large first-floor room contains a mass of documents collected by a local historian, relating to the 1789 Revolution and the Vendée Wars. On the second floor you come face-to-face with some of the Vendean heroes: la Rochejaquelein, d'Elbée, Cathelineau, Stofflet and Charette gathered at an inn; the dying Lescure with his wife; a rebel priest saying an open-air Mass; and Pitt's British troops and those of exiled French aristocrats who were cut down during the disastrous invasion attempt of June 1795 at Quiberon in Brittany. ✱ *1 July-31 Aug, daily 10.30am-noon & 3-7pm. 72 Rue Napoléon (tel: 02 51 21 03 27). Admission charge not available at time of going to press.*

Muséum du Coquillage. A huge collection of shells of all kinds, from familiar cockles and sea-urchins to the colourful and exotic produce of the South Seas. Leaflet available in English to help decipher the chatty descriptions. ● *Tues-Fri 9.30am-noon & 2-7pm; Sat, Sun 2-7pm (1 June-31 Oct, daily 9.30am-noon & 2-7pm; 1 July-31 Aug, daily 9.30am-10.30pm). 8 Rue du Maréchal Leclerc, at eastern end of fishing harbour (tel: 02 51 23 50 00). 30F/4.57€, children 20F/3.04€.*

Jardin Zoologique. Beyond the southernmost end of the Remblai, or promenade, some 2km from the town centre, is a small but delightfully laid out zoo, with a collection of reptiles, exotic birds, big cats, wallabies and other animals in a tree-filled park alongside the river Tanchet. Free-roaming monkeys swing down from the trees to investigate the rubbish bins among the rose bushes and fragrant frangipani trees, and otters dive into a glass-sided pool so you can watch their underwater antics. Feeding times are posted at the gate. It's very family-friendly, with ramps for pushchairs, lots of picnic spots, and notices telling you that the ducks love popcorn (children can buy small bags of grain to feed to animals). ● *Daily 2-6pm (15 Feb-1 Nov, daily 10am-noon & 2-6pm; 1-30 Apr, daily 10am-6.30pm; 1 May-15 Sept, daily 9.30am-7.30pm). Route de Tanchet (tel: 02 51 95 14 10). 60F/9.14€, children 30F/4.57€.*

LES SABLES (LA CHAUME)

Across the channel that links Les Sables' fishing port with the sea is the picturesque former fishing village of La Chaume. You can drive around to it, or take a three-minute ferry ride across the harbour mouth from the Quai Guiné pontoon, on the Les Sables side. Near the market is one of La Chaume's most distinctive pieces of architecture, the square-sided Tour d'Arundel that still serves as a lighthouse. If you make your way to La Chaume's other major landmark, the church, you'll find in the square outside that a dreary blank wall has been transformed with a mural presenting a jokey view of the town.

Market: Tuesday, Thursday, Sunday.

Port Olona. More than 1,000 yachts are moored in this busy marina, full of shops and restaurants and, frequently, live music in the bars during the evenings, near the north end of La Chaume's quay. The port hits the headlines every four years as the start and finish of the single-handed, non-stop, round-the-world sailing race known as the Vendée-Globe Challenge. Brainchild of Les Sables' yachting hero Philippe Jeantot, the event has given rise to some heroic exploits on the high seas. The winner usually accomplishes the gruelling circumnavigation in about 110 days. ●

Les Salines: Embarcadère. This remarkable boat journey gives a real insight into the salt industry that used to flourish in the marshes north of Les Sables, as well as into the fish-farming that has taken over. Don't be put off by the rows of plastic chairs on the flat craft that carries you on the guided, 1hr 45min excursion into the marshes. En route, you disembark and watch the guide pick up a long-handled, rake-like *simouche* to lift the salty crystals from the surface of the salt pans, or demonstrate the sluices and channels that let the salt water in to dry out under the baking sun. (There's no shade on board, so take sunhats, and garments with sleeves in hot weather.)

Today, about 100 *oeillets*, the series of square pans in which the sea water evaporates, remain of the 30,000 that were worked 50 years ago (between June and September, one *oeillet* produces between 15 and 35kg of salt, depending on how much rain falls to hinder the process). The salt pans are flooded for the winter to protect them from the cold, and then drained and tidied up in March. Ask for the explanatory leaflet in English before you set out. ▲ *1 Apr-30 Sept, days and times vary according to tides (booking essential). Port Olona car park, Boulevard de l'Ile Vertime; car park entrance is next to the Bowling building (tel: 02 51 21 01 19). 57F/8.69€, children 35F/5.34€.*

Les Salines: Site Historique. Imaginatively-designed open-air trail that winds among old salt workings at L'Aubraie, 3km north-west of Les Sables. Ask for an English leaflet first, to help understand the taped commentaries at various points that explain the history of the salt industry, so vital for preserving foodstuffs in days before canning and refrigeration. A giant model of the area, comparing Roman times with the present shows how Les Sables grew up long after La Chaume was established; a fully functioning Roman clay oven evaporates salt from seawater; a (human) salt-maker demonstrates how to harvest the "white gold" from his *oeillets* (see above); the crippling salt tax (*la gabelle*), brought in in 1340, is described in fascinating detail; and in a building cleverly designed with ropes and flapping canvas to evoke a sailing ship, is an exhibition on Les Sables' great cod-fishing industry. (Until the time of Louis XIV, the boats went on three-month voyages to fish off Newfoundland, or *Terre-Neuve*, taking salt to preserve the huge catches till they could be sold on return to France.) Allow a couple of hours to see it all. ▲ *1 Apr-30 Sept, Fri-Wed 10am-7pm. 120 Route de l'Aubraie - the D87A, north of the Bowling building (tel: 02 51 90 87 74). 42F/6.40€, children 25F/3.81€.*

Musée de la Mer et de la Pêche. Scale-models, naval objects, plans and documents are on show - though slightly lacking in explanation - at the 12th-century Château St-Clair in a small museum devoted downstairs to nautical matters and, on the floor above, to the town's rich fishing industry. You can also read a little about the local sailor-turned-pirate, the bloodthirsty "Nau l'Olonnois", who mercilessly tortured his victims in the Caribbean and was himself eaten by cannibals in 1671. ▲ *Easter-30 Sept, daily 3-7pm (1 June-15 Sept, daily 10.30am-12.30pm & 3-7pm). Tel: 02 51 95 53 11. 15F/2.29€, children 8F/1.22€.*

Prieuré St-Nicolas. Beautifully restored Romanesque church in a wonderful position on the point overlooking the ocean and the entrance to Les Sables channel. Exhibitions and concerts are held in the summer, giving a chance to view the interior. ●

ST-ÉTIENNE-DU-BOIS

Inexplicably spared by the *colonnes infernales* (see page 27), this small village 19km north-west of La Roche-sur-Yon still has a few Renaissance houses clustered around its church - though one side of the square is blighted by an ultra-modern *mairie*. If you walk down the hill behind the church to the *lavoir*, or washing-place, you'll find a noticeboard with maps of local footpaths: if you've an hour to spare, the Sentier du Coteau - through woodland and across an ancient bridge made of megalithic stones - makes a delightful walk.

Speciality: Gros-Plant wine.

Chapelle de la Tullévrière. A cockerel and a cross decorate the roof of this small chapel in a hamlet 5km north-east of St-Étienne on the D94. It was rebuilt in 1835 on the site of an earlier building where one of the rebel priests (see page 26) celebrated Mass during the Wars of the Vendée. Within the simple interior, two stained-glass windows show clandestine religious services of the time; on the wall is a memorial to 22 local martyrs - men, women and children - slaughtered as they attempted to hide from the Republican soldiers in 1794. ●

ST-RÉVÉREND

If you approach this small village, 8km east of St-Gilles-Croix-de-Vie, from the direction of Coëx in the summer you'll probably make out the white sails of its tall 19th-century windmill turning above the treetops.

Moulin des Gourmands. This restored windmill is an imposing sight from the main D6 road. During the guided tour (in French) visitors are taken from top to bottom, while the miller explains how he controls the sail area by pulling levers from inside, and points out carefully-preserved sketches of mill and donkey, drawn on the wall by a long-forgotten predecessor. There's a *crêperie* nearby; future plans include a museum of bread and baking. ▲ *Late June-mid Sept, daily 10am-7pm. (Tel: 02 51 60 16 72). 20F/3.04€, children 10F/1.52€.*

Roseraie de Vendée. Early June is the best time to catch the flowers in bloom at this garden, 2km to the west of the village, which exhibits 8,000 roses (700 varieties) within its 3 hectares. They are grouped by name (countries, first names, famous people and so on), and also by type - such as perfumed, old-fashioned, and varieties for special situations - and the owners make a virtue of the fact that they don't spray for pests or diseases, so that you can see which varieties are most susceptible. Guided tours available at weekends in May and June; on Saturdays from July to September. Take a sunhat in hot weather, as the grounds have little shade. Rose-flavoured jams, liqueurs and syrup available in the shop. ▲ *Mid May-mid Oct, daily 9.30am-7pm. Rond Point des 4 Chemins, signposted off D6, near the D32 crossroads (tel: 02 51 55 24 03). 15F/2.29€ (1 July-31 Aug 10F/1.52€), children free.*

TALMONT-ST-HILAIRE   **i tel: 02 51 90 65 10/fax: 02 51 20 71 80**

A former port of great charm, nestling at the foot of impressive medieval castle ruins that once belonged to the powerful Princes of Talmont and, between 1152 and 1204, to the English crown. Up the hill behind the castle are some beautiful old, ivy-covered houses. More in keeping with the 21st century perhaps is the Vendée Air Park, 4km along the D4 towards La Roche-sur-Yon - an American-style development where owners of light aircraft can buy a house with a plane-sized garage and a taxiway outside the front door.

The tourist office can advise on tours of nearby oyster beds and salt marshes, held between July and September. There are also guided visits of the dunes and forest around the lovely beach of Le Veillon, 5km to the south-west, where dinosaurs used once to roam (you can see casts of their footprints in the Écomusée at the Puy-du-Fou castle).

Market: Saturday (July and August).

Festivals: Fête de la Vache (working oxen, milking, butter-making) at Grosbreuil, 9km north of Talmont, July. Fête de la Moule (mussel festival), La Guittière, 2km south of Talmont, July; Fête des Huîtres (oyster festival), La Guittière, July; Fête de la Soue (salt festival), La Guittière, August.

Specialities: Oysters.

Crafts: Lead soldiers, and glass-blowing, both near Querry-Pigeon, 6km south-west of Talmont (see below).

Golf: Golf de Port-Bourgenay, 18-hole seaside course 6km south-west of Talmont (see page 15 for Vendée Golf Pass). *Tel: 02 51 23 35 45.*

Château de Talmont. The solidly-built castle ruins are for the most part 12th-century, the work of Richard Coeur-de-Lion (the English king Richard the Lionheart, son of Henry Plantagenet of England and Eleanor of Aquitaine) who spent a good deal of time hunting in the neighbouring forests. It was much fought over during the Wars of Religion, and reduced to its present state in 1628. From the top of the keep there are marvellous views over the town, countryside, marshes and sea. On July and August mornings you can visit the castle with a guide in medieval costume (tours in

English available, June-mid September), and in the afternoons try archery or calligraphy, watch dubbing ceremonies, and learn the steps of medieval dances. ▲ *1 Mar-early Nov, daily 2-6pm (1 May-30 Sept, daily 10am-1pm & 2-7pm). Place du Port (tel: 02 51 90 27 43). 17F/2.59€, children 8F/1.22€ (1-30 June, & mornings 1 July-31 Aug, 23F/3.50€ with guided tour, children 10F/1.52€; 1 July-31 Aug afternoons, 32F/4.87€ with entertainments, children 17F/2.59€).*

Musée Automobile. The more than 150 immaculately-presented vehicles dating from 1885 to the 1960s lined up in this large motor museum 6km west of Talmont, include such makes as De Dion-Bouton, Bugatti and Hispano-Suiza, and a selection of bicycles, motor-bikes and horse-drawn carriages. ▲ *School holiday periods, daily 2-6pm (1 Apr-30 Sept, daily 9.30am-noon & 2-6.30pm; 1 June-31 Aug, daily 9.30am-7pm). Route de Talmont (tel: 02 51 22 05 81). 45F/6.86€, children 20F/3.04€.*

Port-Bourgenay. Traffic-free holiday development and sports complex 5km south-west of Talmont, with plenty of activities ranging from tennis to croquet, swimming to golf (see above). Down on the waterside, beyond a comically-turreted private castle, is a marina, with cafés, restaurants and yacht-orientated shops. ●

Figurines d'Art, Editions Vanot. Patrick Vanot makes exquisitely detailed lead figures in his studio 3km west of Talmont, pouring molten metal into moulds and spinning them to fling the lead into the farthest recesses. Soldiers on sale - painted or plain - range from the Middle Ages, through the Revolution and the Wars of the Vendée to World War I. ✳ *1 July-31 Aug, daily 2-7pm. 207 Rue de la Dagoterie, turn off the D4A opposite the Cave Ferré (tel: 02 51 22 28 28). Free.*

Souffleur de Verre. Jean-Michel Gauthier holds his audience spellbound as he turns glowing lumps of molten glass into fantastic shapes, full of swirling colour. The shelves in this converted barn are full of vases, lamps and figurines for sale. ● *Tues-Sun 2.30-6.30pm. Rue de Chevrefoy, off D4A, 500 metres north of Port Bourgenay (tel: 02 51 22 27 13). Free.*

3. LA TRANCHE, LUÇON AND THE MARAIS POITEVIN

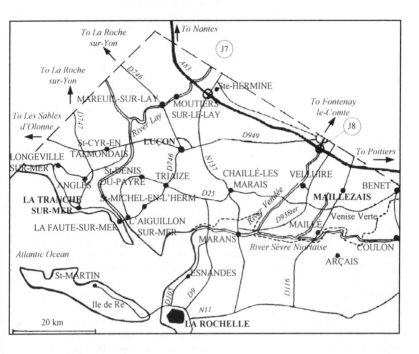

Known for its sunshine, its windsurfing and its spring floral procession, La Tranche has always been a popular holiday destination. If you're looking for relief from the flatness of the surrounding countryside, just head north-east to the village of Mareuil, or visit Luçon - a dignified town that has for centuries been the seat of the bishops of the Vendée. And don't miss a trip east to the magical Marais Poitevin, or "Green Venice" marshland; it's full of picturesque villages where you can travel by boat or bike among a maze of tranquil waterways.

L'AIGUILLON-SUR-MER   **i tel: 02 51 56 43 87/fax: 02 51 27 15 17**

At this former trading port at the mouth of the river Lay, 21km south-west of Luçon, ships once loaded cargoes of cereals cultivated on the reclaimed land of the "dry" marsh, or fenland, that lies to the north and north-east. L'Aiguillon bay is one of the largest shellfish-producing areas of France and oyster- and mussel-farming, plus fishing, are still the livelihoods of those who live in the whitewashed cottages. Legend has it that a shipwrecked Irishman named Patrick Walton was the first to try planting a stake in the water and encouraging mussels to grow on it in 1255. Today, as the tide falls, hundreds of thousands of these *bouchots* are revealed standing in the mud, each one holding a rich crop of shellfish.

Another sort of fishing is practised by the locals on the bridge that links L'Aiguillon to La Faute. Curious constructions of bent poles and square nets - known as *carrelets*, and also seen on many other estuaries in the region - are winched down into the rising tide and up again in the hope of capturing eels, shrimps and other delicacies.

An artificial lake on the waterfront has its own sandy beach for swimming; if you prefer something bigger, you can nip across the bridge and enjoy the vast stretch of fine sand at neighbouring La Faute.

You can spend a day at sea on a *vieux gréement* (traditional sail-powered wooden boat) during July and August, or visit the bay's oyster beds - information and reservations through the tourist office. Other diversions include free evening entertainment on the port each Tuesday and Friday in July and August, with spectacular firework shows on 14 July and 15 August.

Market: Tuesday and Friday. Marché de la Nature (farmers' market) second Saturday of the month.

Specialities: Mussels. Oysters. Eels.

Brocante: Dépôt-Vente Brocante. *Wed, Thurs 10am-noon & 3-7pm; Fri, Sat 3-7pm. Zone Artisanale, Boulevard des Courlis (tel: 06 81 85 68 75).*

Factory shop: Aux P'tites Puces (see below).

Aux P'tites Puces. If you're in search of fabric for upholstery, summer frocks, mackintoshes or lace curtains try the three outlet shops on this site. They sell every conceivable type of material - much of it end-of-range stuff - priced by the *kilogram* - just snip off the length you want and it will be weighed at the checkout! ● *Thurs-Sat 9.30am-12.30pm & 2.30-6.45pm. Zone Artisanale (near Super U), Boulevard des Courlis (tel: 02 51 56 46 97).*

Pointe de L'Aiguillon. A long spit of land juts out into L'Aiguillon Bay, bordered by a concrete dyke built a century ago by Dutch engineers to protect the hard-won fields from the sea. From the road that runs beside it you have views on the eastern side of the wind-carved cliffs of La Dive - a former island rising to the dizzy height of 15 metres above the flat fields - and, to the south, of the gracefully curving bridge linking the city of La Rochelle with the low-lying island known as the Ile de Ré. The high, crumbling wall beside the road blocks the outlook on the seaward side, but you can clamber up primitive steps that stick out of it at intervals to see the mussel-posts stretching away to the horizon at low tide. On the eastern side are the mud-flats of the Anse, or bay, de L'Aiguillon - now a wildfowl reserve visited by vast quantities of avocets and other waders. During peak migration times (mid-August to mid-November) nearly half a million birds pass this way, in greatest numbers just after sunrise; guided walks with ornithologists take place at weekends. ● *Information from Ligue pour la Protection des Oiseaux (tel: 02 51 46 21 91). 30F/4.57€.*

ANGLES   i tel: 02 51 97 56 39

The primitive bear sculpture that peers down from above the west door of the church is the main curiosity of this small village, 20km west of Luçon. According to local folklore the beast was a dangerous animal that abducted and ate the village's youngest and most beautiful maidens, until a holy man turned him to stone.

Market: Saturday.

Festival: Fête de l'Ours (bear festival), July. Fête de la Tour de Moricq at Moricq, 2km east of Angles, August.

Église d'Angles. The interior of the village's handsome church arouses a great deal of interest for the way its design bridges the Romanesque and the later Plantagenet styles. Rounded arches characteristic of the 12th century rub shoulders with the finer, more graceful architecture that followed, and three statues look down on visitors. The simply-carved figure high above the nave is thought to represent Henri Plantagenêt (who, as King Henry II, ruled England from 1154 to 1189); the two more sophistica-ted works are said to be of his wife, Eleanor of Aquitaine, and of their son Richard Coeur-de-Lion (Richard I of England). ●

Église de St-Benoist. Another church with a strange animal on the roof is that of St-Benoist-sur-Mer, a village 3km north-east of Angles. If you stand back far enough (don't worry about falling into the sea; it's retreated 12km over the centuries) you can just make out the figure of a rabbit, apparently placed there as a joke by the original monastic builders, and it's - yes - smoking a pipe! In the stone-flagged 11th-century interior, the church's mossy walls are outshone by a dazzling Renaissance altarpiece. ●

Tour de Moricq. Marooned in the marshland 2km east of Angles, at the eastern end of the village of Moricq, rises a huge, isolated square tower, built in the 15th century on what was then the coast to defend the mouth of the river Lay. During the Wars of Religion, Protestant prisoners were held in it. Since the port of Moricq silted up at the turn of the last century it has fallen into disrepair. At present it is viewable only from the outside, but restoration work is in progress. ●

Cairn du Pé de Fontaine. At the top of the hill behind the village of Fontaine, 3km north-west of Angles, is a surprisingly large neolithic burial chamber, consisting of two dolmens, still surrounded by many of the stones that would have covered them 5,000 years ago. As you are said to be able to see 17 church towers from here, it has been a popular look-out spot through the ages, right down to World War II - as demonstrated by the remains of a huge German bunker nearby. ●

ARÇAIS (Deux-Sèvres)   **i tel: 05 49 35 43 44**

This lovely waterside village in the Marais Poitevin, 10km south-east of Maillezais, was an important trading centre until the railways superseded water transport. Today Arçais is full of shops, pretty *gîtes* and bed-&-breakfast establishments, and dominated by a picturesque 19th-century château alongside the slipway. Beside it you can rent boats to paddle around some 40km of tree-lined waterways dug by hand in the early 19th century. Car-parking is almost impossible in the centre, so it's best to wander the cobbled pavements and explore the craft shops and the winding alleyways on foot. You can also rent boats at a couple of other typical marshland villages: St-Hilaire-la Palud, 4km farther south, and Montfaucon, just off to the west.

Promenade en Barque. Rent a canoe or a flat-bottomed boat, with or without guide, from one of the establishments at the water's edge. ● *From 140F/21.34€ for four people with guide; 90F/13.72€ without.*

Bicyclette Verte. If you'd rather stay on dry land, you can rent bikes from this large cycle-hire centre. ▲ *Easter-Sept. Route de St-Hilaire-la-Palud (tel: 05 49 35 42 56). From 30F/4.57€ an hour; 70F/10.67€ a day.*

CHAILLÉ-LES-MARAIS   **i tel: 02 51 56 71 17/fax: 02 51 56 71 36**

The ancient capital of the "dry" marsh, or drained fenland, area of the Marais Poitevin, 14km south-east of Luçon, was once an island; as you admire the cliffs rising above the D25, you realise you are indeed driving along the former seabed. If you're travelling this way in July and August, you'll get closer to the soul of the region if you take the secondary roads through the little marshland villages - and probably move faster than on the main routes.

The monks from five nearby abbeys who begun drainage work in the 13th century when the estuary that covered this region began to silt up, are commemorated in the Canal des Cinq Abbés - the waterway just south of Chaillé that runs roughly north-east/south-west and divides the fertile, open meadows of the "dry" marsh (*marais desséché*) from the mysterious, tree-lined "wet" marshland (*marais mouillé*) to the west. Another important canal, the Ceinture des Hollandais that separates the marshes from the plain lying to the north, takes its name from the Dutch engineers brought in 350 years later by Henri IV and his successor, Louis XIII, to restore the intricate drainage system after a succession of wars had prevented its upkeep.

All this water makes the area a fishermen's paradise, and the Chaillé tourist office alongside the busy N137 provides especially good information on the subject, with maps and tips on where to look for black-bass, zander, carp and pike, as well as details about permits, shellfish-digging and fishy techniques.

Market: Thursday.

Brocante: Dépot-Vente Sud-Vendée. *Thurs-Sat 2-7pm, Sun 3-7pm. On N137 at entrance to Chaillé (tel: 02 51 56 79 07).*

Maison du Petit Poitou. A charming little museum - one of six *maisons du parc*, or national park visitor centres, in the Marais Poitevin - lying on the N137 just to the south of the village. Local farming traditions are explained, including the making of cowpat fuel that was highly prized for cooking and heating, and the sport of "cow hunting" (going shooting, using an obliging cow as cover so as to be able to approach wild ducks unseen). Snowy-white skeletons of different marshland animals and birds are beautifully displayed, along with dissected pellets revealing the diets of owls, herons and other birds. Outside, are some typical livestock of the region: goats, cows, mules and a rather grumpy *baudet du Poitou* (a shaggy-coated breed of donkey). ▲ *1 April-12 Sept, Mon-Sat 10am-6pm, Sun 2-6pm. Tel: 02 51 56 77 30. 20F/3.05€, children 10F/1.52€; family ticket 60F/9.14€.*

COULON (Deux-Sèvres)   ℹ tel: 05 49 35 99 29/fax: 05 49 35 84 31

Officially categorised as one of "the most beautiful villages of France", this busy little waterside town, 60km south-east of Luçon and 8km west of Niort, really does live up to its classification. The capital of the rural "Green Venice" region, it contains a handsome church, old streets lined with interesting craft shops, and photogenic fishermen's houses reflected in the limpid waters of the Sèvre Niortaise river.

You can rent traditional, flat-bottomed boats called *plates* from several companies along the quayside in which to travel the maze of small canals, roofed with leafy branches, that lead off the main river like a series of green cathedrals. Prices range from around 175F/26.67€ per six- or seven-seater boat per hour with a guide (who does the paddling); 100F/15.24€ for an hour without. Some of the hire companies own waterside sites where you can moor to eat your picnic. Boats may also be rented from the quieter village of La Garette, 3km south of Coulon. And if you prefer to tour on dry land, you can rent bikes or take trips alongside the canals by mini-bus or land-train (details from the tourist office).

Market: Friday and Sunday.

Maison des Marais Mouillés. In one of the village houses you can learn about the history of the "wet" marshland, or "Green Venice", from prehistoric times and how the land was reclaimed from the sea, first by monks and later by Dutch engineers. Also featured are the area's eel-fishing and poplar-wood industries, and its crops - including the *mogettes* that are such an important element in the Vendean diet. You can see a room-setting typical of a marshland house, plus a 20-minute audio-visual show and photographs illustrating how the flat-bottomed boats are used even today to transport everything - including livestock - to and from the little green fields. ▲ *1 Feb-30 Nov, Tues-Sun 10am-noon & 2-7pm (1-30 June, daily 10am-noon & 2-7pm; 1 July-31 Aug, daily 10am-8pm). Place de la Coûtume (tel: 05 49 35 81 04). 28F/4.27€, students 20F/3.05€, children 12F/1.83€.*

Aquarium de la Venise Verte. Allow a good hour to enjoy close-up views of carp, perch, black-bass and some of the other freshwater fish that normally live in the canals, and see a half-hour slide show (with English translation) on the flora and fauna of the Marais Poitevin. ▲ *Easter-31 Oct, daily 10am-noon & 2.30-7pm. Place de l'Église (tel: 05 49 35 90 31). 20F/3.05€, children 12F/1.83€.*

ESNANDES (Charente-Maritime)

Since the 13th century, fishermen from this attractive village 12km north of La Rochelle have used sturdy, flat-bottomed boats called *acons* to collect their daily harvest of mussels from the thousands of stakes planted in L'Aiguillon Bay. If you continue along the road beyond the Maison de la Mytiliculture (see below), past crumbling cliffs and damp salt meadows known as *mizottes*, the road rises to give a wonderful viewpoint. (Keep an eye on tide times, though, as the waters can flood in over the road.) The village's huge, strongly-fortified Romanesque church, with its sentry-way and battlements, is visible for miles; in summer you can climb the tower for a superb view over the village and marshes. Charron, 7km farther north, is the traditional centre of the mussel industry for L'Aiguillon Bay; the waterside to the west of the village seethes with activity when the fishermen come in.

Speciality: *Mouclade* (a creamy, faintly curry-flavoured mussel dish).

Maison de la Mytiliculture. Once you have watched the 20-minute video about the labour-intensive mussel-farming industry, you will be amazed that these succulent shellfish are so inexpensive. Interesting displays on the geography and biology of the area, and a model of L'Aiguillon Bay on which you can press a button to make the tide rise and fall over the mud flats. ▲ *1 Feb-30 Sept, Mon, Wed, Sat 2-6pm (1 Apr-14 Sept, Wed-Mon 2-7pm; 15 June-31 Aug, daily 10am-12.30pm & 2.30-7.30pm); 1 Oct-30 Nov, Sat 2-5pm. Rue de l'Océan (tel: 05 46 01 34 64). 20F/3.05€, children 12F/1.83€.*

Musée des Graffiti Anciens. A curious collection of plaster copies of rough drawings and inscriptions found carved into walls in buildings of the region is on display at the top of the church tower in Marsilly, 3km south-west of Esnandes. The oldest example shows a 12th-century knight with his shield; the most recent is a poignant note from a German soldier in hospital during World War II. Afterwards you can climb a bit farther to enjoy a view across the marshland (don't forget the binoculars; you won't want to go down the 113 stone steps to get them). ▲ *1 Mar-30 Nov, Sat, Sun 2.30-6.30pm (1 Apr-31 Oct, Wed-Sun 2.30-6.30pm). Tel: 05 46 01 36 23). 15F/2.29€, children free.*

LA FAUTE-SUR-MER   i tel: 02 51 56 45 19/fax: 02 51 97 18 08

On a peninsula between the sea and the river Lay, 23km south-west of Luçon, La Faute has a vast beach - with an area given over to sand-yachting - a busy fishing port, and pine woods that anchor the shifting dunes and provide shade on hot summer days. Bird-lovers will find themselves ideally placed between the Pointe d'Arçay, to the south, where thousands of wading birds pause at migration times, and the Belle-Henriette lagoon - a good spot for gulls, terns and plovers in summer, plus migrating chiffchaffs, redstarts and wagtails.

Market: Thursday and Sunday.

Specialities: Oysters. Mussels.

Parcours de Santé. Athletic holidaymakers will find a circuit laid out near the Plage des Chardons, with a selection of wooden obstacles to jump over or swing from that anyone is welcome to use as a fitness aid. You are, however, advised to choose a level appropriate to your physical capabilities, and to spend at least 15 minutes warming up before having a go. ●

LONGEVILLE-SUR-MER   i tel: 02 51 33 34 64/fax: 02 51 33 33 09

A thick band of pine forest shelters the huge sandy beaches that lie 2km south-west of Longeville, the village itself being set slightly inland and 25km west of Luçon. The aptly-named Plage du Rocher is good for rockpools at low tide, and even the occasional fossil, while the wide open space of Les Conches draws numerous surfers. Among the many woodland footpaths is another entertaining *parcours de santé*, or fitness trail (see above), also known as a CRAPA - short for Circuit Rustique d'Activité Physique Aménagé - just south of the turning for Le Rocher beach, with some 20 sturdy obstacles to walk along, jump off or climb over.

Market: Friday.

Festival: Foire à la Brocante (antiques fair), mid-July and mid-August.

Moulin de Bots Pias. Overlooking a sea of maize and sunflowers, some 4km south-east of Longeville, stands a restored windmill - the last of 15 that once operated in the *commune*. Bots Pias (the name is derived from the local patois for *sabots plats*, or worn-down clogs!) - was built in 1819 and remained in service till 1955. The miller takes visitors round, explaining the grinding process and the regulating of the slatted wooden sails, and pointing out the long wooden pole, or *guivre*, that is used to rotate the roof and keep the sails facing the wind. ✳ *1 July-31 Aug, daily 3-7pm. Les Rabouillères (tel: 02 51 90 36 17). 15F/2.29€, children free.*

Pierre qui vire. Unless a farmer has surrounded it with a towering maize crop, you can see a large standing-stone (also known as the Menhir du Russelet) on the skyline amid open fields about 1km west of Longeville. Local legend claims that it spins around each day at midnight. ●

LUÇON   ℹ tel: 02 51 56 36 52/fax: 02 51 56 03 56

This pleasant town at the junction of the plain with the Vendée's southern marshes is rather misrepresented by the garish light-industrial sprawl around its fringes. Artfully-trained trees of green and copper-coloured foliage are trimmed into leafy arches above the roads leading to the centre. The heart of the town is dominated as much by a crazily-decorated concrete water-tower north of the Champ-de-Foire (built in 1912 to supply a regiment of dragoons garrisoned in the town) as by the elegant 85-metre spire of its cathedral. Luçon's most famous inhabitant was the future Cardinal Richelieu, who declared the place on his arrival in 1606 to be "the filthiest and most unpleasant in France". The town suffered a great deal at the hands of the Huguenots during the Wars of Religion but, as a Republican stronghold, escaped relatively unscathed from the later Wars of the Vendée.

Immaculately well-groomed today, Luçon's streets are lined with substantial two-storey houses of solid white stone and organised into an incredibly complicated one-way system. If you want to stop and explore, it's best to leave the car in the huge car park opposite the cathedral. Main shopping areas are Rue Clemenceau and Rue du Président-de-Gaulle; the covered food market is behind the cathedral, off Rue Victor-Hugo.

The tourist office dispenses excellent brochures on the town in English.

Market: Wednesday and Saturday.

Festival: Nocturnes Océanes (concerts of romantic music), July.

Specialities: Liqueurs (see below). Kamok cakes from G. Paquet pâtisserie in Rue Clemenceau.

Brocante: Dépôt-Vente de Vendée. *Thurs-Mon 2-7pm (closed public holidays). Les Quatre Chemins, Ste-Gemme-la-Plaine, on D949, 5km east of Luçon (tel: 02 51 27 00 55).*

Cathedral. Richelieu, who was bishop here from 1606 to 1622, said Mass beneath the graceful spire and soaring white columns of the cathedral, and is said to have preached from the painted wooden pulpit now kept in the north aisle. In a mixture of architectural styles, the interior features Romanesque carved faces of humans and animals alongside 17th-century stone garlands, and the church is linked to the bishops' palace by beautifully-preserved 16th-century cloisters. Concerts are some-times given on the monumental organ, made by the celebrated 19th-century organ-builder Aristide Cavaillé-Coll and presented to the city by the Emperor Napoléon III. ● *Daily 9am-noon & 2-7pm. Tel: 02 51 56 36 52.*

Le Grand Séminaire. The Richelieu Courtyard in this former school for priests is the setting for summer concerts in a season of romantic music known as "Les Nocturnes Océanes". Plans are under way to install a multi-media presentation on the life of Cardinal Richelieu. ✳ *Open only for concerts. Rue du Général-de-Gaulle (tel: 02 51 56 36 52).*

Chapelle des Ursulines. The austerity of the white-painted chapel in this former convent is tempered by a decorative altar-piece and an astonishing 33-metre-long wooden ceiling covered with 17th-century paintings of cherubs and musical instruments. A plaque on the end wall records the sad fate of the convent's nuns during the Vendée Wars, 11 of whom died in the town's prison. ✳ *1 July-31 Aug, Tues-Sat 2.30-6pm. Rue Clemenceau (tel: 02 51 56 36 52). Free.*

Jardin Dumaine. Shady green oasis in the town centre, north-west of the tourist office, where you can wander among gravel paths (but not on the grass!), formal borders, collections of interesting trees and shrubs and an avenue of giant 150-year-old yew hedges (from which strains of recorded music waft in summer). There is also a pretty Victorian-style bandstand for open-air concerts. Youngsters are bound to love the topiary animals on the north lawn that recall the fables of La Fontaine - mostly familiar to British children, as the 17th-century French writer cribbed them from Aesop. ● *Daily 9am-7pm (1 July-31 Aug, daily until 9pm). Access via Rue de l'Hôtel-de-Ville or Allée St-François. Free.*

Centre Boléro. Before or after watching an hour-long performance by Boléro's resident puppet company in a little *"café-théâtre"* just to the south of the cathedral square, you can visit an adjacent museum - small, but charming - showing Guignol, Punchinello, and many different types of marionettes from China, Turkey, Java and elsewhere. ✳ *15 July-15 Aug: museum open 3-6pm; performance 4pm. Museum: 70 Rue du Port; theatre: 2 Rue Traversière (tel: 02 51 56 89 97). 35F/5.34€, children 35F/5.34€; family (2+2) 100F/15.24€.*

H. Vrignaud Fils. Opposite the cathedral is a old-world shop selling the output of a local distillery that manufactures, among other specialities, a tasty coffee-based liqueur called Kamok, a pear-flavoured drink called Liqueur du Puy du Fou, and a blend of orange and brandy known as Liqueur des Vendéens. ● *Mon-Sat 9-11.30am & 2.30-7pm. 2 Place Richelieu (tel: 02 51 56 11 48).*

Church of Les Magnils-Reigniers. This former priory church, in a village 3km north-west of Luçon, is little used today. A light carpet of moss covers the stone-flagged floor in front of three altars, ranged side-by-side. On the west wall some misty-coloured 12th-century frescoes, discovered in 1968, show images believed to be of the resurrected Christ appearing to his disciples. ✳ *1 July-31 Aug, Tues-Fri 3-6pm. Tel: 02 51 97 70 00. Free.*

MAILLÉ

A frozen-in-time atmosphere pervades this marshland village 6km south-west of Maillezais, compounded by the old-fashioned "wind-up" wells that still stand in front of many of the houses on the main street. The west door of the church features some marvellous stone acrobats dating from Romanesque times - though sadly eroded by the centuries.

Market: Sunday in July and August, from 11am - look for the tasty *préfou* (garlic bread) sold from a mobile oven by Denis Bigot.

Electric boats. Follow the Grand'Rue to a canalside quay, from which you can take a trip along the picturesque Marais Poitevin waterways in quiet, electrically-powered boats. ▲ *Easter-30 Sept, daily. Tel: 02 51 87 07 52. From 250F/38.08€ an hour for eight people with guide, 200F/30.48€ without.*

MAILLEZAIS   i tel: 02 51 87 23 01/fax: 02 51 00 72 51

This village on the edge of the Venise Verte, 30km east of Luçon, is famous for the set of ancient monastical ruins (see below) that towers over the countryside to the west. Pause first in the centre, though, to admire the church of St-Nicolas, its main doorway decorated with carved Romanesque birds, serpents and acrobats. As you head along Rue de l'Abbaye in the direction of the abbey, look out for number 74: pieces of grey bone stick out high up in the walls - placed there, legend has it, to protect from illness any animals kept inside.

Between spring and autumn you can hire little boats at a pretty waterside spot just below the abbey, and paddle around a circuit of the canals. You will soon be able to bike along them, too. A new cycle route due to be in place by 2001 will link Maillezais with La Tranche, almost 60km to the west, via a network of towpaths, and thence with the rest of the Vendée's coastal cycleway.

Specialities: *Préfou* (garlic bread). Jams, purées, syrups and fruit products from J-J. Aubert of Liez, 2.5km east of Maillezais.

Abbaye St-Pierre. Just west of the village, where the wind sweeps in exhilaratingly off the marshes, rise the ghostly remains of an early 11th-century abbey, a dazzling example of Romanesque architecture. Some 200 monks lived here in the 13th century, undertaking the first draining of the area to create the productive fields that exist today. A hundred years later, the writer Rabelais (see page 85) spent three years within its walls. During the Wars of Religion the abbey was seized and fortified by the Protestants, then changed hands several times before being burnt down. Its decline continued after the Revolution, when the remains were confiscated by the state and much of the stone sold for demolition.

An excellent visitors' leaflet (available in English) describes the history of the buildings and the life of the resident monks. From the excavations in the uneven ground, you can make out the positions of the cloister and chapter house while, among more intact buildings, you can visit the octagonal kitchen, the monks' and visitors' refectories and a guests' dormitory, and follow stone steps down to vaulted storage spaces that include a magnificently preserved cellarium.

Geoffrey la Grand'Dent ("Longtooth") - half-factual, half-fictional son of the powerful Raymondin de Lusignan and the fairy Mélusine (see page 95) - plundered the place in the 13th century; in 1589 the Calvinist writer Agrippa d'Aubigné turned the abbey into a Protestant stronghold, and remained its governor for 30 years. Costumed guides are shortly to be introduced to plunge visitors into this turbulent history; afterwards there will be half-hour boat trips along the canals created by Maillezais' monks. Occasional concerts and *son-et-lumière* performances are given in summer.
● *Daily 9am-noon & 2-5.30pm, (1 Feb-31 Mar & 1-31 Oct, until 6pm; 1 Apr-30 June & 1-30 Sept, until 7pm; 1 July-31 Aug, daily 9am-8pm). Tel: 02 51 00 70 11. 15F/2.29€, students 11F/1.67€, children 7F/1.07€.*

L'Espace Marais. A delightfully arranged museum in a barn 2.5km south-east of Maillezais gives an excellent idea of the traditional way of life in the marshes. Tools and other objects show how the locals carried on farming, building, eel-fishing and rope-making. Outside, a "Jardin du Diable" (Devil's garden), features a range of surprisingly common poisonous plants ranging from foxgloves to deadly nightshade (ask for the explanatory sheet in English), while a trail laid out through a wooden maze teaches children about the flora and fauna of the marshes. ▲ *1 May-30 Sept, daily 10am-7pm. Anchais (tel: 02 51 00 72 20). 20F/3.05€, children 10F/1.52€.*

MARANS (Charente-Maritime)   **i tel: 05 46 01 12 87/fax: 05 46 01 01 72**
After the flat landscape of the marshes, it comes as a surprise to arrive among dignified three-storey stone buildings and to look down from the bridge on the busy N137, upon an almost Venetian scene of fishing boats and pleasure craft alongside quays bordered by whitewashed houses with coloured shutters.

The name of this extraordinarily attractive town on the river Sèvre Niortaise, 23km north-east of La Rochelle, is synonymous with that of a breed of chicken renowned for its brown speckled eggs - these appealed to no less a connoisseur than James

Bond, who can be heard in *From Russia With Love* to demand "Marans eggs" for breakfast. For more than two centuries, until rail transport superseded that of water, the port was the focus of intense commercial activity. Today Marans' narrow cobbled streets are still busy - especially when the market is in full swing in the pretty glass-sided hall near the quay.

Market: Tuesday and Saturday.

Speciality: Marans eggs.

Embarcadère Le Thalassa. Easy to spot on the east side of the bridge are the little green motor boats moored to the quay, ready to set off on exploratory trips up the Sèvre and along some of the adjacent canals that iron out a few of the river's more eccentric meanders. Possible circuits range in duration from an hour to a whole day. ▲ *Easter-31 Oct, daily 9am-7pm. Quai Joffre (tel: 05 46 35 08 91). From 90F/ 13.72€ an hour for five people.*

MAREUIL-SUR-LAY   **i tel: 02 51 97 30 26/fax: 02 51 30 53 32**

This picturesque wine-producing town, dominated by the spire of its austere Romanesque church and by a slightly dilapidated 16th-century castle, overlooks the river Lay, 10km north-west of Luçon. A list of vineyards offering *dégustations* (tastings) is available from the tourist office, and a signposted *Route des Vins* leads to many of them. The nearby village of Rosnay, 5km to the west, claims the highest wine output per head of population in France - almost 10 per cent of its 452 inhabitants being wine producers.

You can rent boats on the river from the ironmonger at 12 Rue Hervé-de-Mareuil (the main street, north of the bridge), or enjoy fishing and waterside walks, plus a jokey mini-golf with obstacles based on wine-making. In early August a dazzling illuminated procession is held, with spectacular water-borne floats and a superb firework finale.

Market: Thursday. A Marché de la Nature (farmers' market) is held at St-Florent-des-Bois, 10km north-west of Mareuil, on the first Sunday of each month.

Speciality: Fiefs Vendéens wine.

Festival: Fête Nautique (illuminated boat procession), August.

Église de Dissais. This 12th-century church 2km east of Mareuil has been restored as a memorial to 7,500 combattants who lost their lives during the Vendean army's three attempts to take the nearby town of Luçon from the Republicans in 1793. ▲ *Mid May-mid Nov, Sun & public holidays 2.30-6.30pm (1 July-31 Aug, daily 2.30-7pm). Tel: 02 51 97 26 91. Free.*

Pont de Lavaud. This simple iron bridge, 4km south-west of Mareuil, was designed by none other than the great engineer Gustave Eiffel in 1866 to carry traffic on chunky stone pillars across the river Lay. You can inspect the underneath of it, too, if you rent a boat from L'Aubraie restaurant nearby. ●

Parachute memorial. A large granite slab on the D50, just to the west of Eiffel's bridge (see above), commemorates the first Allied parachute drop of arms to Vendean Resistance workers on 14 July 1943. Once they picked up the poetical coded message *"Pourquoi me réveiller au souffle du printemps?"* (Why awaken me at the first breath of spring?) via the BBC from London, the *résistants* prepared to retrieve the precious consignment, which they concealed in the house beside the present monument. ●

MOUTIERS-SUR-LE-LAY

This sleepy village 10km north of Luçon is clustered around a picturesque square overlooked by several superb *maisons bourgeoises* (large houses), a part-Romanesque church containing a colourful 19th-century altarpiece, and a former priory that was once the residence of the bishops of Luçon.

Tour de Bessay. Guided tours are given of this magnificent Renaissance tower attached to a traditional *logis*, or country house, 2km south of Moutiers. After watching a short video, you ascend via a series of big empty rooms towards the bell-shaped, lantern-topped roof, finishing at the *chemin de ronde*, or sentry-way, which is pierced by holes for muskets and offers panoramic views over the surrounding countryside. In the garden, a tumbledown dovecote reveals 3,000 nesting-holes, giving an idea of how many pigeons might have been needed to feed the family and staff. ✳ *Mid July-late Aug, Wed-Mon 2.30-6.30pm. 18F/2.74€, children 12F/1.83€.*

Aire de la Vendée. You don't necessarily have to travel on the A83 motorway to visit the wonderful service area (see page 78) about 4km north-east of Moutiers. It can be reached via the country lanes without having to set foot on the *autoroute* if you follow the signposts to it off the D19, between Ste-Pexine and St-Simon-la-Vineuse. Leave the car in a car park and walk in through the gate. ● *Exhibitions open daily 10am-6pm. Free.*

LA ROCHELLE (Charente-M'time)   ℹ tel: 05 46 41 14 68/fax: 05 46 41 99 85

One of France's best known and most attractive ports, this historic city is within easy reach for anyone staying in the south Vendée. The most interesting shops, streets and sights are conveniently clustered around the picturesque Vieux-Port, where hundreds of yachts float in the shadow of three ancient towers that once guarded the harbour entrance.

The town's layout is quite compact, so it's best to leave the car somewhere (there's a large underground car park on Place de Verdun) and stroll around on foot - wear comfortable shoes, as the cobblestones are hard on the legs.

English, off and on, from the time of Eleanor of Aquitaine until the Hundred Years War, the great salt- and wine-trading port of La Rochelle was fiercely Protestant in the 16th century and was thus bloodily involved in the Wars of Religion. The city successfully resisted a long siege by the Duke of Anjou in 1573, but a subsequent one (1627-28) led by Cardinal Richelieu, who was determined to unify France by stamping out Protestantism, left only 5,000 survivors from a population of 28,000. Ruined for a time, La Rochelle became prosperous once again on the lucrative West Indian sugar and slave trades.

Principal shopping areas are neatly contained within Grande-Rue des Merciers, full of half-timbered buildings, and Rue du Palais, the east and west boundaries of the old town. If you take a stroll through the streets around the fairy-tale-style Hôtel de Ville (town hall) be sure to take in the 16th-century Maison Henri II, the mirrored gilt splendour of the Café de la Paix on Rue Chaudrier, the old arcades that line Rue du Minage, and the Porte de la Grosse Horloge that was formerly the gateway between port and city. The tourist office organises tours of the old town on foot and by horse-drawn carriage.

Across the harbour mouth at Port des Minimes, reached by waterbus from the west side of the old port, you will find a marina, an aquarium and a small sandy beach.

Markets: Daily, Place du Marché. Sunday, La Pallice, 2km west of the town centre. Crafts market (15 June-15 Sept), daily, near the towers.

Brocante: Foire de la Brocante (antiques fair) April/ May. Marché aux Puces (flea market), Rue St-Nicolas, Saturday (1 July-31 Aug, Thursday & Saturday). Salon des Antiquaires (antiques fair), November.

Festivals: Carnival, mid-May. Francofolies (popular French music and culture), July. Le Grand Pavois (large in-water boat show), September.

Specialities: Charentais melons. *Chaudrée* (fish soup with white wine). *Mouclade* (mussels in cream sauce). Pineau des Charentes (a delicious fortified wine, available in amber or rosé versions, drunk as an apéritif).

Tour St-Nicolas/Tour de la Chaîne/Tour de la Lanterne. Of La Rochelle's three famous 14th-century towers, two stand either side of the harbour entrance, one containing models and plans showing the port's history, and the other a mini *son-et-lumière* show explaining the horrendous 1627 siege.

The third - the Tour de la Lanterne, a little farther west and topped with a gothic spire - is a former lighthouse and one-time prison. Its rooms are decorated with some amazing graffiti inscribed by captives, many of them English sailors who carved on to the soft stone walls of their jail the images of the ships in which they had served.

Each tower has identical opening hours and admission charge. ● *Wed-Mon 10am-12.30pm & 2-5.30pm; closed public holidays (1 Apr-30 Sept, daily 10am-7pm). Tel: 05 46 41 74 13. 25F/3.81€, students 15F/2.29€, children free.*

Musée Grévin. La Rochelle's answer to Madame Tussaud's. Waxwork figures convey the history of the town through 15 scenes, from its founding in 1199 by Eleanor of Aquitaine, through siege and slave-trading, to the deportation and execution of a 79-year-old mayor in 1944. ● *Daily 9am-7pm (1 June-30 Sept, daily 9am-11pm). 38 Cours des Dames (tel: 05 46 41 08 71). 29F/4.42€, children 19F/2.90€.*

Musée du Flacon à Parfum. More than 1,000 perfume bottles, miniatures and samples, plus labels and powder boxes in this charming and unusual collection near the Grosse Horloge. ● *Mon 1.30-7pm, Tues-Sat 10.30am-7pm (1 July-31 Aug, Mon 1.30-7pm, Tues-Sat 10.30-7pm, Sun & public holidays 3-6pm). 33 Rue du Temple (tel: 05 46 41 32 40). 25F/3.81€, students 22F/3.34€, children free.*

Musée du Nouveau Monde. A grand 18th-century mansion contains paintings, drawings, sculptures and maps telling the story of the town's links with the New World - America, Canada and, in particular, the West Indies - over the last 400 years, through emigration, plantation-owning and the slave trade. ● *Wed-Sat & Mon 10.30am-12.30pm & 1.30-6pm, Sun 3-6pm. 10 Rue Fleuriau (tel: 05 46 41 46 50). 21F/3.21€, children free.*

ST-CYR-EN-TALMONDAIS

Small village 12km west of Luçon, at the junction of *bocage* and marshes, notable for the dramatic war memorial silhouetted against the sky on the west side, as well as for its wonderful lotus ponds (see below).

Parc Floral de la Court d'Aron. A magnificent garden on the D949 to the east of the village, featuring green lawns, woodland walks, spring bulbs, summer colour from busy-lizzies and, from late June, lakes covered in thousands of exquisite pink lotus flowers on long, elegant, green stems.

Within the garden stands a 17th-century-style mansion, embellished with turrets. Still a private home, it is open during the summer for half-hour guided tours of several rooms containing monumental fireplaces, paintings, porcelain, sculpture and Flemish and Gobelins tapestries, plus a mini-museum of archaeological finds and military decorations (not ideal for unruly children). *Park ▲ Easter-30 Oct, daily 10am-7pm. Tel: 02 51 30 86 74. 44F/6.68€ (until 30 June, 33F/5.02€), children 15F/2.29€; House ✳ 1 July-31 Aug, daily 10am-noon & 2-6pm. 15F/2.29€, children 6F/0.91€ (plus admission to park).*

Église de Curzon. The pride of this simple church in Curzon, a drowsy village 3km south-east of St-Cyr, is its 11th-century crypt. Tug open the trapdoors in the floor, press a button on the right for five minutes' illumination and screw up your courage... Down below, strange faces ogle you from the tops of the carved columns - a spooky experience you'd never expect so close to the seaside razzmatazz of La Tranche, just 15km away. ●

STE-HERMINE
If you arrive from the west at this small town on the edge of the plain, 12km north-east of Luçon, you almost have the impression of falling off the wooded *bocage* on to the hundreds of hectares of crops that roll away to the horizon like an undulating ocean. The central crossroads is dominated by a monumental World War I memorial featuring the politician Georges Clemenceau (see pages 54, 89 and 107) and several *Poilus* - the affectionate nickname for French soldiers of 1914-18.
Market: Friday.

Aire de la Vendée. It may seem bizarre to suggest a motorway service station as a tourist attraction but you could spend a happy couple of hours at this one on the A83, located between junctions 6 and 7, about 4km west of Ste-Hermine: it offers three state-of-the-art museums as showcases for the region. "*La Vendée en Images*" is full of hands-on, multi-language computer screens; the "*Théâtre du Marais*" presents a 10-minute video (in French) about the ecology of L'Aiguillon Bay; and the third, "*La Vie du Marais Poitevin*", plunges you into the beguiling green wilderness of the "Green Venice" marshes - right down to the effect of duckweed under foot. The surroundings have been planted up imaginatively with marshland flora and woven willow. In July and August you may even be offered a free go at some sport, like archery - it's all part of the French motorways' scheme to combat driver fatigue by encouraging motorists to take a break. You can also reach it on foot, without paying a toll (see page 76). ● *Exhibitions open daily 10am-6pm. Free.*

St-Juire-Champgillon. This tongue-twisting *commune* (actually two separate, equally picturesque villages) 4km north-east of Ste-Hermine has turned itself into a summer artistic centre. A stroll around the alleys and lanes of either village reveals lovely houses and mansions of mellow local stone plus other unexpected delights: in Champgillon, a Jardin Blanc and a Jardin Noir (gardens planted with white or dark-coloured plants, respectively); in St-Juire, glimpses of a couple of privately-owned châteaux and, behind the school, a *Jardin des Cinq Sens*, designed to please each of our different senses, as well as a suumer-long series of art exhibitions held in a couple of barns near the *mairie*. ✳ *Exhibitions: July & August, Sun-Fri 3-8pm. Tel: 02 51 27 82 04. Free.*

ST-MICHEL-EN-L'HERM
Though it rises only 17 metres above sea level, this former island of whitewashed houses, 15km south-west of Luçon, seems almost imposing when seen across the flat marshland. From the tourist office in the centre you can take a 2.5km circular walk through the back lanes by following a series of green arrows. If you drive north along the Triaize road, look out on the right, at the hamlet of Les Chaux, for a farmhouse built on an enormous, centuries-old bank of oyster shells thought to have been either a fortification against the sea or protection from invading Normans.
Market: Thursday.
Specialities: Eels. Cheese (Petit-Vendéen, La Micheline).

Abbey ruins. Concealed in the walled gardens of a large house on the main square are the remains of a former royal abbey whose Benedictine monks were among those who undertook the draining of the marshes surrounding the village. First established in the seventh century, it was reconstructed several times after the depredations of the Hundred Years War, the Wars of Religion and, finally, the devastating Wars of the Vendée. Still intact are the 17th-century chapter-house (filled to the ceiling with mud until 1907) and the lofty refectory, while skeletal ribs of vaulting are all that remain of the *chauffoir* where the monks took exercise. Allow a good 45 minutes for this interesting visit. ✳ *1 July-31 Aug, guided tours from tourist office Tues, Thurs & Fri 10-11.30am & 3-4.30pm. Tel: 02 51 30 21 89. 15F/2.29€, students 10F/1.52€, children 5F/0.76€.*

Temple du Soleil. A collection of unusual, classically-inspired stone sculptures by local artist André Deluol. ● *Sat-Mon 3-5pm (15 June-30 Sept, Wed-Mon 3-7pm). 1 Rue de l'Étendard, just north of the church (tel: 02 51 30 25 15). 20F/3.05€, children free.*

LA TRANCHE-SUR-MER   **i tel: 02 51 30 33 96/fax: 02 51 27 78 71**

Its 13km of sandy beaches and dozens of campsites have made La Tranche, 32km south-west of Luçon, a popular family resort that is also a paradise for surfers and windsurfers. The crowds of summer visitors - particularly young people - swell the population from its winter level of around 2,000 to between 80,000 and 100,000. When weather conditions are right, surfers escape to the rollers off La Terrière and the Pointe du Grouin beaches; the less sporty will find some lovely shady walks in the forest of holm oaks and fragrant pines to the west of the town, and plenty of temporary entertainments like paint-ball, amusement parks and street performances to fill the summer days and evenings.

The town has been much rebuilt since World War II, during which many of its buildings were razed by the occupying Germans to improve sightlines for the defence of the important war-time port of La Rochelle. La Tranche has enjoyed a rather more peaceable tradition in recent years, since a couple of Dutch horticulturalists opened the eyes of the townspeople in 1953 to the idea of using their sandy soil to start a bulb industry.

If you crave relief from the flat landscape inland, try heading west to hunt for prehistoric stones in leafier countryside around Avrillé and Le Bernard or to enjoy some medieval fun at Talmont castle; go north to search for stone animals on the churches of Angles and St-Benoist or, slightly farther east, to look round the shops and cathedral in Luçon; or take a boat across the bay (see below) and spend a day in historic La Rochelle. On the other hand the flat countryside can be a positive advantage: by 2001 a 60km cycle route should be in place leading eastward alongside the canals to Maillezais, in the "Green Venice" area.

Markets: Tuesday and Saturday, Place de la Liberté. Wednesday, La Grière car park.
Festival: Parade of flowers, April.
Specialities: Flowering bulbs. Garlic. Onions.

Parc des Floralies. Gusts of perfume welcome you to these gardens, where borders and leafy glades are ablaze with spring colour, dramatic formal patterns of crocuses and narcissi, and rivers of tulips of every shape and hue. The gardens remain bright in the summer months, too, thanks to the begonias, petunias, gladioli and sweet-scented carnations - with not a dead-head in sight. Good children's playground, and some pleasantly shady picnic spots. ▲ *1 Mar-30 Apr & 1 July-30 Sept (seasons may vary according to weather conditions), daily 10am-6pm. Boulevard de la Petite-Hollande (tel: 02 51 30 33 96). Spring: 33F/5.02€, children 17F/2.59€, disabled free. Summer: Free admission for all.*

Croisières Inter-Iles. From near the Grande-Plage you can take excursions to the low-lying island known as the Ile de Ré, or to La Rochelle (see page 76). ▲ *June-Sept. Embarcadère, Parking de la Plage (tel: 02 51 27 43 04).*

TRIAIZE

Attractive marshland village 7.5km south of Luçon, grouped around a restored 12th-century church with an unusual spire that looks like a partially-inflated, wavy sausage-balloon.

The lack of wood in this open landscape meant the inhabitants had to find other methods of cooking and heating, and the village has perpetuated the once-widespread custom of making *bouses*, dung-pats that could be burnt as fuel - even the ash made a valuable fertiliser. At the annual festival of old customs the stuff is put to good use for cooking eels, mussels, *mogettes* and other regional specialities - as well as for throwing, frisbee-style.

Festival: Fête de la Bouse (cowpat festival), July.

Réserve Naturelle. From the observatory of this 200-hectare marshland wildlife reserve on open pastureland 5km north-west of the village, you can peer through telescopes at resident ducks, harriers, curlews and egrets. Winter inhabitants include wigeon, teal and greylag goose; thousands of black-tailed godwits pause here in spring when the wild orchids and irises are in flower; summer sees redshank, storks and the occasional spoonbill; migratory species like garganey and black tern may drop by in autumn. ▲ *1 Dec-28 Feb, first Sun of month, 2-6pm; 1 Mar-30 June, Sun 2-6pm; 1 July-31 Aug, daily 10am-noon & 3-7pm. St-Denis-du-Payré (tel: 02 51 27 23 92). 22F/3.34€, children 14F/2.14€.*

VELLUIRE

A prosperous-looking stone-built village 21km east of Luçon, located at a crossing-point on the Vendée river. Along the road south towards Le Gué-de-Velluire you have the strange impression of being on a cliff overlooking the ocean - indeed, the marshland that lies 40 metres below was once the sea bed.

On the north-west edge of the village is the *communal*, or common grazing land, of Le Poiré-sur-Velluire, last vestige of a tradition whereby farmers turn their animals out in spring and round them up again in December.

Festival: Celebration of new season's grazing, Le Poiré-sur-Velluire, April.

Speciality: Fiefs Vendéens wines from Vix, 5km to the south-east.

Communal. This 250-hectare reserve is being run experimentally on a system of "commons". During winter the pastureland is flooded. Once it dries out and the grass shoots up in spring, farmers turn out their horses, cows and geese - each marked with an identifying number - and the new season is celebrated with a colourful festival. The *communal* is a haven for birds: the occasional pair of storks nest here from early spring; little bustard gather in autumn; and spectacular numbers of lapwing and golden plover visit between September and March. An observatory 2km west of the village, on the poplar-edged road linking l'Anglée and La Tublerie, provides an excellent vantage-point. ●

Château de Chasteliers-Barlot. Its courageous owners are trying to renovate this imposing, white stone stronghold, built in 1593 by Protestants to guard the then mouth of the Vendée river. Although the site is not open to the public, you can have a close-up look from the lane called Chemin de Chastelier (off to the left just as you enter the village of l'Anglée to the north-west of Velluire), which carries you right through the courtyard. ●

Vieille Forge. In a village 3km south of Velluire is an old forge containing an exhibition of equipment used by the blacksmith for making tools, fitting metal rims to wagon wheels and shoeing horses, plus a video show explaining some of the techniques. ▲ *15 Apr-15 Sept, Tues & Thurs 3-5pm. 73 Rue du 8 Mai, La Taillée (tel: 02 51 52 52 05). Free.*

Église de Mouzeuil. At Mouzeuil-St-Martin, 11km north-west of Velluire, restoration of the ancient church after a recent fire has revealed a dense decoration of flower paintings on its wooden ceiling. ●

LA VENISE VERTE

Encroaching on three *départements*, this labyrinth of tranquil, duckweed-covered waterways nicknamed "Green Venice" is one of the region's most entrancing features and by far the prettiest corner of the Marais Poitevin. The vast marshland drained by 12th-century monks and 17th-century Dutch engineers stretches from Marans in the west to Coulon in the east, and from Maillezais down to Arçais.

It is criss-crossed with tiny *rigoles* - canals, edged with rustling poplars or pollarded willows - that run into the Sèvre Niortaise river.

Although it has a vaguely urban sound, the "Green Venice" is actually entirely rural. The tree-lined waterways, which serve partly as drainage for little squares of green pasture and partly as avenues of transport for everything from wedding parties to cattle, are blissfully silent, except for the buzz of dragonflies - and the giggles of incompetent crews of tourists as, unlike the expert locals, they zigzag inelegantly from bank to bank.

Between April and October you can rent canoes or workaday *plates* (flat-bottomed metal boats) from various boat-hiring establishments - with or without a guide to do the paddling. If you prefer to stay on dry land, there are plenty of signposted trails to explore on foot or by bike; cycle rental is on offer in most villages.

Specialities: Eels. *Lumas* (a local word for snails). *Coulonnais* (light, fluffy cakes). Lamb with *mogettes*.

Prettiest spots. Best known of the waterside villages - and, therefore, the most crowded is Coulon (see page 70). If you like a quieter life, it's worth trying such equally picturesque places as Arçais (see page 69), Maillezais (see page 73), Maillé (see page 73), Damvix or St-Sigismond, or exploring other rural havens like Bouillé-Courdault (Courdault has a most unusual, bulb-shaped port), La Garette or Le Mazeau. Since you can fit four to six people into one boat, the hourly hire fee of from about 140F/21.34€ (85F/12.95€ if you forgo the guide) is quite a bargain.

4. FONTENAY-LE-COMTE, POUZAUGES
AND THE HAUT-BOCAGE

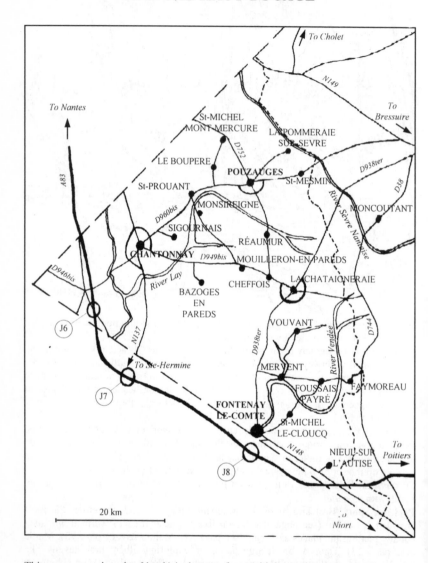

This area contains the Vendée's largest forest, highest village and - from pre-Revolution days when the area was known as Bas-Poitou - its lovely former capital of Fontenay-le-Comte. Wonderful medieval wall-paintings adorn the walls of some ancient churches around Pouzauges. In more futuristic mode, the cinema park of Futuroscope is not far away, while new museums are planned at Réaumur, to look at science, and at Faymoreau, to illustrate the Vendée's former coal industry.

BAZOGES-EN-PAREDS

You can easily spot Bazoges as you drive across the rolling green hills of the bocage; look out for a huge castle keep crowned by a jaunty little pointed watch-tower. With its solid stone buildings looking on to the square that surrounds the fortified stronghold, and its ancient church, this unspoilt village 12km south-east of Chantonnay manages to purvey an old-world atmosphere, yet with a pleasantly unfossilised look.

Festival: Foire aux marrons (chestnut festival) at La Caillère-St-Hilaire, 3km south of Bazoges, October.

Musée d'Arts et Traditions Populaires. Guided tours of Bazoges' excellent museum, housed in one of the cottages in the courtyard of the *donjon*, or keep, give a fascinating glimpse of rural life in the region (descriptive sheet available in English). Fascinating facts are imparted about rural life in former times: people believed dirt prevented disease entering through empty pores, so washed only face and hands; several generations of a family would share the same bedroom; babies old enough to crawl were tightly swaddled and placed upright with their legs in a hollow container during the day, to keep them out of danger while their mothers worked in the fields. ● *Sun 2.30-6.30pm (1 Apr-15 Sept, daily 2.30-6pm). Tel: 02 51 51 23 10. 15F/2.29€ (35F/5.34€ including castle keep and garden), children 10F/1.52€.*

Donjon. The magnificent tower dominating the town dates back to the 14th century. Recently restored and furnished, it has a principal room with a large fireplace, and windows with stone seats. Up the narrow spiral stairs a gallery running round the entire top of the building affords wonderful panoramic views of the surrounding countryside. Down below, in a beautifully laid-out medieval-style garden, fruit-trees, herbs and fragrant old-fashioned roses grow in wattle-edged beds alongside a huge 16th-century *fuie*, or dovecote, which could contain 2,000 pigeons. ● *Sun 2.30-6.30pm (1 Apr-15 Sept, daily 2.30-6.30pm). Tel: 02 51 51 23 10. 20F/3.05€ (35F/5.34€ including museum), children 10F/1.52€.*

Ciste des Cous. About 1km south-west towards La Jaudonnière, and signposted off to the right at a bleak and lonely site, is the Vendée's oldest megalithic monument. Inside an unusual, circular stone-flagged enclosure, dating from 3000BC, a low tunnel leads to a prehistoric burial chamber in which more than 100 skeletons were excavated in 1913. ●

CHANTONNAY　　　　　　　　　**i tel: 02 51 94 46 51/fax: 02 51 46 99 30**

This cheerful market town in the centre of the Vendée, 21km south-west of Pouzauges, is known as "the gateway to the *bocage*". Among its excellent range of shops are an inordinate number of charcuteries and pâtisseries; try the *pain raisonné* (raisin bread) and other goodies from Charbonnier's, on the main street.

Market: Tuesday, Thursday and Saturday.

Lakes. You can swim or fish in the Lac du Moulin-Neuf, 6km south of Chantonnay on the river Lay, follow a signposted walk around the edge or, in summer, try your hand at archery as well as sailing, canoeing and windsurfing. Sailing, fishing, walking, pedaloes and picnics can also be enjoyed at the Lac de Rochereau, 6km east of the town. ●

Château de Sigournais. High stone walls surround an imposing, beautifully restored medieval castle keep with pointed, slate-roofed turrets, in a picturesque village 4km north-east of Chantonnay. Guided tours of the interior explain coats of arms from 34 French provinces and 144 Vendean *communes*, and a collection of before-and-after photographs that show the recent restoration work on the castle. As you would expect, there are magnificent views from the covered *chemin de ronde*, or sentry-way, at the top. ✳ *1 July-early Sept, daily 2.30-6.30pm. Tel: 02 51 40 44 58. 20F/3.05€, children free.*

Puybellard. Although this village lies a mere 20 metres south of the busy D949bis, 2km north-east of Chantonnay, it produces the most astonishing feeling of having stepped back in time. The fortified church still has useful-looking slit openings alongside the front door through which defenders could fire to protect the local populace gathered within; opposite is a venerable prison tower; and behind that are narrow lanes and alleys - particuarly Rue des Dames, near the *mairie* - lined with buildings that display, in the most casual fashion, arched doorways, Renaissance porches and other ancient features. ●

LA CHATAIGNERAIE   i tel: 02 51 52 62 37/fax: 02 51 52 69 20

If you approach this little hillside town from the south-east, by the D19, you see a vast rocky outcrop supporting a handsome stone viaduct. A popular spot for country walks, it is now also the location of a bungee-jumping enterprise (see below). More surprises are in store if you arrive from the west, by the D949bis; the road is lined with a riot of miniature trees in twists and pyramids, advertising a huge horticultural enterprise.

Market: Fourth Monday of the month.

Saut à l'Elastique. If you're crazy enough to contemplate taking the 52-metre plunge above the valley of the river Mère, head for the disused viaduct on the D19, 5km east of La Chataigneraie. ▲ *Late June to early Nov, most Sats & Suns. Viaduc de Coquilleau, Route de Coulonges, near Breuil Barret (tel: 05 56 38 81 48). 300F/ 45.72€ first jump (includes certificate and T-shirt); second on same day 150F/ 22.86€.*

Chapelle de la Brossardière. Pilgrimages still take place to this pretty little Protestant chapel between La Tardière and La Brossardière, 2km north-west of La Chataigneraie, erected on the site of a massacre in 1595. It's usually locked, but you are allowed to walk around the outside of it. ●

St-Pierre-du-Chemin. This large village 6km north-east of La Chataigneraie is known for its special greyish-pink stone, called *pierre des Plochères*, outcrops of which can be seen sticking up through the surface of surrounding fields, and which has been used in the construction of several large buildings. The village's best claim to fame, however, is the relics of third-century martyr St Valentine that have been held in the church - on the left of the nave - since the mid-19th century. For obvious reasons, in mid-February the village is the focus of a "Fête des Amoureux", or Festival of Love. ●

CHEFFOIS

Above the rooftops of this picturesque village 4km north-west of La Chataigneraie towers a fortified gothic church, topped with a *chemin de ronde*, or sentry-way; its sober exterior hardly prepares you for the riot of columns and statues - and even the site of a well - that you find inside.

Rocher de Cheffois. At the top of a hill to the south of the village, behind a small 16th-century chapel, some extraordinarily craggy scenery surrounds a former quartz quarry - now a deep, dark lake. A steep, signposted walk leads around the crater. ● *Head south from the church, and then turn left into the Chemin de la Chapelle, just before the lane rejoins the main road.*

Polissoir de la Vézinière. Another curiosity is a polishing-stone used by neolithic men for sharpening stone weapons and implements 5,000 years ago. Two metres long, it has distinct marks showing where the tools were rubbed, and a panel in French explaining the technique. ● *Leave Cheffois by the St-Pierre-du-Chemin road from near the church, bear left after about 1km and continue until you see a sign to La Vézinière.*

FAYMOREAU-LES-MINES

Village on the eastern border of the Vendée, 16km north-east of Fontenay-le-Comte, in an area rich with memories of the French industrial revolution. Coal was mined in the region from the early 19th century, the industry reaching its peak between 1913 and 1958, when labourers imported from Czechoslovakia and Poland were producing up to 60,000 tonnes of coal a year to fuel a local power station and a glassworks. At the pit village of La Verrerie, 3km north of Faymoreau both miners and mine masters had their homes in three parallel streets known as *corons*, the poorest houses being at the top of the valley and the smartest - known as "Bas de Soie", or "silk stockings" - at the bottom. The restaurant of the village's imposing Hotel des Mines has been restored to its original art deco style, and the chapel built by the mine director's wife to keep the workers more attuned to Catholicism than Communism has been rescued from decline. A few other relics remain, notably the evocative pit-head tower at Epagne, 8km to the west.

Centre Minier. A new museum installed in the old glassworkers' hostel at La Verrerie tells the history of the local industry, using multi-media devices to create the impression of going down a mine. There are displays of mining lamps, tools and documents, a *"salle des pendus"* - where working clothes were hung to dry at the end of the day - plus details about the industry and the East European miners who came to work here. ● *Opens September 2000. Information from Faymoreau mairie, at La Verrerie (tel: 02 51 00 43 76). Admission details not fixed at time of going to press.*

FONTENAY-LE-COMTE   i tel: 02 51 69 44 99/fax: 02 51 50 00 90

Ancient streets lined with Renaissance houses - once the haunt of poets, scientists, philosophers and lawyers - indicate the former importance of a place that, until the French Revolution of 1789, was the capital of Bas-Poitou (as the Vendée region was formerly known). Lying near the south-eastern corner of the *département* at the junction of the plain and the steep, wooded hills of the bocage, the town was razed by the English in the Hundred Years War and later, having a large Protestant population, lived through considerable turmoil during the Wars of Religion.

The writer François Rabelais (c1494-1553) - creator of two legendary giants of French literature - spent almost 16 years in Fontenay as a monk, before moving to the abbey of Maillezais in 1524. In a series of bawdy, satiric allegories with touches of local patois he told of Gargantua, who rode on a mare as big as six elephants, and of his son, Pantagruel, who shattered the mighty ship's chains that bound him into his cradle with one blow of his infant fist, learnt all knowledge and every language, and once sheltered a whole army from the rain beneath his tongue. Some centuries later, another writer - novelist Georges Simenon, who lived in the Château de Terre-Neuve (see below) during World War II - also used the region as a backdrop: in *Maigret a Peur*, his fictional detective tracks a serial killer through the town's uncharacteristically rain-sodden streets.

The status of Fontenay was overturned after the Vendée wars, when Napoleon deemed it be too far from the geographical centre of the *département* to quell any new peasant uprisings, and picked on the then small village of La Roche-sur-Yon as his new capital.

The town is laid out on both sides of the Vendée river. Leafy Place Viète, at the top, is called after a 16th-century mathematician born in Fontenay, who is credited with the creation of modern algebra. This side of the river buzzes with activity on Saturday mornings, when the market is in full swing and stalls fill the streets - the food-hall is by the river, not far from arcaded Place Belliard and Rue du Pont-aux-Chèvres, both lined with interesting old houses. The elegantly-sculpted 16th-century Fontaine des Quatre-Tias, from which the name "Fontenay" derives, is a little to the north of the market-hall. Above it, on the site of the town's long-vanished feudal fortress, is a tree-filled park known as the Parc Baron. On the eastern side of the river, across the Pont aux Sardines, you can stroll along the pedestrianised Rue des Loges which has kept the picturesque shop-fronts and ancient houses (some with plaques outside, giving a little of their history) of stone or half-timbering from the days when this was the town's main street.

The tourist office arranges regular guided tours on foot, including some around the town's Renaissance cellars.

Market: Saturday, throughout streets. Tuesday afternoon (1 July-31 August only), regional specialities on sale near tourist office.

Festival: Les Ricochets (music and storytelling festival), July and August. 48 Heures du Chien, du Chat et du Cheval (two-day dog, cat and horse show) at Marsais-Ste-Radégonde, 6km north-west of Fontenay.

Specialities: Cantreau sponge-finger biscuits. Fiefs Vendéens wines from Pissotte, 4km north of the town.

Musée Vendéen. You should really come here to get a feel for Fontenay's history before walking around its streets. Prehistoric remains and some exquisite gallo-roman glass found locally during archaeological digs fill the ground floor. Above is a display on the region's bird life, examples of furniture typical of the southern Vendée, and pictures of the sure-footed Vendée mules. These beasts, produced by crossing the large *baudet de Poitou* donkey with a female horse, were much sought after by the French military in former times. The second floor contains works by such local artists as Paul Baudry, Charles Milcendeau and wood-engraver and etcher Auguste Lepère (1849-1918), and an interesting illuminated model of the town, complete with sound effects and commentary on its historical development (ask on arrival for headsets with English translation). ● *Wed-Sun 2-6pm (15 June-15 Sept, Tues-Fri 10am-noon & 2-6pm; Sat, Sun & public holidays 2-6pm). Rue du 137e RI, near Place Viète & Notre-Dame church (tel: 02 51 69 31 31). 13F/1.98€, students & children free.*

Église Notre-Dame. The church's slender 15th-century spire, 82.5 metres high, can be seen from almost everywhere in town; for a bird's-eye view, you can climb the tower (enquire at the museum next door). Beneath the church lies a 1,000-year-old crypt, its vaulted ceiling supported by Byzantine-style pillars. ●

Château de Terre-Neuve. Nicolas Rapin, 16th-century poet and magistrate of Fontenay, created this exquisite, fairy-tale-style stately home which he trimmed with pinnacles and turrets and adorned with terracotta statues of the Muses. Today it is a private home, but visitors are given 45-minute guided tours of some of the beautifully-furnished rooms featuring magnificent fireplaces - one depicting the search for the "philosopher's stone" (which alchemists believed would turn base metals into gold) - and mellow wooden panelling from the château of Chambord in the Loire valley, plus collections of keys, ivory, costumes and Old Master paintings. A section is devoted to the etching plates of artist Octave de Rochebrune, who was responsible for restoring the château in the 19th century, and there are collections of gothic keys, flintlock pistols and hundreds of pestles-and-mortars. ▲ *1-31 May, daily 2-6pm; 1 June-30 Sept, daily 9am-noon & 2-7pm. Tel: 02 51 69 99 41. 28F/4.27€, children 9F/1.37€.*

Tour Rivalland. One of the town's lesser-known and rather more modern attractions is located on Rue Rapin just outside the gates of the Château de Terre-Neuve. The strange octagonal spire, built by a rich freemason in 1880, is one of the earliest structures in Europe to be made of poured concrete. ●

Auzay. Picturesque village clinging to the slopes of two hills, 7km south-west of Fontenay. A rich source of neolithic discoveries, it also has a more recent historical treasure in the form of an iron bridge spanning the river Vendée, linking Auzay to the village of Chaix, that was designed by Gustave Eiffel. ●

Pétosse. A curiously quiet village 9km west of Fontenay, strung out along a main street rejoicing in the name of Rue des Chats Ferrés (Street of Iron-shod Cats). Local legend says that witches, disguised as cats, clattered along in metal-soled clogs to attend their sabbaths. Whatever the truth, if you go into the church you will find near the north-east corner of the central cupola a strange little feline figure, set to pounce from the ceiling. ●

FOUSSAIS-PAYRÉ

This picturesque village, 16km north-east of Fontenay-le-Comte, is renowned for its ancient church, and Renaissance buildings. Opposite the church are the Auberge Ste-Catherine (St Catherine's Inn), former family home of 16th-century mathematician François Viète, and a tiny 17th-century market-hall.

Market: Wednesday (July and August only).

Église. Admirers come from afar to marvel at the sculpted façade of the 11th-century church. Although the wall has had to be reinforced with buttresses, these have been ingeniously designed not to obscure the beautifully carved panels either side of the doorway that show a Crucifixion scene and the risen Christ with the disciples at Emmaus. Over the doorway you can make out weird animals, and the figure of Jesus between the symbols of the four Evangelists. Concerts are often held in the church in summer. ●

MERVENT   **i tel: 02 51 00 20 97/fax: 02 51 00 20 97**

Hillside village in the heart of the vast Mervent-Vouvant forest, 7km north of Fontenay-le-Comte. In summer the lake created by dams across the Mère and Vendée rivers is a popular spot for swimming, canoeing and windsurfing. Signposted walks lead through 5,000 hectares of oak and chestnut - especially beautiful in autumn - that are home to red deer and wild boar.

Specialities: Fiefs Vendéens wines from Pissotte, 5km south-west of Mervent.

Zoo de Mervent. Reptiles, monkeys, big cats and other animals are on view in enclosures on the wooded slopes at the edge of the forest, 3km south-east of the village. ● *The zoo is undergoing modernisation and should reopen early in 2000. Information from the tourist office (see above).*

Parc de Pierre-Brune. A beautiful drive on the D99A through the woods brings you to a large, shady, pleasantly old-fashioned leisure park in the heart of the forest, 2km north of Mervent. Once you get used to the razzmatazzy music, you'll find plenty to amuse the children in the way of adventure playground, train-rides, mini-golf, chair-o-planes, bumper-boats, mini-karting and the Vallée Enchantée, full of colourful swings, slides, roundabouts, crazy bikes, bouncy castle and seesaws. ▲ *Easter-1 Nov, Mon-Fri 2-7pm; Sat, Sun & public holidays 10am-7pm (1 June-31 Aug, daily 10am-8pm). Tel: 02 51 00 20 18. 57F/8.69€, children 57F/8.69€.*

Grotte du Père Montfort. Candles burn inside a little cave some 3km north-west of Mervent village, in which St Louis-Marie Grignion de Montfort lived for a time in about 1715, during a mission to convert the region's many Protestants to Catholicism. The cave is signposted to the east, off the D938ter; once you park and follow guiding marks painted on the rocks, you'll find the place halfway-down a precipitous slope in the forest, overlooking the river Mère. Père Montfort is buried at St-Laurent-sur-Sèvre (see page 108), where he founded several religious orders. ●

Château de la Citardière. A curiously low, solid, moated Renaissance castle, its top decorated with impressive stone spouts that look like cannons, stands in the woods 2km north-east of Mervent. On the pretext of visiting one of its temporary exhibitions, you can go inside one or two of the vaulted rooms (one contains an excellent example of a *potager*, or stone range, formerly heated by hot embers) or enjoy a snack at the *crêperie* on the ground floor. Concerts and other cultural events take place in summer. ● *Sat 5-8pm; Sun and public holidays noon-8pm (1 June-30 Sept, Thurs-Tues noon-10.30pm). Tel: 02 51 00 27 04. Free.*

Maison des Amis de la Forêt. Good tableaux of stuffed birds, boar and deer, and displays of mushrooms, tools and wooden objects show life in the forest and the uses made of the wood and other materials harvested in it. There's also a video on woodland life - to the slightly incongruous accompaniment of *Chariots of Fire* music. The museum is beside a small lake, some 2km north-east of Mervent. Children love the adventure playground with its daredevil "death-slide" and other wood-built amusements, as well as the mini-golf where each hole is designed to represent a different local tourist attraction. ▲ *Easter-31 Oct, Mon-Fri 9am-noon & 2-5.30pm, Sun 2-5.30pm. La Jamonière (tel: 02 51 00 00 87). 13F/1.98€, children 10F/1.52€.*

MONCOUTANT (Deux-Sèvres)

Lying in the wide valley of the Sèvre Nantaise, this large village 20km south-east of Pouzauges is about to become an important item on the angling map.

Centre International de la Pêche. From 2001, a huge new tourism development to the south of Moncoutant will offer lakes and rivers stocked with black-bass, trout, carp, pike and other freshwater fish - even sturgeon - each providing a different fishing challenge; aquariums, both real and "virtual"; and the last word in tackle shops. It's designed for every level of angler, from beginners to champions. English-speaking staff will be on hand to help, and country walks, geology workshops and children's fun and games are planned to entertain accompanying members of the family who might be less piscatorially inclined. Day, weekend and week-long passes available. ● *Opens spring 2001. Information from the Hotel de Ville at Moncoutant (tel: 05 49 72 60 44/fax: 05 49 72 84 76). Admission details not fixed at time of going to press.*

MONSIREIGNE

This small village is perched on a hilltop overlooking the green valleys of the bocage, 10km south-west of Pouzauges.

Musée de la France Protestante de l'Ouest. Guided tours of a museum, in a country house 3km north-east of the village, explain three centuries of Protestantism in western France. Historic items on show include photographs, documents and such objects as the metal tokens that admitted clandestine worshippers to secretly-held services during the times of religious intolerance. Jean Calvin (1509-64), the French Reformist and disciple of Martin Luther, spent some time spreading his doctrine in Poitiers, giving western France a strong Huguenot (as Calvin's brand of Protestantism was described) tradition. The Wars of Religion (1562-98) pitched Catholics against Protestants, causing death and the destruction of religious buildings on a grand scale. Eventually Henri IV (who had been himself a Protestant) converted to Catholicism on his accession to the French throne, in 1589, and nine years later issued the Edict of Nantes which brought the long religious struggle to an end. This law allowing Protestants freedom of worship endured for almost a century, until it was revoked by Louis XIV causing more than 400,000 Huguenots to flee overseas (many to Britain). Only with the Revolution in 1789 were their political and civil rights restored.

Many Protestants still live in this area - you will see in St-Prouant, Mouilleron-en-Pareds and other villages, streets named Rue du Temple (after the name given to an *église réformée* or French Protestant church). ▲ *15 June-15 Sept, Mon-Sat 10am-1pm & 2-7pm, Sun 2-7pm. Le Bois-Tiffrais (tel: 02 51 66 41 03). 15F/2.29€, children 10F/1.52€.*

MOUILLERON-EN-PAREDS

If you are in the picturesque main square around noon, you can hear the 13 bells from the Romanesque church play *Ave Maria* before the midday chimes. Incredibly, this unspoilt village, 16km east of Chantonnay, is the birthplace of not just one, but two of France's most famous wartime heroes: Georges Clemenceau (1841-1929), who was born above a baker's shop; and Jean de Lattre de Tassigny (1889-1952), who drew his first breath at the home of his prosperous grandparents.

Musée National des Deux Victoires: Maison Natale du Maréchal de Lattre de Tassigny. Cosy, 19th-century middle-class house, home of the maternal grandparents of distinguished French soldier Jean de Lattre and still furnished in comfortable bourgeois style. Decorated eight times in World War I, de Lattre became a general at the start of World War II but was imprisoned by the Vichy government. He later escaped, took command of a unit in north Africa, led the French First Army that landed in Provence in August 1944, liberated Alsace, crossed the Rhine and the Danube rivers, and accepted the surrender of Germany in Berlin on 8 May 1945. The three floors of the house are filled with family furniture and mementoes, and details of the Marshal's career, including his later service as commander-in-chief of the French forces in Indo-China in the early 1950s. Part of the display is devoted to his only son, who was killed in Indo-China in 1951 and who lies buried beside his father in the village cemetery - their graves marked with simple white crosses. ● *Wed-Mon, 10am-noon & 2-5pm (15 Apr-15 Oct, Wed-Mon 9.30am-noon & 2-6pm). Rue de Lattre (tel: 02 51 00 31 49). 22F/3.34€ (Sun, 15F/2.29€), children free. Admits to both museums.*

Musée National des Deux Victoires: Clemenceau-de Lattre. Personal relics, photographs and documents on show in the former *mairie* draw parallels between these two famous sons of Mouilleron, especially relating to the signing by Georges Clemenceau of the Treaty of Versailles on 28 June 1919, and Jean de Lattre's signature in Berlin on behalf of France at the conclusion of World War II. Look for a large stone eagle that once stood in the Reichstag in Berlin, and for a piece of used blotting-paper kept by Clemenceau as a souvenir of the 1919 treaty - Hitler had the original document destroyed, so this collection of "mirror-image" signatures is all that survives. ● *Admission details as above.*

Rochers de Mouilleron. On the eastern edge of the village, starting from the ancient pump and washing-place, you can take the Sentier des Meuniers (the Millers' Path), once busy with donkeys carrying bags of corn and flour. Splashes of paint on the ground guide you up past trees and rocks to a windy ridge where you find three majestic windmills, one now an oratory to the remembrance of Maréchal de Lattre de Tassigny, and an imposing memorial showing the Marshal with his troops. Like those on the Mont des Alouettes (see page 103), these mills and 11 others that once stood beside them played an important signalling role in the Wars of the Vendée. ●

NIEUL-SUR-L'AUTISE　　　　**i tel: 02 51 52 49 03/fax: 02 51 52 43 23**

Eleanor (Aliénor, to the French) of Aquitaine, queen of France through her first marriage to Louis VII and later queen of England after becoming the wife of Henry Plantagenet, is said to have been born at her father's castle here, 10km south-east of Fontenay-le-Comte. The group of monastic buildings that make up the abbey in the heart of the village is the most intact to survive in the whole of Poitou.

Festival: Fête de la Meunerie (milling festival), Whitsun in odd-numbered years.

Crafts: Handmade willow baskets, Daniel Breillat, Rue de l'Abbaye.

Abbaye Royale St-Vincent. Wonderful animal faces decorate the façade of the restored 11th-century abbey church. The Augustinian monks who lived here were involved in the draining of the marshland to the south, particularly in the digging of the Canal des Cinq Abbés (see page 69) around 1217. The abbey's pride is the magnificently complete cloister of white stone, dating from 1068 , where you will see the gravestone of Aénor of Chatellrault, mother of Eleanor of Aquitaine. Above the chapter house, in the former dormitory, is an evocative sound and light show about monastic life (though the illuminated captions superimpose three versions of biblical texts so artily that it's impossible to read them). Information on the abbey's history is given in an excellent leaflet handed to all visitors (available in English). In summer there are often plays, concerts and *son-et-lumière* performances. ● *Daily 9am-noon & 2-5.30pm, (1 Feb-31 Mar & 1-31 Oct, until 6pm; 1 Apr-30 June & 1-30 Sept, until 7pm; 1 July-31 Aug, 9am-8pm). Tel: 02 51 52 49 03. 15F/2.29€, students 11F/1.67€, children 7F/1.07€.*

Maison de la Meunerie. With chickens and rabbits outside, this picturesque watermill has a homely feel - though keep an eye on small children, as the floating weed makes the surface of the millpond appear solid enough to be walked on. A 45-minute sound-and-light presentation gives detailed information on the working of the mill - there's an English translation available, which you have time to read during the musical interludes. You can also visit the living-quarters of the miller and his family, charmingly furnished in traditional Vendean style. ▲ *1 May-15 Oct, Sat, Sun 3-6pm (1 June-30 Sept, daily 10.30am-12.30pm & 2-7pm). 16 Rue du Moulin (tel: 02 51 52 47 43). 20F/3.05€, children 10F/1.52€.*

Site Néolithique Champ-Durand. Early men used deer-antlers and the shoulder-blades of cattle to dig the 2km of ditches and stone walls, arranged in three concentric rings to create this earth-and-stone fortification at a windswept site just south of the village, on the Oulmes road. Discovered from aerial views in 1971, it dates from around 2400BC; research has shown it was probably also a meeting-place, a market and a graveyard. ●

NIORT (Deux-Sèvres)　　　　**i tel: 05 49 24 18 79/fax: 05 49 24 98 90**

The large, flower-decorated town straddling the lovely Sèvre Niortaise river is dominated by three features: the twin spires of the Église St-André, a sturdy castle keep and a delicate glass market-hall. Formerly renowned for tanning and glove-making, Niort is known today as the centre of the French insurance industry.

It's best to head straight for the huge open-air parking area in Place de la Breche, to the east of the old centre, and then begin exploring on foot. If you start along Rue Ricard you'll be welcomed by a pair of bronze dragons, whose sinuous bodies perform the useful function of keeping cars to the centre of the street and pedestrians to the side.

The smartest shops are on Rue du Rabot/Rue Sainte-Marthe, which lie one block south, while to the north you will easily spot the intricately-decorated 14th-century Pilori - once the town hall, but now home to a changing series of exhibitions. Other picturesque streets, many with half-timbered buildings, include Rue du Pont (Madame de Maintenon, mistress and later wife of Louis XIV - whom she is said to have pressured into revoking the Edict of Nantes (see page 88) - was born in a house on the site of number 5).

Market: Food-hall, daily; plus outdoor stalls Thursday and Saturday.

Specialities: Angelica in many forms - candied or made into jams, sweets and liqueur. *Tourteau fromagé* (a sort of cheesecake made from goat's cheese).

Halles. One of the most noticeable buildings in town is the wonderful 19th-century glass-and-metal market hall by the river. It's busy every morning - especially so on Thursdays and Saturdays. If the sight of all that food makes you hungry there's a friendly bar among the stalls, serving hearty portions of excellent *plats du jour* (dishes of the day). ●

Musée du Donjon. The vast, grey, Romanesque keep looming above the river, constructed by the English kings Henry II and Richard I, contains a museum of archaeological discoveries - including a chariot wheel found recently in the marshes, and a beautiful gold necklace dating from 2000BC. Steep flights of stone spiral steps lead upward to rooms full of local costumes, furniture and an authentic-looking Poitevin interior, plus descriptions of the glove and tanning industries, and eventually to the roof, from which you can enjoy panoramic views of the town. ● *Wed-Mon 9am-noon & 2-5pm (2 May-15 Sept, Wed-Mon 9am-noon & 2-6pm). Closed on winter & spring public holidays. Quai de la Préfecture (tel: 05 49 28 14 28). 17F/2.59€, children free (everybody free on Wed).*

Musée Bernard d'Agesci. The town's municipal museum, housed in a former girls' school, has a Beaux-Arts section that is strong on Spanish and Dutch 17th- and 18th-century paintings, plus ivories, enamels and tapestries. Other exhibitions include a collection of stuffed birds, and work by local sculptor Pierre-Marie Poisson, who created decorative pieces for some of the great French ocean liners of the 1920s and 30s. A museum devoted to schools and education is planned for the rest of the buildings. ● *Wed-Mon 9am-noon & 2-5pm (2 May-15 Sept, Wed-Mon 9am-noon & 2-6pm). Closed on winter & spring public holidays. 28 Avenue de Limoges (tel: 05 49 77 16 70). Admission free.*

POITIERS (Vienne)   **i** tel: 05 49 41 21 24/fax: 05 49 88 65 84

Although this city is some 80km from the eastern edge of the Vendée, the theme park of Futuroscope that lies 8km to the north, near the A10 autoroute, draws holiday-makers from far afield. Art historians will find much to admire in the old part of the town, almost encircled by the Clain and Boivre rivers. If you venture into the centre don't miss the Romanesque church of Notre-Dame with its intricately-sculpted façade, the gothic cathedral of St-Pierre decorated with 12th-century stained glass in vibrant reds and blues, or the Romanesque and gothic wall-paintings in the Baptistère St-Jean.

Futuroscope. In contrast to the medieval splendours of Poitiers, the architecture of this "European cinema park" is a riot of glass and strangely-angled buildings. You really need more than a day to visit everything here - not so much because of its size (the site is surprisingly compact), but because of the time spent queuing for the most popular attractions (take snacks to eat while you wait; they'll be better than the on-site ones).

The history of sound and pictures is explained through state-of-the-art visual images in the Communication Pavilion. The very latest in screen entertainment includes 3D, 360-degree cinema, and Europe's largest flat screen. You can "take off" on a space mission, "ride" a swooping rollercoaster, or "drive" a racing car in cinemas where the seats move under you. In others you can try a "magic carpet", with images projected simultaneously in front of your eyes and beneath your feet, or experience virtual reality behind a pair of special electronic spectacles. Open-air family attractions inclue bumper-boats, remote-controlled cars, slides, adventure playgrounds and a maze whose "paths" are delineated by jets of water, while indoors you can watch animated Lego models, create harmony in the "musical house" or influence the outcome of interactive cinema shows by pressing a button. On some spring and summer evenings visitors can also see a spectacular laser show.

The tourist office just inside the park can help arrange overnight accommodation, either in the adjacent modern hotels or in local *chambres d'hôte* (B&Bs); you can also borrow simultaneous-translation headsets (but must leave identification documents as a deposit). Note that children measuring less than 1m 20cm in height are not allowed in the shows where seats move with the action. ▲ *Mon-Fri 9am-6pm; Sat, Sun 9am-7pm (slightly longer hours in summer); laser shows early Apr-end Oct, Sat (July and Aug, daily) 10pm. Tel: 05 49 49 30 80. Low/mid/high season: 145F/ 22.10€, 175F/26.67€, 195F/29.72€; children 100F/15.24€, 120F/18.29€, 140F/ 21.34€; under-fives free.*

POUZAUGES   i tel: 02 51 91 82 46/fax: 02 51 57 01 69

You need to be extremely adept at hill-starts to drive around the narrow streets in the centre of this attractive town nicknamed "the pearl of the bocage" - even the buildings seem to have difficulty clinging to the rocky slopes.

A better idea is to park near the church and wander round on foot, following a painted green line that leads you on a roughly 90-minute tour via shops and major points of interest (accompanying leaflet available from tourist office).

Market: Thursday and Saturday.

Specialities: Fleury-Michon meat products (obtainable in supermarkets everywhere - even Britain).

Château de Pouzauges. Occupying the highest point in the town is the ruined, 13th-century stronghold that once belonged to the notorious Gilles de Rais (see page 110). Today pigeons are the only residents of the imposing square keep, currently undergoing restoration; you can share their bird's-eye view of the countryside if you climb the steep wooden steps to the top. ▲ *1 May-14 June, Sun & public holidays 2.30-6pm; 15 June-15 Sept, daily 10am-1pm & 2.15-7pm. Tel: 02 51 57 01 37. 15F/2.29€, children 5F/0.76€.*

Église Notre-Dame du Vieux-Pouzauges. Well signposted, about 1km south-east of the town, the church of Notre-Dame (completed in around 1066) stands in a grassy churchyard. Once inside, press a button for a seven-minute *son-et-lumière* display, with French commentary, highlighting the magnificent wall-paintings on the north side of the nave - a sort of medieval strip-cartoon. A symphony of terracotta and ochre, they are thought to date from the 13th century and were discovered under layers of paint in 1948. Five scenes on the lower level depict episodes in the the life of the Virgin Mary and her parents. Above are friezes of grotesque animals, and illustrations representing different months of the year; over the west door, are more-recently uncovered frescoes showing Cain and Abel. ●

Bois de la Folie. Druids once worshipped the mistletoe at this mysterious, distinctively-shaped clump of trees, which is reputed to be inhabited by the fairy Mélusine (see page 95) as well as by numerous pixies and goblins. You reach the hilltop wood by footpath from an exposed ridge, near the two privately-owned windmills of Terrier-Marteau that peep tantalisingly over the treetops 1km north of the town, off the Les Herbiers road. ●

Puy Crapaud. Signposted from the roundabout off the eastern side of the Pouzauges bypass, this 269-metre hill is one of the highest points in the Vendée - the locals claim that on a clear night you can see the beams of coastal lighthouses, 80km to the west. At the summit, an old windmill emerges incongruously from the roof of a restaurant; if you climb the precarious steps to the top, you are rewarded with a superb view of the Vendean hills and *bocage*. ●

Église de La Pommeraie-sur-Sèvre. The church of this time-warped village 9km north-east of Pouzauges is known for a series of Renaissance frescoes that depict in witty style, along the south wall, the Seven Deadly Sins. The procession of colourfully-clad people mounted on life-sized animals being carted off to Hell by an extravagently-horned demon was intended to remind the village's inhabitants to attend confession. Press a button for a free mini sound-and-light show in French that explains the sequence. ●

Manoir de Réaumur. A 17th-century manor house in the village of Réaumur, 8km south of Pouzauges, contains a permanent exhibition on the life of René-Antoine Ferchault de Réaumur (1683-1757), and on his achievements.

Born in La Rochelle, the versatile French scientist spent holidays at this country mansion which belonged to his family. As well as inventing the thermometer that bears his name (on which freezing-point is 0 degrees and boiling-point 80 degrees) Réaumur developed a method of making steel, attempted to cross rabbits with chickens, and carried out studies of insect life that earned him a reputation as the father of French entomology.

A major refit is under way, and the museum is due to reopen in 2001 with guided tours, multi-media presentations and plenty of hands-on scientific activities. ● *Opening 2001. Information from Réaumur mairie (tel: 02 51 57 90 99). Admission details not fixed at time of going to press.*

Château de St-Mesmin-la-Ville. A magnificent, partly-ruined, 14th-century castle overlooks a tributary of the Sèvre Nantaise river at the hamlet of La Ville, just beyond St-Mesmin and about 8km east of Pouzauges. Its walls and five towers seem to grow from the very rock, and you wonder how anybody could ever have contemplated attacking such an apparently impregnable building.

From its six-sided inner courtyard a guide takes visitors round the chapel and some of the rooms in the tower above, and points out the view from the rampart that runs around the top. (Holidaymaking health inspectors and DIY plumbers will be intrigued by the diagram of the sewage-disposal system - ultra-modern for its time - that led directly into the moat.)

Summer entertainment on the theme of feudal life is planned once restoration work is sufficiently advanced. ▲ *1 May-11 Nov, Sun & public holidays 2-6pm (late June to late Aug, daily 2.30-6.30pm). Tel: 02 51 91 24 61. 20F/3.05€, children 10F/1.52€.*

ST-MICHEL-LE-CLOUCQ

Small village 6km north-east of Fontenay-le-Comte. If you are in the area at a mealtime, check out the menu of the excellent *ferme-auberge* in a classily converted barn on Place de la Maison-Neuve - though not cheap, it offers home-produced dishes of high quality - including a garlic-rich *grillée de mogettes* (beans on toast, to the uninitiated!).

Brocante: Emmaüs (see page 60). *Mon 2-6pm, Tues-Sat 8am-noon & 2-6pm (tel: 02 51 51 01 10).*

Parc Ornithologique de Pagnolle. Everything that chirrups or twitters - from a miaowing mynah bird to cassowaries, cranes, ducks and chickens - can be seen in this attractive flower-filled garden, 3km north of the village. The shady enclosures have informative labels to describe the occupants - which also include wallabies, deer, a camel, and some shaggy *baudet* donkeys. You need a good couple of hours to take it all in. ▲ *1 Apr-30 Nov, daily 10am-dusk (until 8pm in summer). La Braud (tel: 02 51 69 02 55). 35F/5.34€, children 15F/2.29€.*

Lac d'Albert. Swim, windsurf or rent pedaloes in the summer months at this large lake on the river Vendée, 4km east of the village towards Chassenon-le-Bourg. ▲ *1 May-30 June, Sun; 1 July-31 Aug, daily.*

ST-MICHEL-MONT-MERCURE

Its dizzy altitude of 285 metres makes this picturesque village 14km north-west of Pouzauges the highest in the Vendée. A massive copper statue of St Michael, the patron saint of high places, crowns the late-19th-century church - you can climb 194 steps inside the steeple for a wonderful panorama on a clear day across five *départements*.

Festival: Fête des battages (old-time harvest day), Moulin des Justices, 15 August.

Moulin des Justices. This stocky 19th-century stone windmill, 3km north-west of St-Michel still produces wholemeal flour. Its adjustable slatted sails creak like the mast of a yacht as they turn in the wind - they're not very protected outside, so keep well away if they are in motion. During a half-hour guided tour, the miller explains the finer points of operation, and you can buy bread, flour and biscuits to take away. Nearby are some sturdy wooden climbing frames for the children, several rusty items of farm machinery and a few incongruously exotic pheasants and other birds, plus a *crêperie* with a wonderful view over the hills and valleys of the *bocage* from the grassy terrace in front. ▲ *15 Mar-30 Sept, Sat, Sun & public holidays 3-7pm (16 June-15 Sept, daily 10am-noon & 2.30-7pm). Tel: 02 51 57 79 09. 15F/2.29€, children 10F/1.52€.*

Chapelle de Lorette. In the extremely pretty village of La Flocellière, 2km east of St-Michel, is an unusual small church the interior of which is modelled exactly on the Santa Casa in the Italian town of Lorette (angels were supposed to have transported this "holy house", birthplace of the Virgin Mary, to Italy from Nazareth in 1294). The streets around the *mairie* are especially picturesque; sneak a look into some of the walled gardens and through the gates of the village's privately-owned château that has now been transformed into an elegant B&B. ●

Maison de la Vie Rurale. Welcoming farm museum 1.5km south-east of St-Michel, strong on milk production and poultry. There are explanatory panels in French on aspects of farming life, plus a plywood cow and some friendly (real) calves and chickens. An area is also devoted to vegetables, flowers and other plants - such as willow - that were an important part of rural life. Exhibitions, concerts and events on folk and countryside themes are held in summer, and you are allowed to picnic in the grounds. ▲ *1 May-15 Oct, daily 2.30-6.30pm (15 June-14 Sept, daily 10.30am-6.30pm). Ferme de la Bernardière, off D752 (tel: 02 51 57 77 14). 20F/3.05€, children free.*

ST-PROUANT

Village 10km south-west of Pouzauges, on the edge of La Pélissonnière forest. Summer sunlight filters through the trees alongside the D23 and illuminates the woodland walks; in autumn, the woods are a favourite haunt of mushroom-hunters searching for ceps and other delectable fungi.

Prieuré de Chassay-Grammont. A small, but extraordinarily well preserved 12th-century monastery - founded by Richard the Lionheart in 1196 for some 10 monks of the Grandmontine order - is signposted off the D960bis 3km south-west of St-Prouant. Having fallen into disuse long before the Revolution and been used as farm buildings until as recently as 1983, it escaped the usual wholesale destruction. Today, the tall chapel and abbey buildings still form a complete, harmonious group around the cloister, including a chapter-house and restored refectory with elegantly vaulted Plantagenet-style ceilings. The abbey contains an exhibition on the history of the hermit-like monks, who took vows of poverty, humility and chastity, and existed on a near-vegan diet of fruit, vegetables and bread. Concerts of classical music are held during the summer. ▲ *1 May-11 Nov, Sun & public holidays 2.30-6.30pm (1 July-31 Aug, daily 2.30-7.30pm). Tel: 02 51 66 40 96. 20F/3.05€, students 15F/2.29€, children free.*

Church of Le Boupère. The 12th-century church of a pretty hilltop village 5km north-east of St-Prouant looks from some angles more like a castle. Three centuries after its construction, imposing fortifications were added to protect church and villagers during the Wars of Religion, including loopholes and machicolations (openings at the top of the building, through which stones and other unwelcoming objects could be dropped on attackers). ●

VOUVANT   i tel: 02 51 00 86 80

With its postern gate and cobbled streets, this attractive fortified place 12km north of Fontenay-le-Comte could almost be a film set, and certainly deserves its title of one of the most beautiful villages in France. High on a promontory in a crook of the river Mère, Vouvant is surrounded by stout defensive walls from which you can look down on the meandering waterway below, and is filled with allusions to the region's most famous inhabitant, the mythical Mélusine (see below). Crowds throng here in the summer to admire the façade of the church, drink in the medieval atmosphere and to buy interesting crafts. On the other side of the river, pedaloes may be rented at the Pic Vert *crêperie*.

Festival: Fête folklorique (festival of folk-dancing and traditions), August.

Tour Mélusine. Ancient watch-tower that dominates the village and surrounding countryside built, according to folklore, in 1242 by the fairy Mélusine.

This legendary creature, who had been sentenced by a curse to become half-serpent each Saturday, has been credited with the construction of several mighty castles, each within the space of a single night. Some say her name is a corruption of "Mère Lusignan", and that she married into a powerful local family of that name. Before agreeing to marriage, however, she made it a condition that her husband, Raymondin, should never see her on Saturday evenings. He agreed but one day, mad with jealousy, he spied on his naked wife as she was bathing. To his amazement, he saw she had a serpent's tail. Realising that her secret was out, the distraught Mélusine flew through the window, never to be seen again, and all her works crumbled... though enough of the stone steps remain in this case to allow you a spectacular view from the top. ●

Romanesque church. The richly-sculpted 11th-century decoration on the north front of the church is one of the marvels of the Vendée. Fantastical animals surround the twin doorways, and high above them is a series of magnificent life-sized statues dating from the 15th century. Inside the church the ornamentation is simpler, and you can have a closer look at some stone carvings that repose in the 11th-century crypt. In the south aisle, a stone slab commemorates Geoffroy la Grand'Dent (Geoffrey Longtooth), supposedly the son of Mélusine and her human husband, who repented from his warmongering (see page 74) in time to ensure a Christian burial. ●

Maison de Mélusine. The artily-lit basement of the tourist office building contains a few artistic representations of the famous Vendean fairy. Among them is a copy of the sculpture commissioned from the Martel brothers (see page 33) to decorate the huge dam that holds back the Mère river. ● *Mon, Tues, Thurs, Fri 1.30-4.30pm (mid-June-mid-Sept, daily 10am-noon & 3-6pm). Place du Bail (tel: 02 51 00 86 80). Free.*

Cour des Miracles. Pretty courtyard behind the Café de la Tour, its name alluding to the story that one December day in 1715 a terminally sick child begged visiting missionary, and future saint, Père de Montfort (see page 108) for cherries. The priest told the boy's grandmother to go out and pick some - to her astonishment the tree in this little yard was bowed down with fruit. ●

5. LES HERBIERS, CLISSON AND THE VENDÉE WARS

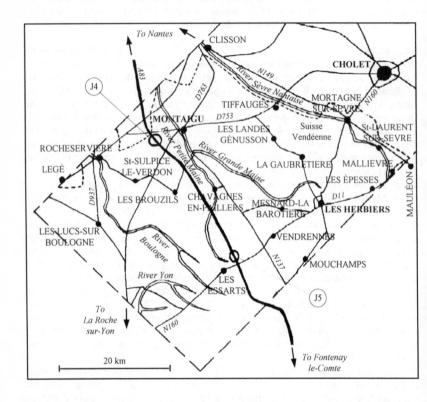

With the superb daytime and evening attractions of Puy-du-Fou, displays of medieval seige weaponry at the castle of the evil Bluebeard at Tiffauges and eloquent reminders of the Vendée Wars at the Logis of La Chabotterie, Les Lucs-sur-Boulogne and Les Brouzils, there is no shortage of interesting historical entertainment in the *bocage*. A more tranquil mood is guaranteed along the valley of the picturesque Sèvre Nantaise river, or in some of the region's tiny chapels.

LES BROUZILS
On the edge of one of the Vendée's rare forested areas, 12km south of Montaigu, this small village is one of the centres of cultivation for the Vendean food staple, the *mogette*.
Festival: Foire à la Mogette (haricot bean festival), October.
Refuge de Grasla. In 1794, almost 2,500 survivors from local families sought safety each night from the *colonnes infernales* (see page 27) at a site deep in a forest where the Vendean leader Charette often concealed his troops. Today, signposts guide you from the D7, 2km south-east of the village, to an area where the atmosphere of those times has been brilliantly reconstructed. As the lookout's horn toots from the treetops, you experience the surprise felt by the Republican General Terrand when he

stumbled upon an empty encampment after eventually venturing into this dangerous area - that was then still roamed by wolves as well as by hostile Vendeans. Today's reconstitution shows shelters improvised from wood and bracken, similar to those discovered by the Republicans, plus chapel, smithy, saw-yard and workshops, complete with appropriate sound effects and a gently smoking charcoal kiln.

Maps and a couple of videos (the first, running 20 minutes, gives an excellent explanation of the Vendée Wars) help to put you in the picture before you are taken on a short guided tour. At camouflaged information points you can press buttons to hear additional French commentary on certain aspects of the refugees' lives (explanatory sheets are available in English). You could easily spend a couple of hours in this lovely spot - especially enjoyable on a hot day when the leafy glades and picnic areas provide welcome shade. Combined with a visit to the Chabotterie (see page 109), it makes a good way of getting to grips with the Vendée Wars. ▲ *15 Apr-30 Sept, daily 2-6pm (15 June-14 Sept, Mon-Sat 11am-1pm & 2-6pm, Sun & public holidays 11am-1pm & 2-7pm). Tel: 02 51 42 96 20. 20F/3.04€, children 10F/1.52€.*

Musée des Ustensiles de Cuisine. France's only museum devoted to kitchen utensils is managed with charm and enthusiasm by the ladies of a village 8km south-west of Les Brouzils. Beautifully presented on two floors is everything from cooking stoves to potato-peelers and coffee-roasters to yoghurt-makers; dating from 1850 to 1960. Don't miss the old pressure-cookers - they were as deadly as they look! ▲ *Easter-end Oct, Sun & public holidays 2.30-6.30pm (1 July-early Sept, Wed-Mon 2.30-6.30pm). 25 Rue Georges-Clemenceau (opposite the post office), St-Denis-la-Chevasse (tel: 02 51 41 48 48). 15F/2.29€, children 5F/0.76€.*

CHAVAGNES-EN-PAILLERS   **i tel: 02 51 42 27 75**

A profusion of bell-towers and churches indicates that this small town 12km south-east of Montaigu is one of the Vendée's "holy places". In 1801 a local priest, Father Baudouin, founded its imposing seminary and two convents.

Market: Wednesday and Saturday.

Festival: Foire à la Brioche, May.

Sanctuaire de Notre-Dame-de-Salette. Built on an impossibly steep slope about 5km south of the town stands the most extraordinary sight. Just off the D17 between La Rabatelière and St-Fulgent teeter some 20 towers and turrets of stone and brick, built in 1889 and interspersed with colourfully-painted figures representing visions that appeared to two children in eastern France 43 years earlier. If you're nimble, you can scramble up past the Stations of the Cross to the simple chapel, built like a castle keep. It's safer to descend by the steps, which also give you an opportunity to look more closely at the statues. A leafy picnic area by a pretty, tree-lined stream awaits you at the bottom. Notices remind you to respect this holy place so, however tempting the idea, children should not make unseemly noise or climb on the monuments. ●

Chapelle de la Sainte Famille du Chêne. Another extraordinary religious structure is this little stone chapel built in 1874 by the same priest who erected the sanctuary above. Signposted off the D6 at La Haie, 2km south of Chavagnes and just before the junction with the D17, it is marked by a large bell dangling outside. Push open the chapel door to look at the altar; hollowed out from a tree that forms the back of the building, it has a base worn smooth by countless hands and knees. ●

CHOLET (Maine-et-Loire)   **i tel: 02 41 62 22 35/fax: 02 41 49 80 09**

Although lying outside the Vendée's eastern boundary, the town of Cholet declares itself to be the "*capitale historique de la Vendée militaire*" (historic capital of military Vendée), for the ferocious Vendean wars also involved much of the *département* of Maine-et-Loire. In spite of being sacked and burnt three times during the troubled post-Revolution years, the town centre retains a number of picturesque mansions with ironwork balconies, once the homes of wealthy cloth merchants. Principal shopping streets are clustered around the twin-spired 19th-century church of Notre-Dame on the rather bleak main square; look for the far more atmospheric Place Rougé, just to the side.

Toiles (textiles) made the city's fortune in the 18th century; today the emphasis is on the manufacture of ready-to-wear garments and shoes. The curious additional claim to be France's "*capitale du mouchoir*" (handkerchief capital) comes from the heyday · of the town's textile industry when this was one of the specialities manufactured. The humble product shot to prominence in 1900 when Théodore Botrel, a celebrated Breton cabaret artist, created a stirring romantic song called *Le Mouchoir rouge de Cholet* (The Red Handkerchief of Cholet), in which he sang of a soldier who bought three white Cholet handkerchiefs as a present for his true love. Before he could give them to her, they were requisitioned by General Charette (see pages 26, 27 and 109) - one to wear on his head, one to hold his sword, and the third to pin over his heart and staunch the flow of blood. Such was the success of the song, that the town began to turn out handkerchiefs of blood-red, woven with white (the identifying colour worn by the Vendeans); these can still be bought today from many shops, including La Bonne Toile de Cholet at 2 Avenue Gambetta.

Market: Saturday, 8am-5pm.

Festival: Carnival, second Sunday in April (illuminated procession on the following Saturday).

Musée d'Art et d'Histoire. Ultra-modern museum, devoted largely to the Vendée wars and the city's role in them - more than 50 per cent of its population was killed in · the four years of fighting (a good explanatory leaflet about the wars is available in English). Among some fascinating exhibits are weapons, objects, and a series of dramatic 19th-century paintings commissioned by Louis XVIII of both Republican and Vendean leaders. Other displays feature 18th- and 19th-century sculpture, and a large collection of contemporary abstract works. The museum, up a rather precipitous flight of steps, is not too well indicated but is on a boulevard immediately south of the town centre, just beyond the gardens of the Palais de Justice; try parking in one of the little streets across the river. ● *Wed-Mon 10am-noon & 2-6pm. Closed on public holidays. 2 Avenue de l'Abreuvoir (tel: 02 41 49 29 00). 20F/3.04€, students and children free (admission free for all on Sat, from Oct to May).*

Musée du Textile. The brick chimneys of this former bleaching-house dating from 1881, located 1.5km from the town centre on the D752, are visible from afar. The building is now beautifully restored as a museum, showing stages in the manufacture of Cholet's famous textiles. A new, glass-roofed section contains some huge *metiers*, or looms, which the guide sets in motion, making a wonderful clatter. In an old engine shed nearby you can feel the texture of cotton, linen and hemp; outside is a garden full of plants used for dying (e.g. woad) or carding (teasels). ● *Wed-Mon 2-6pm (1 June-30 Sept, Wed-Mon 2-6.30pm). Closed public holidays. Route de Beaupréau (tel: 02 41 75 25 40). 10F/1.52€, children free.*

Parc Oriental. Created in 1900 by a Paris architect who adored the Far East, this amazing Japanese-style garden, 13km south-east of Cholet, fell into oblivion during the 1940s until rescued by local horticultural enthusiasts in 1980. Many of its sculptures and temples were found to have been recycled from the 1900 Paris Exposition Universelle; the layout, symbolising the four seasons of life, is inspired by Edo designs of 16th to 19th centuries. Around the lake a tranquil effect is created by the pagoda, the curved bridges and the 120 species of trees and shrubs - including magnolias, maples and pines - complemented by delicate, Japanese-inspired work on sale in a pottery studio within the grounds. Though lovely at any time of year, the garden is, of course, is at its absolute best in April at the time of the cherry blossom. ▲ *1 Mar-15 Nov, Tues-Sat 2-6pm, Sun & public holidays 2-7pm (1 July-31 Aug, daily 10.30am-7.30pm). Beside Château Colbert hotel, Maulévrier (tel: 02 41 55 50 14). 30F/4.57€, disabled 18F/2.74€, children free.*

CLISSON (Loire-Atlantique)   **i tel: 02 40 54 02 95/fax: 02 40 54 07 77**

Your first impression on glimpsing this captivating town on the banks of the Sèvre Nantaise river, some 25km west of Cholet and on the northernmost border of the Vendée, is of having somehow strayed into a corner of Tuscany - an unexpected side-effect of the Vendée Wars. The Republicans' fire-and-sword policy ruined the castle in 1794 and flattened Clisson, leaving just two ancient bridges across the Sèvre and its tributary the Moine. Rebuilding was started in Italianate style by the wealthy Cacault brothers - Pierre and François - and Frédéric Lemot, a sculptor whom they had known in Italy. The idea caught local imagination and from the early 19th century a harmonious collection of buildings grew up on the slopes above the two rivers - even influencing the design of some of the factories along the banks. Floodlit on summer nights, Clisson's steep cobbled streets and stairways take on an even more magical quality. Friday mornings are fun, because of the busy market (try to avoid visiting between Sunday and Tuesday, though, as either shops or castle are closed). There are restaurants to suit every taste and pocket, and shady picnic places near the Moulin Plessard watersports base, about 500m south-east.

Signposted footpaths lead along the banks of the Sèvre from Le Pallet in the north to Tiffauges in the south. The tourist office arranges guided tours of the town and some of its local industries, or you could follow the *"Route Touristique du Vignoble du Val de Loire"* (a trail through the wine-producing areas of the Loire Valley), visiting vineyards producing Muscadet, Gros-Plant du Pays Nantais and Coteaux d'Ancenis between Clisson and Saumur, 100km to the east. Since this is serious Muscadet country, you might want to buy the *Guide Pratique des Étapes en Muscadet*, a book listing wine producers and places where you can enjoy a few *dégustations* (wine-tastings). You may need cash for any wine purchases you intend to make.

It's a little-known fact that Clisson is the home of *The Magic Roundabout*. Eric Thompson's laconic style and English scripts were a perfect match for the drily witty French commentaries written by the late Serge Danot, creator of these much-loved children's programmes. All the episodes of *Le Manège Enchanté*, as the television series is better known in France, were filmed in one of the waterside Italianate buildings between Moulin-Plessard and Gétigné, where Margote and Zébulon (sorry: Florence and Zebedee!) took their first steps, and a heavily English-accented Pollux (Dougal) nibbled his first lump of sugar.

Market: Friday (throughout the streets).

Festival: Baroque music in the town's churches and in the Villa Lemot (see below), July and August. Les Mediévales (medieval entertainment), August.

Specialities: Muscadet de Sèvre-et-Maine and Gros-Plant wines.

Château de Clisson. The successive enclosures and improvements carried out between the 12th and 16th centuries make this impregnable-looking stronghold - now a dramatic ruin overlooking the town - a fascinating example of the different styles of military architecture. In one of the courtyards, 18 of the town's inhabitants perished when they were thrown into a well by Republicans in 1794. ▲ *1 Mar-30 Nov, Wed-Mon 9.30am-noon & 2-6pm. Tel: 02 40 54 02 22. 15F/2.29€, children 10F/1.52€.*

Les Halles. Wander inside the town's market hall, between the castle and the nearby church, and look up at the incredible network of 15th-century wooden beams that support its roof. The building survived the town's destruction only because of its usefulness as a temporary barracks during the Vendean wars. ●

Garenne Lemot. Large, steeply sloping park studded with follies, statues, temples and grottoes on the east bank of the Sèvre, designed by the sculptor Frédéric Lemot (1771-1827) as his own country retreat. ● *Daily 9.30am-6.30pm (1 Apr-30 Sept, daily 9am-8pm). Free.*

Maison du Jardinier. Charming, Italian-style, rustic building near one of the park entrances containing an exhibition showing the Italian influences on the town's architecture. ● *Tues-Sun 10am-noon & 2-5.30pm (1 Apr-30 Sept, daily 9.30am-12.30pm & 2-7pm). Tel: 02 40 54 75 85. Free.*

Villa Lemot. An elegant building inside the park, open for temporary art exhibitions. From the villa's terrace you look straight across the river towards the Temple de l'Amitié, burial place of Frédéric Lemot whose vision is so indelibly stamped on the town. ● *During exhibitions, Tues-Sun 2-5.30pm. Tel: 02 40 54 75 85. Free.*

LES ÉPESSES

This small village in the haut-bocage, 10km north-east of Les Herbiers, is the focus for some of the *département*'s best-known entertainment at the world-famous castle of Le Puy-du-Fou (see below).

Factory shop: France Mode (women's shoes). *Tues-Fri 2-6pm, Sat 10am-noon & 2-7pm. Rue de l'Industrie, signposted, on the southern edge of the town (tel: 02 51 57 30 58).*

Musée de la Voiture à Cheval. Around 50 horse-drawn vehicles, from 18th to 20th centuries, most of them beautifully restored, make up this surprisingly fascinating collection near the village centre. Many have hidden details like pull-out tables, cunningly-concealed holders for revolvers, convertible roofs, and spikes on the runners at the backs of carriages to discourage robbers from jumping aboard. ▲ *1 Apr-31 Oct, Sun 2.30-6pm (1 May-30 Sept, daily 9am-noon & 2-6pm). Tel: 02 51 57 39 04. 38F/5.79€, students & children 20F/3.04€.*

Puy-du-Fou. The name of the ruined granite-and-brick Renaissance castle 2km north-west of Les Épesses, burnt down by Republicans in 1794, is now synonymous with the dazzling *"Cinéscénie"* sound and light show staged there during the summer months. In addition, there is a museum and a theme park (see below), so plenty to entertain the whole family day or night (though it's probably a bit exhausting to try and cram everything into the same day).

Écomusée de la Vendée. In the surviving wing of Puy-du-Fou castle is a museum of Vendean history from prehistoric times to the present. There are fine examples of Romanesque stone-carving, and explanations of the Wars of Religion that pitched Catholics against Protestants throughout the Renaissance period in the Bas-Poitou (as the Vendée was known until the time of the Revolution). An ingeniously illuminated model of the Vendée, Brittany and Maine-et-Loire gives a 20-minute explanation, with sound effects and French commentary, on the start of the uprising that evolved into the Vendée wars (you will get more from this if you first read the section on page 25). The museum's air-conditioning makes this a wonderful place to spend an hour or two on a scorching day. Across the courtyard is an interesting collection recalling the industries of the Vendée, from bicycles to tileworks, Lussault clocks to Cantreau sponge fingers. ▲ *1 Feb-31 Dec, Tues-Sun 10am-noon, 2-6pm (1 May-30 Sept, Tues-Sun 10am-7pm). Tel: 02 51 57 60 60. 15F/2.29€, children free. (Note: The museum will be moving to the grand new Historial due to open at Les Lucs-sur-Boulogne in 2003.)*

Grand Parc. A whole day is hardly enough to take in all the entertainment on offer at this impeccably organised "historical theme park". Arrive as early as possible, and plan your day around the various performance times: the falconry, jousting, storming of the medieval keep and legend of St-Philibert are the most spectacular; chariot-racing is due to be added to the menu in 2001 and a brilliant new children's play feature in 2002. The rest of the time there will never be a dull moment, as you wander round a reconstructed 18th-century Vendean village (including an scarily gloomy tunnel with recreations of scenes of the Vendée Wars), pass through the medieval township full of costumed entertainers and wandering animals, look around a typical fort and thatched village of the year 1000, and appreciate the immaculately-kept gardens. Don't forget sun hats and other protective clothing; though many of the paths are through shady woodland, the main shows are in the open, with little shelter. Drinks and snacks are on sale (you are not allowed to take picnics into the grounds, though you may leave to eat your sandwiches in the car park, and be re-admitted later), and there are a couple of atmospheric restaurants on site offering meals with period entertainment thrown in for around 105F/16€, children 45F/6.86€. ▲ *1-31 May, Sat, Sun & public holidays 10am-7pm; 1 June-mid Sept, daily 10am-7pm. Tel: 02 51 64 11 11. 115F/17.53€, children 50F/7.62€.*

Cinéscénie: *Jacques Maupillier, paysan vendéen.* Some 200,000 spectators a year come to see this incredible open-air, night-time show, first performed in 1977. More than 800 local people and 50 horsemen act out the history of the Vendée through the life of "Jacques Maupillier", an archetypal Vendean, to the accompaniment of lasers, fountains, fireworks and the most sophisticated of sound and lighting techniques. The commentary, using the voices of Philippe Noiret and other famous actors, is entirely in French; although foreign-language translations are available through special headsets, these do tend to detract from the atmosphere of the event. Anyway, after a slightly slow start the overall visual effect is so breathtaking that total understanding of the story hardly matters. Galloping horses thunder out of the castle to fall over at your feet, ballet dancers perform seemingly upon the very surface of the lake, and sudden bursts of light reveal hundreds of actors who have composed themselves into living tableaux in the darkness. The picturesque castle and its lake provide the backdrop to this thrilling spectacle, the ultimate in *son-et-lumière* performances.

As two-thirds of the seats tend to be sold by January, you do need to apply early (reservation office staff speak English, and it's possible to book by credit card) since there are only about 20 performances a year, but note that the show continues whatever the weather and absolutely no refunds are made. Once the sun sets, night breezes can whistle across the lake even on the warmest evening, so dress warmly and take rugs or sleeping-bags to cover legs - large plastic bin-liners for each member of the family are a wise standby if it looks like rain. Arrive at least one hour before the start to find your places in the grandstand. If you have difficulty obtaining seats, it's worth trying tourist offices anywhere in the Vendée for coach packages, which may have some of their block bookings left. It's no good relying on buying a ticket at the gate. Astonishingly, once the performance ends there seem to be no traffic jams; somehow all those thousands of vehicles just melt into the night. ▲ *Late May-early Sept, mostly Fri & Sat. June/July starts 10.30pm; Aug/Sept starts 10pm; the show runs about 1hr 40 mins. Tel: 02 51 64 11 11. 125F/19.05€, children 45F/6.86€.*

Maison de la Mariée. Local volunteers give a guided tour of a house on the main square of a pretty village 8km north-east of Les Épesses, now transformed into an interesting museum of marriage customs and costumes. Bulging wardrobes upstairs are full of hats, *coiffes*, dresses and shawls, giving a flavour of 19th-century life; downstairs is a reconstituted schoolroom, with old desks, maps and some model pupils. ▲ *1-30 June, Sat, Sun 9am-noon & 3-7pm (1 July-31 Aug, Tues-Sun 9am-noon & 4-8pm). Chambretaud (tel: 02 51 91 50 38/02 51 61 50 93). Free.*

LES ESSARTS
i tel: 02 51 62 85 96

Industrial and market town 20km south-west of Les Herbiers, dominated by the romantic ruins of its feudal castle.

Market: Wednesday and Saturday.

Brocante: Emmaüs (see page 60). *Tues, Wed, Fri 2.30-6pm; Sat 9am-noon & 2.30-6pm. Bois-Jaulin, off N160 2km south-west of Les Essarts (tel: 02 51 06 06 85).*

Château des Essarts. Henri of Navarre (later King Henri IV) is said to have slept at this now-ruined castle in 1588. Of the *logis*, or main house, little remains but a Renaissance fireplace hanging precariously at second-floor height. A climb up the spiral stairs of the square, 11th-century Tour de la Sarrazine gives a good view over the town and, on the edge of the grounds, near a holy statue, you can see an earth-covered tumulus thought to be an ancient Gallic burial mound. ▲ *15 June-15 Sept, daily 10am-noon & 2-6pm. Tel: 02 51 62 88 86. 10F/1.52€, children free.*

Parish church. Beneath the huge 19th-century church is the Romanesque crypt of an ancient priory. Enter through the south door and go down a little stone stairway on the south side of the church (press a button for lighting, and another to illuminate the crypt). A French commentary tells you the crypt's history while you admire the sculpted pillars and vestiges of wall-paintings. ●

Château de la Grève. Interesting 12th-century castle at St-Martin-des-Noyers, 8km south-east of Les Essarts, that was fortified during the Hundred Years War. Over the last 150 years the château has been used as farm buildings, but it is gradually being restored; a guided tour features the moat, turrets, mullioned windows, granite fireplaces and vaulted cellars. ✱ *1 July-31 Aug, daily 3-7pm; 1-25 Sept, Sun 3-7pm. Tel: 02 51 07 86 36. 15F/2.29€, students 10F/1.52€, children free.*

LA GAUBRETIERE

Known as the "Pantheon of the Vendée", this village 9km north-west of Les Herbiers is the last resting-place of many who served in the Vendean uprising; during the war and its reprisals La Gaubretière lost 1,200 of its 1,700 population. In the centre of the village is a memorial to General Charles-Henri Sapinaud, one of the Vendean generals, who miraculously survived the troubles and died in 1829 after having been the village's first mayor.

Factory shop: Rautureau Apple Shoes (see below).

Cimetière. The local victims, and some of the counter-revolutionary Vendean leaders, are buried either in family tombs or in a mass grave beneath a large granite obelisk. The cemetery is not very well signposted, but is off to the right after the church, about halfway down the hill on the D9 Tiffauges road. ●

Château de Landebaudière. Somewhat austere 18th-century mansion, now municipal offices, surrounded by a park of peaceful, tree-lined avenues on the Tiffauges road, north-west of the village. The Duc d'Elbée (see page 38) was married here in 1788, and the château also sheltered the Marquis de Bonchamps (see page 27) after he had been wounded in battle. ● *Park only.*

Rautureau Apple Shoes. This brightly decorated factory shop selling jazzy footwear for men, women and children strikes a distinctly upbeat note. Gaudy modern scarecrows are painted on the outside; inside is full of zany shoes, as featured in *Vogue, Elle* and other magazines. Even if you can't see yourself in their way-out designs, it's worth visiting just to admire the trendy clientele, and such items as patchwork suede boots and leopardskin-patterned kids' wellies. ● *Mon-Fri 10am-noon & 2-7pm; Sat 10am-6pm. 38 Rue Commandant Sauvageot, D9 between cemetery and château (tel: 02 51 66 36 65).*

LES HERBIERS   **i** tel: 02 51 92 92 92/fax: 02 51 92 93 70

Busy little town overlooking the Grand Maine river, at the north-west end of the Vendean hills and 25km south-west of Cholet. Among its many industries are several nationally-known clothing manufacturers and the Jeanneau boat-building company (now part of Bénéteau, see page 40). Les Herbiers' disused station building, now a fashionable bar, is the southern terminus for the steam train that runs in summer from Mortagne-sur-Sèvre (see page 107).

Market: Thursday and Saturday.

Specialities: Jeanneau boats. Ready-to-wear clothing. Albert chocolates.

Factory shops. Vecopri (children's clothes); *Mon-Fri 9.30am-12.30pm & 2.30-7pm, Sat 9.30am-7pm; Route de La Roche-sur-Yon (tel: 02 51 66 91 00).* Alain Manoukian (men's and women's clothes); *Mon-Sat 10am-7pm; Route de La Roche-sur-Yon (tel: 02 51 64 92 39).*

Mont des Alouettes. This windy ridge, at a high point (231 metres) on the Cholet road 3km north of Les Herbiers, was considered in pre-motorway days the gateway to the Vendée. The three windmills that stand here today (along with four others, now demolished) were important semaphores for the Vendean forces during the 18th-century uprising. Hidden in the leafy *bocage* below, royalist sympathisers could be told of the enemy's movements through the position in which the mills' sails were parked: signals included x for "all clear" and + for "alert". A chapel completed in 1823 by the Duchesse de Berry (see page 28) commemorates the wars (though you take your life in your hands crossing the busy N160 for a closer look). One mill has been restored, and is once again grinding corn. ▲ *Windmill: 1 Apr-30 Sept, Tues, Thurs-Sun 10am-1pm & 3-7pm (1 July-1 Aug, daily 10am-1pm & 3-7pm). On N160 (tel: 06 14 41 62 40/02 51 67 16 66). 15F/2.29€, children 10F/1.52€.*

Château d'Ardelay. A striking, square tower with a distinctive, red-tiled, pointed roof dominates the village of Ardelay, 3km south of Les Herbiers. You can tramp into the walled courtyard over the wooden drawbridge spanning the dry moat. During temporary exhibitions, you can also visit the elegantly-restored 15th-century rooms - empty but for some magnificent granite fireplaces - and admire the array of timbers that support the steeply-pitched roof. ▲ *During exhibitions, Sat, Sun 2.30-6.30pm. Tel: 02 51 66 95 41. Free.*

Abbaye de Notre-Dame de la Grainetière. Founded in 1130 by Benedictine monks, this abbey 8km south-west of Les Herbiers was fortified, and withstood an English seige in 1372. (Students of French literature may like to know that Abbé Prévost wrote several chapters of his sentimental novel *Manon Lescaut* here, around 1731.) The abbey's fortunes declined, and after being severely damaged by Protestants during the Wars of Religion the building was reduced to further ruin in the aftermath of the Revolution and the Vendée Wars, when it was sold off for use as a quarry and farm. Today it is a peaceful place. One side of its stone-flagged gothic cloister, supported on a series of graceful twin columns, remains intact; the only other surviving feature is a magnificent vaulted *salle capitulaire* (chapter-house). Since the late 1970s, the abbey is home once again to a small group of Benedictine monks who offer guided tours by appointment, though you can also wander around and admire the buildings by yourself. ● *Tues-Sun 2.30-5.30pm. Tel: 02 51 67 21 19. 10F/1.52€, children free.*

Vieille Église St-Christophe. On the edge of Mesnard-la-Barotière, a village 8km west of Les Herbiers, is a pretty 11th-century church that contains some wonderful medieval wall-paintings - best seen in broad daylight, since there is no electric lighting in the church. Even the most bloodthirsty child may flinch at the 13th-century depictions of poor St Laurent being barbecued over blazing logs, or the beheading of John the Baptist. Less gruesome panels include the Annunciation, the Nativity and the Last Supper, and a scene thought to show the paintings' wealthy sponsors. Tops of columns around the chancel are decorated with primitive stone carvings of leaves and roughly-hewn beasts. Some descriptive notes lie on the altar.●

Lac de la Tricherie. This open expanse of water 1km south-west of Mesnard is a popular place in summer for swimming, boating and fishing, with additional attractions of a mini-golf, *crêperie* and some shady picnic tables. ●

LEGÉ (Loire-Atlantique)
A tall cyclindrical water tower that - along with a lofty chapel commemorating the Vendean leader Charette - dominates the skyline, proclaims the name of this town mid-way between Nantes and Les Sables-d'Olonne long before you arrive. Legé became prosperous as part of the "Marches of Brittany", a free-trade zone between the former dukedom of Brittany and the kingdom of France. However, since Charette made his base here - at 2 Rue Madame de la Rochefoucauld, south-east of Legé's massive church - the town suffered cruelly at the hands of the *colonnes infernales* (see page 27) in 1794.

L'Enclos de la Colonne. This strange garden behind the Super U car park is full of grottoes and religious statues. A place of pilgrimage, it is located just off the Rocheservière road; turn left immediately after the shopping centre. ●

Château du Bois-Chevalier. This charming, moated house, signposted off the Rocheservière road, 3km north-east of Legé, is a rarity - a stately home that has emerged unscathed from the troubles of the late-18th century. Built in 1655, the house has slate roofs and brick chimneys that are mirrored in the still waters that surround it. During the Wars of the Vendée it belonged to royalist sympathisers and General Charette, a frequent visitor, used to hold parties in the drawing-room. A 45-minute guided tour (with accompanying notes in English) takes you from dining-room to attics of what is still essentially a family home. ▲ *1 June-30 Sept, Mon, Wed-Sat 10am-noon & 2-6pm, Sun 2-6pm. Tel: 02 40 26 62 18. 25F/3.81€, children 20F/3.04€.*

LES LUCS-SUR-BOULOGNE   **i tel: 02 51 46 51 28/fax: 02 51 46 51 20**
On 23 February 1794 the Republican *colonnes infernales* (see page 27) wiped out 564 women, children and old people who had sought sanctuary in a hilltop chapel. Today the village, 23km north of La Roche-sur-Yon, contains a shrine to not only the local victims but to all who fell in the post-Revolution civil war. Due to open at Les Lucs in 2003 is the Historial de la Vendée, a new museum that will present the entire history of the *département* from neolithic times to its 20th-century agricultural, fishing and other industries.

Mémorial de Vendée: Chemin de la Mémoire. Alexander Solzhenitsyn performed the opening ceremony for this hall of memory, 1km north-east of the village centre, in 1993 - the bicentenary of the Vendée Wars. Situated at the foot of the hill crowned by the Petit-Luc chapel, the low, slab-sided building arouses mixed reactions, yet the mistake is to think of it as a museum.

Small, knee-high panels identifying some of the wars' leading figures line the path to a wooden footbridge that spans a moat surrounding the sombre memorial building. Inside, a few, exquisitely-chosen items are spotlit - though you need a torch to read the tiny labels that lurk in the dark beside them, and certainly would find it helpful to know something about the characters and events beforehand (see page 25). However, once you let the hypnotic music seep in, the overall effect is extremely moving. Roughly-crayoned abstract sketches are projected, suggesting the murders, fire and pillage of this march of terror; real examples of the menacing weapons that the peasants improvised from their scythes and hedging tools (they turned around the blades to convert them into lethal bayonets) look as chilling now as they did two centuries ago.

After you emerge into the daylight, blinking and somewhat subdued, you can climb a steep wooded slope to the chapel of Petit-Luc (see below). ● *Wed-Mon 10am-6pm (1 Apr-31 Oct, daily 10am-6pm; 1 May-31 Aug, daily 10am-7pm). Tel: 02 51 42 81 00. Free.*

Chapelle du Petit-Luc. At the top of the hill (see above) stands a chapel built on the site of the massacre from the stones of the original church and containing marble panels bearing the names and ages of each of the 563 dead. (It is also possible to reach the chapel by road; drive back into the village, then out again on the D39 towards St-Denis-la-Chevasse, and turn left where indicated.) The 564th victim, Abbé Voyneau the village priest, is commemorated by a simple stone column: walk down from the chapel to the D39, go straight across and past the old presbytery; the memorial marking the spot where he was put to death stands near a little stream. ●

Église St-Pierre. The 20th-century stained-glass windows in the church on the crossroads at the centre of Les Lucs tell the tale of the tragic events that took place in the chapel on the hill (see above), as related by the *curé* Barbedette, a local priest who noted the names and ages of all the dead. To hear a French commentary on the pictures, look behind the organ for a set of coloured buttons; press the yellow one, wait five seconds, and then press the green. ●

MALLIÈVRE

The last vestiges of a feudal castle overlook this attractive, granite-built village on the Sèvre Nantaise river 15km north-east of Les Herbiers that - with an area of just 17 hectares - has the distinction of being the Vendée's smallest *commune*. It's best to park on the west side of the river, and walk in over the bridge. The narrow, sloping streets are bordered by large houses once inhabited by weavers and weaving-masters, who installed their workers in cellars beneath their homes; guided tours in summer from Friday to Sunday at 3.30pm. A trail called the Circuit des Fontaines (map from the Maison de l'Eau, see below) is punctuated by occasional commentary points, marked with blue plaques, where you can press a button to hear more about the industry. Nearby are the picturesque hills and dales of the "Suisse Vendéenne" (see page 109), which stretches from Mallièvre north-west to Tiffauges.

Factory shop: Société Cardin (household linen, from towels and dressing-gowns to tea towels and the famous red handkerchiefs of Cholet). *Mon-Fri 9am-noon & 3-6pm; closed 1-15 Aug. By river, on D11 (tel: 02 51 65 36 30).*

Maison de l'Eau. After standing in the dark listening to a long and rather portentous introduction on the theme of water, you progress to more enjoyable films, models and aquariums among a series of rooms, upstairs and down, in the house of a former weaving-master. Aspects covered include water-fuelled industries such as fulling, degreasing, paper-making and flour-grinding, as well as defensive moats, leisure activities and spectacular fountains.

You can also sniff different "*eaux*" - *eau de javel* (bleach), *eau écarlate* (grease-spot remover), *eau de vie* (alcohol), *eau de cologne* and so on, guess whether it requires more water to grow 100g of rice or to make 100g of paper (answer: yes, 17 times as much!), and see how much water is consumed by various domestic appliances. English leaflet available. ▲ *1 Apr-15 Oct, Sun & public holidays 2-7pm (15 June-15 Sept, daily 10am-noon & 2-7pm). 7 Rue de la Poterne (tel: 02 51 65 33 99). 30F/4.57€, children 15F/2.29€.*

Vitrine du Pêcheur. In a small street alongside the Maison de l'Eau (see above) are beautiful displays of fishing tackle, with examples of oxygenating plants and some handsome stuffed zander, perch and tench, as well as videos about angling. ▲ *As Maison de l'Eau, above. Free.*

La Cave du Tisserand. One cottage near Mallievre's market square has been equipped with a loom and has a mini *son-et-lumière* giving an idea of a weaver's life a century or more ago. ▲ *As Maison de l'Eau, above. Free.*

MAULÉON (Deux-Sèvres)   **i tel: 05 49 81 95 22**

Small town on a rocky spur above the river Ouin, 23km south-east of Cholet. From the esplanade of the ruined castle, there's a great view over the valley of the river Ouin, where a bloody battle took place between Vendeans and Republicans in 1793.

La Vie des Jouets. Hundreds of shiny-cheeked dolls are arrayed alongside model aeroplanes and fire-engines, board games and lead soldiers in a fantastic museum, featuring more than 3,000 toys from 1830 to the present day. ● *Wed-Sat 2-6pm; Sun & public holidays 2.30-7pm (1 July-31 Aug, Mon-Sat 10am-1pm & 2-7pm; Sun 2.30-7pm). 6 Rue du Château (tel: 05 49 81 64 12). 25F/3.81€, children 15F/2.29€; family (2+3 or more) 80F/12.19€.*

MONTAIGU   i tel: 02 51 06 39 17

This attractive town overlooking the confluence of the Maine and Asson rivers, 52km south-west of Cholet, is still partly surrounded by solid medieval ramparts. Little remains of the 12th- to 15th-century castle, fortified and moated by Louis XI. It was dismantled on orders from Henri III to prevent it becoming strategically useful to Protestants. However, there are pleasant pathways in the gardens around the fortifications, and shady picnic spots alongside the Maine river or in the Parc des Rochettes a little way along Rue de Nantes, full of lawns and trees considered by the locals to typify an English parkland. Narrow streets off Rue Clemenceau, the main shopping thoroughfare, wind alongside ancient walls past some picturesque old houses. Montaigu's tourist office is particularly well supplied with information on the Vendée, as well as on neighbouring Loire-Atlantique and the Muscadet region, and organises occasional guided walks around the town. Try and avoid visiting on Sunday or Monday, though, as shops and museum are closed.

Market: Saturday.

Festival: Literary festival, June.

Musée de Nord-Vendée. A collection of objects and documents illustrating the history of the northern part of the *département*, is housed in a pretty stone pavilion - the oldest building in the town - on the site of the medieval castle. The cellar holds glass, pottery & sarcophaguses; the ground floor presents domestic objects. At the top of the building, among the *coiffes* (head-dresses) and agricultural implements, is the strangest exhibit of all - a stuffed calf with two heads, two tails and six legs. ▲ *1 June-30 Sept, Tues-Sun 10am-12.30pm & 2.30-6.30pm. Pavillon des Nourrices (tel: 02 51 94 02 71). Free.*

Maison de la Rivière et du Pêcheur. In an old watermill 4km south of Montaigu is this museum on three levels, devoted to freshwater fish, plants and insects. Among its attractions are a game-fishing simulator, and a system of "smellyscopes" - as you peer through each of three telescopes trained on different plants outside you can actually smell the different perfumes. There are quite a few buttons to press, levers to move and drawers to open; outside, by the millwheel, you will find waterside trails and canoe hire. It can be hard to find; park by the *mairie*, on the main street, and walk down a steep road opposite. ▲ *1 Apr-30 Sept, Sun & public holidays 2-6pm (16 June-15 Sept, daily 11am-7pm). St-Georges-de-Montaigu (tel: 02 51 46 44 67). 22F/3.34€, children 16F/2.44€.*

Château de la Preuille. A small wine museum at a vineyard located beside a picturesque 13th- to 15th-century castle 6km north-west of Montaigu, near St-Hilaire-de-Loulay. You can admire a huge wine-press as well as sample - and buy - Muscadet-sur-Lie, Gros-Plant, and Loire Gamay and Chardonnay wines. ● *Tues-Sat 10am-12.30pm & 2-6pm (15 June-15 Sept, daily 10am-12.30pm & 2-6pm). Signposted from the D93 as you leave the N137 and head towards Clisson (tel: 02 51 46 32 32). 15F/2.29€.*

MORTAGNE-SUR-SEVRE   i tel: 02 51 65 11 32

Quiet town on the Sèvre Nantaise river, 15km north-east of Les Herbiers, at the eastern boundary of the Vendée, and in English hands for half of the 14th century. It is dominated by the ivy-covered ruins of a fortress, said to have been built by the brother of William the Conqueror, which includes the remains of a circular tower called the Tour des Anglais. The castle was torn down on the orders of Cardinal Richelieu in 1626.

A *Circuit Historique* brochure, free from the tourist office, guides you around shady squares, steep little alleys and historic houses - including one that claims to be the cradle of the Maupillier family immortalised in the grand night-time Puy-du-Fou spectacle (see page 101). Have a look inside the lofty church: its north side features Romanesque columns and, in a little gothic-style chapel, there are stone effigies and the remains of medieval wall paintings.

Market: Tuesday.

Train à Vapeur. For an afternoon ride on the Vendée's last remaining steam train, follow signs for the tourist office (which is located in the railway station), near the level crossing on the Cholet road. The three-hour excursion takes you - at a leisurely 40kph - along a 22km section of track between Mortagne and Les Herbiers and back, past green fields, across dizzying viaducts over rivers and streams, and through the Vendean hills. During a 30-minute turnround at Les Herbiers you can watch the train being manoeuvred to face in the opposite direction. No advance booking possible, so arrive at Mortagne station in good time; ticket office opens 1.30pm. ▲ *1 June-15 Sept, Sun 3pm (1 July-31 Aug, Wed, Fri, Sat, Sun & public holidays 3pm). Tel: 02 51 63 02 01. Single Mortagne-Les Herbiers: 55F/8.38€, children 40F/6.10€, family (2+3 or more) 190F/28.96€; return: 70F/10.67€, 50F/ 7.62€ & 240F/36.56€.*

MOUCHAMPS

Don't be tempted to use the car to explore this picturesque small town clinging to a hillside above the river Lay, 13km south of Les Herbiers. The steep streets drop away, revealing endless misty views of the hills beyond, and the side alleys are so precipitous and twisty that you could easily get stuck fast. In the stocky Romanesque church is a memorial to Vendeans who died during the post-Revolutionary wars, meticulously categorised according to whether they were guillotined, massacred or shot.

Local history. A simple but fascinating exhibition on the first floor of the *mairie* recounts the history of the town and of its two most famous sons, airman René Guilbaud (1890-1928) and politician Georges Clemenceau (1841-1929); more details on both below. ● *Mon-Fri 8am-noon & 1-5.30pm. Free.*

René Guilbaud memorial. Admire the sleek lines of the monument, by twin Vendean sculptors Jan and Joel Martel (see page 33) that commemorates the local aviator who disappeared with Norwegian explorer Roald Amundsen over the North Pole in 1928 while on a mission to rescue the stranded crew of an Italian airship. ● *Avenue des Marronniers.*

Le Colombier. The body of the French politician Georges Clemenceau was buried in 1929 next to that of his father in the grounds of the family's mellow 16th-century manor house (not open to the public), with turrets sprouting from its corners, signposted off the D13 to the east of the village. As a ferocious left-wing politician Clemenceau was dubbed "*le Tigre*" (the Tiger). After his successful negotiation of the Treaty of Versailles, after the end of World War I, he received the additional nickname of "*Père la Victoire*" (Father of Victory). He was born at Mouilleron-en-Pareds (see page 89), 20 km to the south-east, and spent his retirement years in his Vendean seaside home at St Vincent-sur-Jard (see page 54). Beyond a little wooden gate, you can follow a short woodland path to the tomb of the distinguished statesman, under a cedar overlooking the Petit-Lay river, with the grave of his father just beyond. ●

ROCHESERVIERE   **i tel: 02 51 94 94 28/fax: 02 51 94 94 29**

This attractive village in the valley of the Boulogne 15km west of Montaigu is easily missed since the D937 sweeps past it over an enormous viaduct. The ancient packhorse bridge across the river was the site of a fierce battle between royalists and Republicans in 1793 and of a further round of bitter fighting in June 1815; the stained-glass windows of the church illustrate another bloody episode of the Vendée Wars, a massacre on 27 February 1794.

Today, the spruced-up square around the *mairie* gives due prominence to a few 16th- and 17th-century houses, and overlooking it all is the fairy-tale Renaissance-style Château de la Touche (not open to the public), a 19th-century explosion of slate-covered pinnacles and towers. There are pleasant walks along the banks of the Boulogne to the north.

Market: Second Wednesday of the month.

Festival: Festival d'Artistes (painters at work near the old bridge), Whitsuntide.

Specialities: Gros-Plant, Muscadet & Gamay wines. *Cerviérois* and *Elysée* desserts from pâtissier Pierre-Yves Charriau in Rue de Nantes.

Brocante: Dépôt-Vente Rocheservices. *Mon, Wed-Sat 10am-12.30pm & 2-7pm, Sun 3-7pm. Just east of D937 (tel: 02 51 06 55 88).*

ST-LAURENT-SUR-SEVRE   **i tel: 02 51 64 63 47**

Since the death here in 1716 of St Louis-Marie Grignion de Montfort, St-Laurent has become a place of pilgrimage and a centre for the religious groups, which today number some 430, founded by this Breton missionary priest. Located 11km south of Cholet, this "holy town" of the Vendée lies in a curve of the Sèvre Nantaise river, on the eastern edge of the *département*. Apart from the basilica (see below), notable buildings include the Maison du St-Esprit, home to an order of Montfortian missionaries and, across the way, the Maison Mère des Filles de la Sagesse - the headquarters of an order of nuns who care for the sick. A calvary on the La Verrie road, its steep steps lined with enormous white angels, affords a wonderful view of the hills.

The saint also founded the Frères de St-Gabriel, a teaching order whose members work in schools all around the world from the shanty towns of South America to underprivileged villages of Africa. At the other end of the scale, the brothers run, in St-Laurent, the Vendée's top educational establishment, the 2,500-pupil Institution St-Gabriel.

As the central area of the town is pedestrianised, you need to park before starting to explore. The tourist office organises free guided walks and provides information on the lovely "Suisse Vendéenne" region nearby (see below).

Basilique. Among a forest of marble columns in the huge 19th-century basilica is the tomb of St Louis-Marie Grignion de Montfort, alongside that of Marie-Louise Trichet, the nun who founded the Filles de la Sagesse. Born in 1673 in Brittany, the newly-ordained Montfort became a chaplain at a hospital in Poitiers in 1700 and three years later founded, with the young Marie-Louise Trichet, a nursing order of nuns. Keen to rekindle religious ardour in a world he saw as full of vice and materialism, he took his missionary fervour to the countryside, visiting the poor and the sick and training others to spread the word. In Rome, he asked Pope Clement XI to send him to Japan as a missionary. The pontiff refused, and instructed him instead to evangelise his own region. The zealous Grignion de Montfort returned to France but found himself expelled by the bishops of Normandy, Brittany and Saintonge. Made more welcome in the west, he based himself at St-Laurent, and in 1715 spent time living as a hermit at Mervent (see page 87). He was canonised in 1927. The saint's writings were an early source of inspiration to Pope Jean-Paul II, who paid homage to his hero at the basilica in 1996. ● *Daily 8am-7pm. Free.*

La Suisse Vendéenne. Strangely, the "Vendean Switzerland" does not take in the Collines Vendéennes (Vendean Hills), but rather the beautiful valley of the Sèvre Nantaise river on the eastern border of the *département*, whose energy was once harnessed by a host of watermills. For a glimpse of the valley's industrial past, try and find the picturesquely-sited village of Rochard, 2km north-west of St-Laurent, where a papermill once functioned. An equal distance to the south of St-Laurent is the Vallée de Poupet, a delightfully verdant bit of countryside on the banks of the river, signposted off the D72 some 3km north of Mallièvre. At Poupet, near a former watermill you can rent canoes, picnic, fish, or eat in a pretty restaurant. On summer Sundays a popular festival, Les Arts de la Campagne, brings well-known comedy, variety and rock performers to an open-air theatre nearby. ●

ST-SULPICE-LE-VERDON

Because of the capture of General Charette in 1796 in woods near the country house of La Chabotterie (see below), which marked the end of the long-drawn-out civil war, this village 13.5km south-west of Montaigu is an important point on the Vendée Memorial map.

Festival: Musique Baroque, at La Chabotterie, 2.5km south-east, July.

Tract'Expo. Open-air display in the village centre of more than 75 tractors dating from between 1938 and 1960 - Massey-Harris, Ferguson, Fordson Major, even Porsche - set up by a group of passionate collectors who have painstakingly restored most of the vehicles. Also on show are threshing-machines and harvesters. ▲ *1 June-15 Oct, Sat, Sun & public holidays 3-7pm. Rue de l'Église (tel: 02 51 42 81 92). 10F/1.52€.*

Logis de la Chabotterie. To get the most out of your visit to this exquisitely restored manor house, whose history is inextricably linked to that of the revered Vendean leader Charette, you need to allow a good couple of hours, and to have done a bit of homework on the Vendean uprising (see page 25). The building, 2.5km south-east of the village, has been totally refurbished, its rooms ingeniously lit and furnished in impeccable 18th-century style, with murmuring voices and other background sounds making you feel you have only just missed actually seeing the occupants. An English leaflet available at the desk describes the self-guided tour. The kitchen contains the very table on which the Vendean chief was laid to have his wounds dressed after his capture by General Travot's exultant Republican troops; in another room you can watch a 12-minute video about the arrest and execution of the charismatic leader. Afterwards you embark on a 16-minute "Parcours", an atmospheric automated history trail in and out of a series of rooms that display episodes from the events of the 1790s. The tableaux and dioramas are excellent and the semi-animated waxworks that tell the story are suitably realistic-looking. However, the quality of the French commentary - delivered as if spoken by Charette himself - often suffers from poor acoustics, and can be hard to understand even for French-speakers. In the adjoining exhibition hall are held serious, well-documented exhibitions on some Vendée-related theme, changing each year.

Outside is an immaculately-replanted garden of flowers and vegetables, arranged in geometric borders, and an arbour of deliciously perfumed old-fashioned roses. You can enjoy strolls and picnics in the wider grounds, and follow the "*chemin de Charette*" to the granite cross marking the exact spot where the Vendean leader was taken. Events with an appropriately period flavour are organised on summer afternoons, as well as a regular festival of baroque music. ● *Mon-Sat 9.30am-6pm, Sun 10am-7pm (1 July-31 Aug, daily 10am-7pm. Closed three last weeks of January. Tel: 02 51 42 81 00. 30F/4.57€, children free.*

Chêne-Chapèlle. Sandwiched between the roadside and the front garden of a normal house is a tiny chapel grafted onto a hollow oak tree. Signposted from the round-about on the D763 at La Grande Chevasse, just to the south-east of La Chabotterie and about 3km south-east of St-Sulpice, this fairyland-scale place of worship, was erected in the early 19th century. ●

TIFFAUGES

Towering over the little town 20km south-west of Cholet is the substantial ruined castle of "*Barbe-bleue*", or Bluebeard - in reality, the infamous Gilles de Rais, or Retz (different spelling, same pronounciation) on whom Charles Perrault's fairytale character is based. As an antidote to the chilling tales of Bluebeard's appalling crimes, you can take pleasant walks by the Sèvre Nantaise river, roam along miller's tracks and sunken lanes, or set off by car or bicycle on the signposted "Circuit de la Suisse Vendéenne" (see page 109) that winds southwards to Mallièvre. Among local industries, the name of Lussault might seem familiar; the company makes clocks for churches - just notice how often you see the name (sometimes reduced to just LT for Lussault; Tiffauges) on such timepieces, both in the Vendée and beyond.

Factory shop: Mulliez (luxury household linen, at a huge mill in a beautiful riverside setting). *Mon-Sat 2-6pm. Route de St-Aubin, Le Longeron, 6km east of Tiffauges, signposted off the D111 south of the Sèvre (tel: 02 41 63 78 10).*

Château de Gilles de Rais. Having fought alongside Charles VII and Joan of Arc against the English in the Hundred Years War and reached the rank of field-marshal at the age of only 25, Gilles de Rais (1404-40) seemed set for a glittering military career. But after the English burnt Joan at the stake for witchcraft in 1431 he retired to his castle at Tiffauges and dissipated his fortune with high living. He turned to alchemy and, believing gold could be made from the blood of young children, seized and murdered more than 200 from around his many properties - including the castles of Pornic and Machecoul - before justice caught up with him and he was tried and hanged in Nantes.

You need two or three hours to take in all of the castle - reduced to its present state largely on orders from Cardinal Richelieu more than 300 years ago. Tours by guides in medieval garb take in the Romanesque crypt (site of many terrible deeds) supported by a forest of sturdy columns; the *oubliettes* (secret dungeons below the round tower, in which prisoners could be "forgotten") and, near the top of the Vidame's Tower, a whispering gallery with 37 half-moon machicolations (the semi-circular holes in the floor through which missiles could be dropped on invaders).

Hold on to small children here, if you don't want them to fall on later arrivals! In the basement of this spooky structure is an eerie, reconstructed laboratory of alchemy, complete with entertainment from a costumed magician and his assistant. A shadow-puppet show (2-7pm) in another building tells the well-known fairy story about Bluebeard's unfortunate young bride discovering her murdered predecessors.

The most popular entertainment is the fantastic display of full-sized working recons-tructions of 15th-century siege machinery operated around noon, and again around 3.30pm, from May to September by "warriors" in medieval costume. To the accom-paniment of a witty French commentary and some deafening bangs they load and fire stone cannonballs and large bags of water over 150-metre distances, and offer goggle-eyed children the chance to cross (wooden) swords with them, fire a cross-bow or be put in the stocks. ▲ *1 Mar-30 Sept. Mon, Tues, Thurs, Fri 10am-12.30pm & 2-6pm (ticket readmits after lunch); Sat, Sun & public holidays 2-7pm (1 July-31 Aug, daily 11am-7pm). Tel: 02 51 65 70 51. 40F/6.10€, children 25F/3.81€; family ticket (2+2 or more) 110F/16.77€.*

Village Vendéen Miniature. Exquisitely detailed houses, churches, windmills, farms and other buildings, painstakingly created from wood, tiles and local stone by a former cabinet-maker. ▲ *1 Mar-31 May, Sun & public holidays 2-7pm; 1-30 June & 1-30 Sept, Mon-Fri 10am-noon & 2-6pm, Sat, Sun 2-7pm; 1 July-31 Aug, daily 10am-noon & 2-7pm; 1 Dec-mid-Feb, Mon-Sat 2-6pm, Sun 2-7pm. Rue du Moulin-Vieux, 100m north of castle on D753 (tel: 02 41 30 22 25). 25F/3.81€, children 15F/2.29€.*

Cité des Oiseaux. Ornithological centre 6km south of Tiffauges, on the edge of three lakes. The 30 hectares of water, an important staging-post for migrating waterfowl, are home to ducks, coots and moorhens; spring brings warblers and golden orioles; grebes and cormorants take up residence in summer; and quantities of waders in autumn. In the exhibition centre on the west side of the reserve, videos and dioramas explain bird evolution, migration and habits, with a closed-circuit camera bringing some of the residents onto a screen indoors. Near the lakeside visitor centre, if you go around to the right on leaving the car park you will find a wooden hide among the trees. ● *Lakeside visitor centre: daily 8am-noon & 1.30pm-dusk (outside visiting hours take your own binoculars). Free.* ▲ *Exhibition centre: 1 Apr-31 May, Sun-Fri & public holidays 2-6pm; 1 June-15 Sept, daily 10am-noon & 2-7pm; 16 Sept-15 Oct, Sun 2.30-6pm. Etangs des Boucheries, Les Landes-Genusson (tel: 02 51 91 72 25). 30F/4.57€, children 15F/2.29€.*

VENDRENNES

Renowned as the birthplace of the fluffy Vendean brioche (a sweet, delicately-flavoured bread), this village on the busy N160 road 9.5km south-west of Les Herbiers is a hallowed stopping-place for everyone anxious to take home a taste of the real thing. About 2km north of Vendrennes is a rather different local curiosity: turn right off the N160 by a sign for a *pension canine* (boarding kennels) and, about 200m into the forest, you'll see an oak tree with 13 trunks.

Festivals: Fête de la Chasse (game fair) at Parc Soubise, 3km south-east, July.

Factory shop: Brosset (brioche has been made here since 1932). *Daily 7am-9pm; on N160 in village - be careful if crossing the road (tel: 02 51 66 09 25).*

Château du Parc Soubise. Between forest and lake, off the Mouchamps road 3km south-east of Vendrennes, is an interesting collection of buildings. (Though not open to the public, they can be viewed from the lane.) The gloomy slate-roofed mansion, built around 1780 by an Italian architect, was torched by the *colonnes infernales* almost before it was lived in. Beside it is a mellow, red-tiled *logis* with outbuildings that include a 14th-century barn and a long building that was once used as a granary above and salting-house below. ●

6. THE PAYS DE RETZ, NANTES
AND MUSCADET COUNTRY

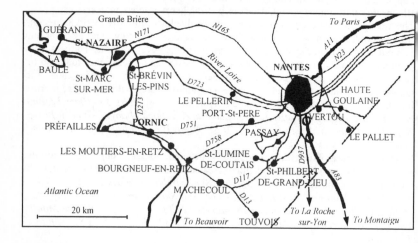

The charms of the Pays de Retz, part of the *département* of Loire-Atlantique that lies sandwiched between the river Loire and the Vendée, are often overlooked. On the north side of the river, the city of Nantes is well worth a day's exploration, as are the temptations of Muscadet wine country to the east. Unless otherwise stated, all the following places are Loire-Atlantique.

LA BAULE **i tel: 02 40 24 34 44/fax: 02 40 11 08 10**
The superb houses and hotels built between the 1890s and the 1930s, and its 9km sweep of beach, made this large resort 25km west of St-Nazaire at one time one of the most glamorous destinations in France.
Today, modern apartment blocks and mass tourism have somewhat marred La Baule's seafront, but just a couple of blocks inland the elegant villas of days gone by still nestle among the pine woods. Avenue de Gaulle, linking the beach to the railway station, is the principal thoroughfare; some of the town's other avenues ramble in slightly eccentric directions, following the lines of paths in the grounds of the resort's original grand houses.

BOURGNEUF-EN-RETZ **i tel: 02 40 21 93 63**
On the frontier between Brittany and the Vendée stands this village, 33km south east of the St-Nazaire bridge. Bird-lovers should check out the tide-tables and make their way west towards Port du Collet to watch thousands of egrets and other wading birds moving inshore to feed as the tide comes in.
Market: Tuesday and Saturday.
Musée du Pays de Retz. Housed in an 18th-century convent building opposite the church, this fascinating museum shows the history of the region: from fossils to folk traditions, salt-production to shopping, plus local costume (including head-dresses) and some typical room-settings. A good video is shown, in French, on the region, and some excellent English notes on the museum's collection are available on request.
▲ *Late Mar-mid Nov, Wed-Mon 10am-noon & 2-6pm (1 July-31 Aug, daily 10.30am-6.30pm). 6 Rue des Moines (tel: 02 40 21 40 83). 20F/3.04€, children 10F/1.52€.*

Table d'orientation. A beautifully-made ceramic table on a ridge above the Machecoul marshes identifies the steeples and other features spread below you. Turn north off the D13, 4km south-east of Bourgneuf, and follow "*point de vue*" signs through the village of St-Cyr-en-Retz. ●

LA GRANDE BRIERE   **i tel: 02 40 66 85 01**
A marshy, secretive landscape of peat bog, wildfowl and thatched cottages just to the north of St-Nazaire, this 40,000-hectare nature reserve is surprisingly difficult to get to by car. From the St-Nazaire bridge, take the Nantes direction at the first major intersection and turn off after 4km, at Montoir-de-Bretagne to reach the eastern edge; for the west side, take the main road towards Guérande and follow signs for St-André-des-Eaux and St-Lyphard. Using flat-bottomed boats known as *blins*, the locals paddle along the canals to catch fish and eels, and to cut reeds for thatching their low, whitewashed cottages. Guided tours of the wildlife-rich marshes are available by boat, by horsedrawn cart, on foot or on horseback. The prettiest spots (and of course the busiest in the peak tourist season) are the village of Kerhinet on the west side of the reserve, between Guérande and St-Lyphard, and the Ile de Fédrun, exactly opposite, on the east.
Market: Thursday in July and August, at Kerhinet.
Specialities: Eels. Frogs' legs. Freshwater fish.
Ile de Fédrun. The island of Fédrun, on the east side of the park, lies a couple of kilometres south-west of the village of St-Joachim, to which it is linked by a raised causeway across the marsh. Lining Fédrun's roughly circular road system is a collection of typical dwellings, mostly thatched, including the Maison de la Mariée, full of wedding souvenirs (nearby St-Joachim was renowned throughout Europe a century ago for the manufacture of artificial orange-blossom) and a visitor centre, where you can pick up information on how to enjoy the rest of this peatland wilderness. ▲ *Maison du Parc (visitor centre): 1 June-30 Sept, 10am-noon & 3-7pm. 180 Ile de Fédrun (tel: 02 40 88 42 72). Free.*
Kerhinet. This picturesque village is hard to locate, as it's completely invisible from the road. A discreet car park is sited behind a hedge on the north side of the lane linking the D51 and the D47, about mid-way between Kerbourg and Breca. From here you can walk 100 metres or so into Kerhinet and admire its 18 thatched, stone-built cottages, which have been beautifully restored. Some are now exhibition centres and craft workshops, and one - the Auberge de Kerhinet - is a hotel. ▲ *Museum: 1 June-30 Sept, daily 10am-noon & 2.30-6.30pm. Kerhinet (tel: 02 40 66 85 01). 15F/2.29€, children 15F/2.29€.*

GUÉRANDE   **i tel: 02 40 24 96 71 / fax: 02 40 62 04 24**
Sturdy stone ramparts completely encircle this medieval town, 20km west of St-Nazaire. Its fortune was founded on the produce of the vast salt marshes that lie to the west (until canning evolved as a more convenient way of preserving food). Park outside, and then stroll around the maze of picturesque streets, full of restaurants, *crêperies* and shops, and a beautiful collegiate church with Romanesque decoration on the pillars inside.
Market: Wednesday and Saturday.
Specialities: Sea salt.
Musée Régional. The museum of local history is housed in one of the town's massive, 15th-century gatehouses. Furnished interiors illustrate domestic life on the Guérande peninsula; other exhibits include porcelain from nearby Le Croisic, paintings, pottery, crafts, and information about the salt and the linen-weaving industries. ▲ *Easter-30 Sept, daily 10am-12.30pm & 2.30-7pm. Porte St-Michel (tel: 02 40 42 96 52). 20F/3.04€, children 10F/1.52€.*

Musée des Marais Salants. The salt industry explained in the village of Batz-sur-Mer, 8km south-west of Guérande. A video shows how the white crystals are harvested by evaporation of seawater. Attractively-presented pictures, tools, clothes, and furniture painted in traditional blood-coloured "Guérande red" give an idea of the saltworkers' way of life. ● *Sat, Sun 3-7pm (1 June-30 Sept, daily 10am-noon & 3-7pm). 29 bis Rue Pasteur, Batz-sur-Mer (tel: 02 40 23 82 79). 21F/3.21€, children 15F/2.29€.*

Grand Blockhaus. Everyday items from toothbrushes to phrase books, lent by American, British, French and German war veterans, form part of the collection amassed in this fascinating museum 8km south-west of Guérande. Inside an impregnable-looking World War II German artillery and observation post, over three levels, you can see dormitories as well as radio, weaponry and machine rooms. An English leaflet is provided, plus a good explanation of the 1942 St-Nazaire Raid and details of the St-Nazaire Pocket - the German forces' last outpost in Europe, which was not liberated until three days after VE Day. The bizarre *trompe-l'oeil* windows on the outside were part of the wartime camouflage, designed to convince Allied reconnaissance planes that the blockhouse was a harmless seaside villa. ▲ *1 Apr-mid Nov, Wed-Mon 10am-7pm (1 July-31 Aug, daily 10am-7pm). On coast road, between Batz and Le Pouliguen (tel: 02 40 23 88 29). 30F/4.57€, children 20F/3.04€.*

HAUTE-GOULAINE

The marshes to the east of this village, 7km south-east of Nantes, were once an important source of frogs' legs for local gourmets. Among present-day attractions are the Château de Goulaine, a hill known as the Butte de la Roche - from which you have an excellent view of Nantes - and a strange, castle-like former lime kiln at Le Montru, 3km south-east of the castle.

Château de Goulaine. One of the border fortresses that defended the dukedom of Brittany against the kingdom of France, this handsome, moated, tufa-built castle is the most westerly of the great "châteaux of the Loire". In the hands of the Goulaine family for more than 1,000 years (a 70-year period of Dutch ownership from 1788 meant that it escaped destruction in the French Revolution), it is said to have welcomed French kings Henri IV and Louis XIV. Guided tours are given of the three *salons*, full of painted ceilings, tapestries and monumental fireplaces. Outside, box-edged beds are arranged in fleur-de-lys patterns, and the tour continues during the warmer months with a walk through a mist-filled glasshouse among some 200 fluttering tropical butterflies. The estate is renowned for two gastronomic items: *beurre-blanc*, the buttery, shallot-flavoured sauce created a century or so ago by one of the family's cooks that accompanies so many fish dishes in the Nantes region; and the Marquis de Goulaine wine - a Muscadet de Sèvre-et-Maine on sale in the castle shop. ▲ *Easter-31 Oct, Sat, Sun & public holidays 2-6pm (15 June-15 Sept, Wed-Mon 2-6pm). Tel: 02 40 54 91 42. 40F/6.10€, children 15F/2.29€.*

MACHECOUL   **i tel: 02 40 31 42 87/fax: 02 40 02 31 28**

This attractive market town on the edge of the Marais Breton, near the border of the Vendée and Loire-Atlantique and 40km south-west of Nantes, is dominated by the twin spires of its large 19th-century church.

At the start of the Vendée Wars, Machecoul saw one of the first risings against the Republicans, on 11 March 1793, when 3,000 Vendeans massacred those whose sympathies lay with the new régime (see page 26). Apart from the enjoyable Wednesday market, there is strangely little to visit in the town today. The jagged silhouette of a ruined castle that once belonged to the sadistic Gilles de Rais, or Bluebeard (see pages 110 and 115), can be glimpsed among the trees bordering the old Rue de Nantes. The locals use the sinister theme as the subject of medieval dinners in May and for an excellent *son-et-lumière* in July.

Rue du Marché, leading from the picturesque market hall, is lined with interesting shops (as well as some paintwork-scraping concrete bollards). The tourist office can advise on local footpaths and cycle trails, and provide a list of wine producers in the surrounding Pays de Retz. Try and make a trip around the marshes to the west - by car, bike, canoe or on foot (see Port-La-Roche, page 33); it's particularly beautiful towards sunset when herons flap languidly across the landscape and keen-eyed hawks hover above unsuspecting wildlife.

Market: Wednesday, throughout the streets.

Festival: Son-et-lumière presentation about Gilles de Rais, July.

Specialities: Séguin, a brandy-type *eau-de-vie*. Gitane bicycles. Goat's cheeses from Fromagerie Beilvert. *Mâche* (winter leaves known as lamb's lettuce, or corn salad). *Muguet* (lilies-of-the-valley, a traditional French 1 May gift).

Factory shop: Micmo (Gitane bicycles, a changing selection on sale each day). *Mon-Fri 9am-noon & 2-5pm; west of Challans-to-Machecoul road; follow "vélos déclassés" signs around to back of factory (tel: 02 40 78 23 23).*

St-Etienne-de-Mer-Morte. In this picturesque village, perched above the Falleron river 9km south-east of Machecoul, is a pretty, free-standing bell-tower with a pointed spire. It is the remains of a much earlier church into which Gilles de Rais stormed on Whit Sunday 1440, at the head of a band of men. In the middle of High Mass, he seized Jean le Ferron, one of the congregation, and dragged him to his nearby castle at Machecoul. For this act of sacrilege, he was later arrested and taken to Nantes, where he confessed to his many horrible crimes before being hanged on 26 October 1440 and then burnt at the stake. ●

LES MOUTIERS-EN-RETZ   **i tel: 02 40 82 74 00/fax: 02 40 82 74 00**

Some particularly intriguing ecclesiastical features may be found in the leafy centre of this appealing village 7km south-east of Pornic. On the beach at low tide, locals root among the rockpools or push giant shrimping nets through the shallows. Another sort of fishing is practised from the stilt-legged wooden *pêcheries* (see page 121) along the windswept southbound coast road, opposite the establishments of some of the region's oyster producers. A signposted *Route de l'Huître Vendée-Atlantique* follows the region's oyster-raising industry south from La Bernerie-en-Retz, 3km north of Moutiers, to Fromentine and Noirmoutier. Local tourist offices have leaflets showing the establishments that welcome visitors for a 90-minute tour, followed by a tasting of half a dozen oysters and a glass of wine.

Market: Thursday and Saturday.

Église. In the cool interior of the village church a handsome model sailing ship hangs below a ceiling lined with wood like the hull of a boat. A one-franc piece placed in the box behind the pulpit will start a light show about the huge 17th-century altar-piece. If you understand French, you can also read about the *Lancastria* (see page 121), sunk in June 1940 while evacuating Allied servicemen, 60 of whom are commemorated in the local cemetery. ●

Lanterne des Morts. In the shady square outside the church stands a stone column dating from the 11th century, a rare structure known as a "lantern of the dead". Whenever a death occurs in the parish, a lamp is lit inside and glows day and night through the slit windows until the burial has taken place. ●

Chapelle de Prigny. Guided tours are given of a tiny 11th-century chapel, on the eastern side of the D13, built in primitive Romanesque style. The pretty slate-covered bell-tower also features a chimney, indicating that the original priest probably lived on the spot. ▲ *1 May-30 Sept, Sat-Sun 3-5pm (1 July-31 Aug, Fri-Sun 3-6pm).*

Shipbuilding, biscuit-manufacturing, sugar-refining and food-canning are the liveli-hoods of this pleasant river port of 250,000 inhabitants, straddling the Loire. The city grew rich in the 17th and 18th centuries on the proceeds of the sugar and slave trades. During the Wars of the Vendée it was the site of a ferocious battle - during which the Vendean leader Cathelineau was mortally wounded - and later the headquarters for the notorious Republican General Carrier who instituted the horrific drownings of prisoners in the Loire. Though you would not guess it from the profusion of old buildings, some dating back to the Middle Ages, the town was heavily bombed by the Allies in 1943.

The big-city smartness and bustle may come as something of a shock after you have spent a tranquil week or two buried in the Vendean countryside. To get the best out of a day trip, try and visit between Wednesday and Saturday - too many shops are closed on Mondays, and most museums are shut on Tuesdays (as well as on public holidays). Driving around the confusing one-way system can be tricky, so abandon the car as soon as possible and visit on foot, or by tram and bus. Easy-to-spot car parks are a multi-storey one beneath the Tour de Bretagne - a skyscraper visible from almost anywhere in town - and another near the railway station; or try the pay-&-display parking on the streets north of the station. Alternatively, travel in by train; if you leave the station by the north exit, (*sortie nord*) you will be right opposite the tram station and the Jardin des Plantes (see below), ready to start exploring.

Shortly to acquire its third line, the city's tram system runs east-west and north-south. Some doors of each tram have special ramps to admit wheelchairs. Tickets, including good-value one-day ones that are also valid on the town's buses, can be bought from slot machines at main tram stops. The ticket must be punched, or *composté*, on entering the tram to validate it (for an all-day ticket, you do this just on the first trip). A good first stop is the (disappointingly small) tourist office within the FNAC bookshop in Place du Commerce, where you can pick up a town plan and browse through brochures. Near the west corner of Place du Commerce you will find Passage Pommeraye, an unusual, 19th-century shopping arcade on different levels linked by decorated steps that rise steeply to finish at Rue Crébillon, where many of the town's smartest shops are located. Turn south-west on Rue Crébillon for Place Graslin, with its beautiful, turn-of-the-century brasserie La Cigale and, just beyond, an elegant, traffic-free avenue of 18th-century houses known as Cours Cambronne. Alternatively, if you cross Rue Crébillon and turn north you come to Rue du Calvaire, home of the Galeries Lafayette department store and of the region's branch of Marks and Spencer.

Just to the south of Place du Commerce, across the tram tracks, is the attractive "Ile Feydeau" (Feydeau island) district, once surrounded by the Loire, but now land-locked in a tide of swirling traffic. Rue Kervégan, the "island's" narrow, cobbled, central street, is lined with the homes of 18th-century shipowners, each house embellished by ornate balconies and carved stone decoration over its doors and windows. Several small restaurants or *crêperies* along here offer a chance to enjoy a budget meal in an atmospheric setting.

To the east of the central north-south boulevard called Cours des 50 Otages, a series of picturesque, pedestrianised streets around the Église Ste-Croix contain 15th- and 16th-century houses and many unusual shops. A more modern retail centre is the huge shopping mall known as the Centre Beaulieu, on a real island that lies between the two branches of the river Loire.

Nantes has an international airport with flights from London, and a regular TGV rail service from Lille, making a useful link with Eurostar. If you arrange to meet anyone at Nantes railway station, make sure you specify the north or south exit (*sortie nord* or *sortie sud*) - or you might have a long and frustrating wait.

Markets: Rue Talensac & Place du Bouffay, Tuesday-Sunday. Place du Ralliement. Wednesday. Place Ste-Anne, Thursday. Place de la Petite-Hollande, Saturday.
Flea market: Place Viarme, Saturday.
Festivals: Carnival, March. International summer festival of world music, July. Festival of the Atlantic (music), July.
Specialities: *Beurre-blanc nantais* (a rich, buttery sauce to accompany fish). *Berlingots nantais* (pyramid-shaped boiled sweets). *Canard nantais* (duck). Biscuits (BN and Belin brands). Market-gardening - carrots, leeks, and *muguet* (lily-of-the-valley, traditionally purchased throughout France on 1 May).

Musée du Château des Ducs de Bretagne. The majestic castle lying between the Ile Feydeau and the railway station, formerly the residence of the dukes of Brittany and kings of France, is undergoing a vast renovation programme. At present, one building welcomes a changing series of temporary exhibitions. The museum dealing with the commercial and industrial history of Nantes is due to reopen in 2003; the remainder of the works, including the archaeological section, are scheduled to be completed in 2006. ● *Wed-Mon 10am-noon & 2-6pm (1 July-31 Aug, daily 10am-7pm). Cours John-Kennedy (tel: 02 40 41 56 56). Temporary exhibitions 20F/3.05€, children free.*

Cathédrale St-Pierre et St-Paul. Within the lofty, white stone interior of the city's flamboyant-gothic cathedral is the spectacularly decorated tomb of Duke François II of Brittany and his wife, commissioned in 1502 by their daughter, Anne of Brittany. ● *Daily 8.30am-7pm. Place St-Pierre. Free.*

Musée des Beaux-Arts. Western painting from the 13th century to the present, including some fine works by Georges de la Tour, a strong showing of 19th-century French artists and a large collection of contemporary art that includes 11 abstract paintings by Vasily Kandinsky. Don't miss the unusual sight of an immense Rubens hanging above the museum's subterranean lavatories. ● *Wed, Thurs 10am-6pm, Fri 10am-9pm, Sat 10am-6pm, Sun 11am-6pm, Mon 10-am-6pm. 10 Rue Georges-Clemenceau (tel: 02 40 41 65 65). 20F/3.04€, children 10F/1.52€.*

Musée de l'Imprimerie. Interesting displays on the history of printing, showing the materials needed for illumination, woodcuts and other techniques. A two-hour tour is given daily at 2.30pm, during which the guide explains how the machines in the adjacent printshop work, and even puts a few of them in motion - though what you are shown depends on whether the main tour party consists of primary school children, or school-leavers about to embark on a printing career. ▲ *1 Sept-28 Feb, Tues-Fri 10am-noon & 2-6pm, Sat 10am-noon & 2-7pm; 1 Mar-31 July, Mon-Fri 10am-noon & 2-6pm. Closed throughout August. 24 Quai de la Fosse (tel: 02 40 73 26 55). 30F/4.57€, children 20F/3.04€.*

Jardin des Plantes. Birdsong drowns out the hum of traffic once you step inside the city's delightful botanical gardens opposite the railway station (a marvellous open-air "waiting room", if you have time to kill between trains). Wonderful spring displays of magnolias, camellias and rhododendrons, and medicinal plants - all clearly labelled - plus green lawns, summer colour, and plenty of entertainment for small children - roundabout, climbing frame and sandy play area. ● *Daily 8am-dusk (greenhouses closed on Tuesdays). Free.*

Ile de Versailles. Tranquil, pretty Japanese-style gardens on an island in the river Erdre, just north of the city centre, and easily accessible by tram. Camellias, azaleas, rhododendrons and cherry trees flower in spring; year-round attractions include bamboos, reeds, cloud-pruned pines and, in the Maison de l'Erdre (closed Tues), aquariums containing freshwater fish. ● *Daily, 8am-dusk (8pm in summer). Free.*

Muséum d'Histoire Naturelle. Comprehensive natural history museum, full of stuffed animals and skeletons of every description. Among its more unusual features are a vivarium housing live snakes, scorpions, stick-insects, toads and other creatures and, between the mummies and the monkeys on the first floor, the grisly sight of a tanned human skin (its original owner, an 18th-century-soldier desired it to be used after his death to cover a military drum, but its resonating quality proved inadequate). ● *Tues-Sat 10am-noon & 2-6pm, Sun 2-6pm. 12 Rue Voltaire (tel: 02 40 99 26 20). 20F/3.04€, children free.*

Musée Dobrée. Thomas Dobrée (1810-95), son of a rich Nantes shipowner, built this granite palace to house his collections of furniture, prints, enamels, porcelain, sculpture and curiosities. They include the heart of Anne, the 15th-century duchess of Brittany who became twice queen of France (by marrying first Charles VIII and, later, Louis XII). ● *Tues-Sun 10am-noon & 1.30-5.30pm. Rue Voltaire (tel: 02 40 71 03 50). 20F/3.04€, children 10F/1.52€.*

Musée Jules Verne. Although he was born in Nantes, the great visionary writer never actually lived in this late-19th-century house on a hill overlooking the river. Though the collection of different editions of his many works would interest serious students, its distinctly "glass-case" feel is not guaranteed to thrill children. The only sparks of life are some of the spin-offs from *Around the World in 80 Days*. These include magic-lantern slides and puzzles; a small room-setting using Verne's own furniture, and a cosily-carpeted spacecraft complete with a stuffed dog. ● *Wed-Mon 10am-noon & 2-5pm. 3 Rue de l'Hermitage (tel: 02 40 69 72 52). 8F/1.22€, concessions 4F/0.61€.*

***Maillé-Brezé*: escorteur d'escadre.** Guided visits are given of a 1950s' French destroyer, bristling with rocket- and missile-launchers, that lies moored on the Loire as a floating museum. ● *Wed, Sat, Sun, 2-5pm (1 Apr-30 Sept, Wed-Mon 2-5pm). Quai de la Fosse (tel: 02 40 69 56 82). 45F/6.86€, children 25F/3.81€.*

L'Erdre et ses Châteaux. Hidden away to the north of Nantes, the Erdre is a breathtakingly beautiful river lined with green fields and decorated with country mansions dating from Renaissance times. You can take enjoyable cruises, with commentary, along this peaceful waterway aboard rather grotesque, glass-sided boats (fortunately you can't see them once you're on board); the prices for the three-hour lunch or dinner cruises include a meal. ▲ *1 Apr-30 Nov (detailed timetable from tourist offices). Sightseeing cruises 55F-95F/8.39€-14.49€ (according to journey length), children 25F/3.81€. Lunch cruises noon; dinner cruises 8pm (advance booking essential). Bateaux Nantais, Quai de la Motte Rouge, Place Waldeck-Rousseau (tel: 02 40 14 51 14). Lunch cruise 255F/38.88€, dinner cruise 295F/44.98€; children 160F/24.40€.*

LE PALLET   **i tel: 02 40 80 41 33**

There's plenty of opportunity to taste Muscadet at vineyards around this village 20km south-east of Nantes, or to walk or go boating on the Sèvre Nantaise river. The importance of the wine industry is underlined across the river at Monnières, where the modern stained-glass windows of the 15th-century village church are full of depictions of vines and wine-making.

Le Pallet is also noteworthy as being the birthplace in 1079 of the philosopher and theologian Pierre Abelard, the subject of scandal for having fallen in love with, and secretly married, his young pupil Héloïse. She later entered a convent from which she wrote him a series of celebrated love-letters and he, having suffered intense persecution, became first a monk and then a hermit before taking up the post of abbot at a monastery in Brittany. Héloïse died 22 years after Abélard, in 1164, and was buried beside him.

Festivals: Jazz-sur-Lie (exhibitions and open-air jazz concerts), August.

Musée du Vignoble. Superb presentation - including a tasting - of everything to do with Muscadet production, displayed in a modern building on the southern edge of the village. A video is screened about Abélard and Héloïse (see above); a version with an English commentary is available on request. ▲ *15 May-15 Nov, daily 10.30am-1pm & 2.30-6pm. Tel: 02 40 80 90 13. 25F/3.81€, students & children 15F/2.29€; children under 12 free.*

Château de la Galissonnière. Botanist Barrin de la Galissonnière, a former resident of this château 1km north of the village and governor of Quebec under Louis XV, is credited with the introduction of many rare trees to France,·including magnolia grandiflora. Today the outbuildings are part of a vineyard; if you drive into the farmyard and ring the bell on the winery door you can try - and also buy - some of the Muscadet produced. Note, however, that credit cards are not accepted for purchases, so you'll need cash or a French cheque. ● *Mon-Fri 9am-12.30pm & 2-6pm. Entrance opposite Le Pallet station, or off the Monnières road (tel: 02 40 80 42 03).*

PASSAY

Only if you arrive at Nantes by plane have you a chance to really appreciate the vastness of the 6,300-hectare Lac de Grand-Lieu, 17km south of the city, the area of which literally doubles during the winter months. At the fishing village of Passay, on the eastern edge of the lake, long, black-netting·eel-traps lie on the rush-fringed shores, and tarred boxes for storing catches float like miniature wartime·landing-craft. This secret wetland contains Europe's largest heron colony - more than 1,000 pairs - and is an important staging-post for migrating birds. Visitors are allowed to penetrate the interior only during the summer fishing festival when, if you turn up before 8.30am, you can accompany the dozen or so local fishermen on a 1½-hour trip into the interior by *plate* (a flat-bottomed boat) and then wade into the water to help pull in the long *senne* nets full of fish to be sold off in aid of fishermen's charities.

Market: Wednesday at La Chevrolière, 3km to the east.

Festivals: Fête des Anguilles (eel festival), April. Fête de la Pêche (fishing festival, see above), 15 August and following Sunday.

Speciality: Eels.

Maison du Pêcheur. A lighthouse-like observatory looms above the village, marking the position of this museum of local life among the low, white-painted fishermen's cottages. From the top.you can look through telescopes at the distant lake, or watch the wildlife on a television monitor that brings live pictures from several kilometres away. Most interesting is the museum at the far end of the garden. Large wall-panels carry explanations on the fragile ecosystem of this watery environment; there are displays showing local fishing equipment and, as a grand finale, a wonderful aquarium of eels, carp, pike and other freshwater fish.· ● *Tues-Sat 10am-noon & 3-6pm, Sun & Mon 3-6pm (1 April-31 Oct, daily 10am-noon & 2.30-6.30pm). 16 Rue Yves-Brisson (tel: 02 40 31 36 46). 13F/1.98€, children 7F/1.07€.*

LE PELLERIN

Something of a seaside atmosphere pervades this little town on the south bank of the Loire, 14km west of Nantes, named for the pilgrims (*pèlerins*) that would arrive here on cargo boats to begin their walk to Santiago de Compostela. Across the river, on the Couëron side, the waving reeds and occasional church tower evoke the scenery painted by JMW Turner on his journey up the Loire in 1826 - it is easy to imagine how these marshes might also have inspired the great 18th-century bird painter John James Audubon, who spent part of his childhood at Couëron.

A ferry service runs across the fast-flowing river, a 10-minute trip that saves a long drive to St Nazaire or Nantes for anyone wanting to cross the Loire. Boats run daily between 6am and 8pm: 18F/2.74€ per vehicle; foot passengers free.

Market: Saturday.

Planète Sauvage. Lions, tigers, bears and zebras are among the 2,000 animal residents of this drive-through safari park 8km south of Le Pellerin. The driving trail winds for 10km - a two-hour run - so it's wise to take something with you to drink on a hot day. Later, on foot, you can visit a reconstructed African village, look at reptiles and monkeys, and see sealions being fed in the dolphinarium. If you'd rather let someone else do the driving, there is also a little land-train. ▲ *Early March-mid Nov, daily 10am-last admission time 4pm (1 June-31 Aug, 10am-last admission 5.30pm). Port-St-Père (tel: 02 40 04 82 82). 90F/13.72€, children 50F/7.62€; land train supplement 28F/4.27€, children 22F/3.34€.*

PORNIC **i tel: 02 40 82 04 40/fax: 02 40 82 90 12**

There is a real Breton flavour to this chic seaside resort full of narrow lanes and steep steps, that was a favourite of Gustave Flaubert, George Sand and other 19th-century literary celebrities. Some 18km south of the St-Nazaire bridge, Pornic has a rocky coastline dominated by a fairy-tale castle with pointed slate roofs, whose prettiness belies the fact that it once belonged to the infamous Gilles de Rais (see pages 110 and 114). The sandiest beach is the Plage de la Noëveillard, just beyond the marina. Farther west, some exquisite villas look over the sea in the smart Ste-Marie district.

If you ramble north along some of the Grande-Randonnée footpaths - or even drive up the D213 - be sure to breathe deeply as you come abreast of St-Michel-Chef-Chef. The town is the home of the St-Michel biscuit factory, whose products you will find laid out in rows on supermarket shelves, and you can't fail to catch the wonderful smell of baking.

Market: Thursday and Sunday.

Specialities: Curé Nantais cheese.

Festival: Spectacular carnivals, April and August.

Factory shop: Faïencerie de Pornic (see below).

Golf: Golf de Pornic. 18-hole golf course to the north-west of the town centre. *49 bis Boulevard de l'Océan (tel: 02 40 82 06 69).*

Faïencerie de Pornic. Inside the factory shop, where you can pick up half-price bargains of some of France's favourite pottery designs, you can view a half-hour video about the industry, watch an expert decorating plates, or even have a go yourself at painting anything from ramekins to tankards (collect the finished product a few days later, after firing). ● *Mon-Sat 10am-12.30pm & 2-6pm (1 July-31 Aug, until 7.30pm). Chemin du Cracaud (tel: 02 51 74 19 10). Admission free; plate painting from 25F/3.81€, according to object chosen.*

Iles Enchantées. Beneath overgrown foliage in dense woodland 11km east of Pornic and a little way north of Chéméré, you can just make out the structure of an 18th-century pleasure garden. A series of concentric canals crossed by little wooden bridges, illuminated by sunlight filtering through the leaves, it is dotted with bits of box hedging and the remains of former pavilions. Spring is the best time to visit;

the canals tend to dry out in hot weather. It's hard to spot, but is signposted on the eastern side of the D66, opposite a farm. ●

PRÉFAILLES　　　　　　　　　　　i tel: 02 40 21 62 22/fax: 02 40 64 53 45

This attractively old-fashioned resort 12km west of Pornic became famous a century ago for the healing properties of an iron-rich spring. Among the pretty, fretwork-decorated villas near the beach is one that was the holiday home and wartime residence of the much-lamented sailor Eric Tabarly and his family; the great yachtsman is now commemorated in the name of the street.

Market: Wednesday and Saturday.

Exposition Cerfs-Volants. Dangling from the ceiling of the century-old Grand Bazar general store is a collection of historic kites (*cerfs-volants*), including hundred-year-old examples that carried advertisements, cameras, and wireless and meteorological equipment. Among the fish-hooks, pottery, stationery and household items on sale beneath them, you can also buy more modern kites to fly on the headlands nearby. ● *Mon-Sat 9am-12.30pm & 2.30-7pm; Sun 9.30am-12.30pm. 31 Grande Rue (tel: 02 40 21 61 22). Free.*

Pointe St-Gildas. This windswept point, 3km west of Préfailles, is the westernmost tip of the Pays de Retz. From the roof of a German blockhouse you can look south towards the flat silhouette of the island of Noirmoutier, north across the Loire estuary, or straight ahead - towards Miami. The nearby semaphore station is shortly to be transformed into a centre that will demonstrate signalling techniques between ships and shore, and also explain the construction of the World War II Atlantic defences. ●

ST-BRÉVIN-LES-PINS　　　　　　i tel: 02 40 27 24 32/fax: 02 40 39 10 34

The most popular holiday centre on this part of the coast, on the south side of the St-Nazaire bridge, St-Brévin is divided into two districts: a northern part full of shady pine trees, and the more open, south-west-facing beach area known as St-Brévin-l'Océan. Lining the north shoreline, around the village of Mindin, are weird constructions of spindly-legged wooden *pêcheries*, with dangling poles supporting horizontal nets that are lowered as the tide rises in the hope of capturing mullet, plaice, and other tasty fish.

Just off Mindin occurred one of the greatest maritime disasters in history. At least 3,000 Allied troops and civilians were drowned on 17 June 1940 when the *Lancastria*, a merchant ship evacuating them to Britain following the fall of France, was sunk by enemy bombing. Commonwealth War Graves Commission headstones in many cemeteries up and down the coast, mark the places where the unfortunate victims were washed ashore and, later, buried.

Market: Thursday and Sunday, at St-Brévin-les-Pins.

Musée de la Marine. Inside a 19th-century fort almost directly under the south approach road to the St-Nazaire bridge is an interesting museum of the sea. The rooms are full of model boats of all scales and types, deep-sea diving gear, histories of local nautical disasters and an informative display about the slave trade that enriched the city of Nantes in the 18th century. ▲ *Mid June-mid Sept, Tues-Sun 3-7pm. Fort de Mindin (tel: 02 40 27 00 64). 15F/2.29€, children under 12 free.*

Le Jardin du Moine. A small private garden whose meandering pathways manage to give the impression of size in a limited space. The creative owner has installed several huge concrete sculptures alongside hundreds of plants and several water features - including a fish-filled pond and a model watermill. ▲ *1 April-30 Sept, Thurs-Mon 10am-noon & 3-7pm. 32 Avenue du 11 Novembre, close to the water tower on the west side of the Route Bleue, near the St-Brévin-l'Océan exit (tel: 02 40 27 07 03). Free, but donations welcome.*

ST-LUMINE-DE-COUTAIS

Some 30km south-west of Nantes as the heron flies, this small village on the edge of the Lac de Grand-Lieu offers a spectacular view of the lake and surrounding villages from the top of its 40-metre-high church tower.

A strange village custom is the Whitsuntide *"cheval mallet"* procession (featuring a wooden hobby-horse rather like those of West Country May-Day celebrations in Britain). A rather lengthy video of this event is on view at the village's museum (see below).

Musée d'art sacré. Banners, chalices, sumptuously-embroidered copes and other examples of religious art are displayed in a 16th-century chapel with a lovely painted ceiling. Many of the items survived the post-Revolutionary conflicts thanks to the ingenuity of a local priest who hid them inside a barrel. Outside, look for the box trees, some more than 10 metres high. According to legend they were planted more than 2,000 years ago by the Romans. ▲ *1 May-30 Sept, Sun & public holidays 3-7pm; 1-31 Oct, Sun 2-6pm. Tel: 02 40 02 90 25. 15F/2.29€ (includes church tower), children 9F/1.37€.*

ST-MARC-SUR-MER   **i tel: 02 40 91 76 84**

Devotees of the 1953 classic film *Les Vacances de Monsieur Hulot* can have fun trying to spot the locations used in the movie at this seaside village 11km south-west of St-Nazaire. The beachside Hotel de la Plage is still in action, and a bronze statue of Jacques Tati's comic hero now stands forever gazing down onto the sands. Strangely, the French seem baffled by the British reverence for Tati's engaging fictional character - for really side-splitting entertainment they much prefer re-runs of Benny Hill. St-Marc can be hard to find - if you don't see signs to it, try aiming for the better-marked resort of Ste-Marguerite which lies to the west. And be prepared for a bit of walking: the village is incredibly busy on summer weekends, and parking can be a problem. ●

ST-NAZAIRE   **i tel: 02 40 22 40 65/fax: 02 40 22 19 80**

As you cross the beautiful, curved 3.35km bridge over the Loire, you see the rooftops below change from curved Roman tiles to the more businesslike slate of Brittany. A heavily-fortified German U-boat port during World War II (the submarine base was the target of a 1942 Anglo-Canadian commando raid), St-Nazaire was 85 per cent flattened by Allied bombing and has been entirely rebuilt since. Its shipbuilding industry still dominates the northern shore of the estuary; the tourist office runs regular two-hour guided tours of the dockyards.

Écomusée et visite du sous-marin *Espadon*. If you telephone ahead to book a precise time, you can set foot on a real 1950s' French submarine. Picking your way over the ropes and cables slung around the water's edge near the war-time submarine pens, you cannot refrain from a shudder when you catch your first glimpse of the *Espadon*'s sinister silhouette as she floats in the impregnable German-built, concrete-roofed submarine lock. An enthusiastic ex-submariner takes groups of 15 up and down the narrow companionways and steep ladders (ladies would be well advised to wear trousers), cheerfully describing life aboard when there were bunks for only two-thirds of the crew (the other third was on duty), and just two lavatories for the 65 men aboard. It's all in French, but you can ask for an English text to read up on the details. After the submarine, the Ecomusée is a bit of an anticlimax. It contains information on birdlife, the shipbuilding industry (including some splendid models), prisms from a lighthouse, and photographs of the wartime devastation of the town and its reconstruction (many inhabitants lived for 30 years in pre-fabricated buildings). ● *Museum and submarine: Wed & Sun 10am-noon & 2-6pm (15 Mar-31 Oct, Wed-Sun 10am-noon & 2-6pm; 1 June-12 Sept, daily 10am-6pm); booking* *tel: 08 00 44 10 00; 45F/6.86€, children 25F/3.81€. Museum only: Wed-Mon 10am-noon & 2-6pm (1 June-15 Sept, daily 9.30am-6.30pm), Rue du Bac de Mindin (tel: 02 40 66 79 66); 20F/3.04€, children 15F/2.29€.*

ST-PHILBERT-DE-GRAND-LIEU   **i tel: 02 40 78 73 88**

In a pretty village 23km south of Nantes, near the southern limit of the great wetland known as the Lac de Grand-Lieu, stands one of the oldest churches in France (see below). You can rent boats, or fish in the calm waters of the Boulogne, or go for walks along a disused railway line to the east of the abbey church. Opposite the campsite just to the north of the river is a cheery playground equipped with bouncy castles, mini-golf and other delights, and you can also learn to play swin-golf (see page 15) on a 14-hole course.

Market: Sunday.

Festival: Medieval-style market day, September.

Specialities: Muscadet and Gros-Plant wines.

Brocante: St-Philbert Brocante. *Fri-Tues 10am-1pm & 2.30-7pm. La Chaussée, on northern edge of village: heading north, turn downhill off the roundabout, just before joining the D117 (tel: 02 40 78 72 16).*

Abbatiale St-Philbert. More than 20,000 visitors flock each year to this ancient Carolingian church built in 815 by monks from St Philbert's Abbey, on the island of Noirmoutier, to keep the relics of their founder safe from repeated Norman invasions. Though the saint's remains had eventually to be carried on to Tournus in Burgundy in 858, you can still see his sarcophagus in the crypt. The church's interior is decorated with alternating bands of white stone and warm brick creating a surprising chequerboard effect. A medieval garden has been laid out behind it, and concerts and exhibitions are held in summer. ● *Mon-Sat 10am-noon & 2.30-5.30pm, Sun 2-5.30pm (1 Apr-30 Sept, daily 10am-12.30pm & 2.30-6.30pm). Tel: 02 40 78 73 88. Entrance via tourist office. 16F/2.44€ (includes garden and bird museum), children 10F/1.52€.*

Maison de l'Avifaune du Lac. Museum devoted to more than 200 types of bird that live near, or pass through, the great wetland to the north. As well as an audio-visual presentation about the flora and fauna of the Lac de Grand-Lieu, you can see live television pictures of the lake and, beautifully displayed behind glass, stuffed spoonbills, kingfishers, curlews, coots and herons. Pressing buttons to try to identify the different species is an ideal way of extending one's French vocabulary. ● *Mon-Sat 10am-noon & 2.30-5.30pm, Sun 2-5.30pm (1 Apr-30 Sept, daily 10am-12.30pm & 2.30-6.30pm). Tel: 02 40 78 73 88. 16F/2.44€ (includes church, see above), children 10F/1.52€.*

Musée de la Chanson Française. The locals of this village 15km east of St-Philbert, and just to the west of the A83 motorway, have pooled their collections of books, posters and record sleeves to remind visitors of the great names of French popular music. This curious little museum, near the village church, consists mostly of items in glass cases, but the volunteer staff also play old records by Brel, Brassens, Piaf and others, and let you choose pieces to hear on the barrel organ. ▲ *1 May-30 Sept, Sat, Sun 2.30-6pm. 8 Rue Paul Joyau, La Planche (tel: 02 40 26 52 15). 20F/3.04€, children 10F/1.52€.*

TOUVOIS

Village 40km south of Nantes, formerly an important centre of poultry-rearing, that lay on the old pilgrim route to Santiago de Compostela (see page 24).

Market: Second and fourth Mondays of the month.

Brocante: Broc'Ouest. *Tues-Sat 10am-12.30pm & 2.30-7pm; Sun 2.30-7pm. 44 Rue Nationale, Falleron; 2 km south of Touvois (tel: 02 51 68 45 45).*

Factory shop: Maillet (ladies' knitted skirts, jackets and sweaters). *Wed, Fri 2-6.30pm; Sat 9am-noon & 2-6.30pm. On D90A Palluau road at Falleron, 2km south of Touvois (tel: 02 51 93 10 03).*

Maison du Paysan. A large building near the church and adjacent to the village campsite contains an assortment of items showing the village's heritage. As well as an interesting collection of agricultural implements, you will find a reconstructed classroom - including rows of desks from the village school - a peasant interior complete with typical *lits à rouleaux* that could be trundled away from the wall for bedmaking and a delightful reconstitution of a general store full of period buttons and other haberdashery. ▲ *15 June-30 Sept, Sat, Sun 2.30-7pm (15 July-31 Aug, Wed 3-7pm; Sat, Sun 2.30-7pm). Tel: 02 40 31 64 05. 15F/2.29€, children 5F/0.76€.*

Chapelle de Fréligné. The delicate spire visible across a field, 2km south of Touvois, tempts you to stop and explore this charming 17th-century chapel. Said to have been built by English sea-captains returning from the Crusades, it was severely damaged during the Wars of the Vendée and has been much restored. A couple of hundred metres north is a little garden containing a holy spring that is the centre for a pilgrimage in early September. ●

VERTOU **i tel: 02 40 34 12 22 / fax: 02 40 34 06 86**

Pretty village on the Sèvre Nantaise river, 7km south-east of Nantes and just off the south-east side of the expressway that hurtles around the city (leave it at junction 47). Attractions at this peaceful spot include waterside restaurants, hire of canoes or small electric boats, and a long-distance footpath that leads walkers along the Sèvre as far as Clisson.

La Sèvre au fil de l'eau. Ninety-minute cruises on a glass-roofed boat along the picturesque river Sèvre. As the vessel travels through Muscadet vineyards and negotiates a lock, the French commentary points out 18th-century waterside mansions known as "*folies nantaises*", reputed to have been built for their mistresses by rich Nantes shipowners. The ticket office opens 30 minutes before departure, though it's best to book places by phone first. The departure point is unsignposted, so follow road signs to the Parc de la Sèvre car park and then walk from there to the right along the river, till you reach the landing-stage. ▲ *Easter-30 Sept, Sun & public holidays 4pm (1 June-31 Aug, Sat, Sun & public holidays 4pm). Bateaux Nantais, Parc de la Sèvre (tel: 02 40 14 51 14). 45F/6.86€, children 25F/3.81€.*

Maison des Vins de Nantes. Serious connoisseurs can compare and contrast the wines of the Nantes area near La Haie-Fouassière, some 6km east of Vertou, from where signs point to this excellent oenological centre. Amid fantastic views across the vineyards of the Muscadet region, which produce 85 million bottles a year, you can learn about the local wine and try more than 200 different labels. These range from sharp white Gros-Plants and local Gamays, through the light wines of the Coteaux d'Ancenis, to Muscadets of the Coteaux de la Loire, Sèvre-et-Maine and of the central area south of Nantes. Maps are available of the *Route Touristique du Vignoble Nantais*, a trail signposted with a grape logo indicating places where you can sample and buy wines. ● *Mon-Fri 8.30am-12.30pm & 2-5.45pm (1 July-31 Aug, daily 10am-12.30pm & 2-6pm). Tel: 02 40 36 90 10. Free; charge for tastings.*

Château-Thébaud. For a view of the rocky Maine river valley that resembles the Grand Canyon, follow the "*belvédère*" sign from the car park by the *mairie* in this village 7km south-east of Vertou. Down below, at the old bridge known as Pont-Caffino, locals go fishing and boating on the river and walking in the woods, scale the craggy cliffs of a former schist quarry, or enjoy live music on summer evenings in a cheerfully noisy bar and *crêperie*. ●

126

Achevé d'imprimer en mars 2000 sur les presses de
l'Imprimerie Graphique de l'Ouest au Poiré-sur-Vie (Vendée)
Dépôt légal : mars 2000 - Imprimé en France